TWO TREES, TWO KINGDOMS, TWO KINGS

"What is truth?" - Pontius Pilate, John 18:38

An Important and Timely Perspective for the Modern Believer

VOLUME 1: TWO TREES

By: Bill and Karen Bishop

WingSpan Press

Published in the United States and the United Kingdom
by WingSpan Press, Livermore, CA

The WingSpan name, logo and colophon are the trademarks of
WingSpan Publishing.

Names: Bishop, Bill, 1945- | Bishop, Karen.
Title: Two trees, two kingdoms, two kings : an important and timely perspective for the modern believer / Bill Bishop [and] Karen Bishop.
Description: Livermore, CA : Wingspan Press, 2016.
Identifiers: ISBN 978-1-59594-588-4 (pbk.) |
ISBN 978-1-59594-911-0 (ebook)
Subjects: LCSH: Bible--Criticism, interpretation, etc. | Bible--Evidences, authority, etc. | Bible--Study and teaching. | BISAC: RELIGION / Biblical Criticism & Interpretation / General. | RELIGION / Biblical Studies / General.
Classification: LCC BS511.3 .B57 2016 (print) | LCC BS511.3 (ebook) | DDC 220.6--dc23.

First edition 2016

Printed in the United States of America

www.wingspanpress.com

1 2 3 4 5 6 7 8 9 10

This two volume set is progressive - designed as a single book.

Part 1 is in Volume 1, and Parts 2 and 3 are in Volume 2.

Please begin with Volume 1.

TABLE OF CONTENTS

VOLUME 1: TWO TREES

Part 2   **TWO KINGDOMS** - Not a part of this Volume. Please find this in Volume 2.

Part 3   **TWO KINGS** - Not a part of this Volume. Please find this in Volume 2.

Preface and Notice to the Reader

This book is based upon dialogue between Bill and Karen Bishop - the result of the twining of two hearts that love God and seek to more fully understand His ways. This book is not intended as a teaching, but rather <u>as merely an extensive study</u>. Neither of us are ordained by any theological institution or even affiliated with any organized church, and nothing we write has been given to us as a "thus saith the Lord" word. We simply try to abide in Christ and bring our hearts and minds to Him as empty slates upon which He can write, relying upon the Holy Spirit to teach us all things and bring us to all truth as we study and try to rightly divide the Word of Truth.

> [27] But the anointing which ye have received of him abideth in you, and <u>ye</u> need <u>not that any man teach you</u>: but as the same anointing <u>teacheth you of all things</u>, and <u>is truth</u>, and is no lie, and even as it hath taught you, <u>ye shall abide in him</u>. - 1 John 2:27

> [13] Howbeit when he, the Spirit of truth, is come, he will guide you into all truth: for he shall not speak of himself; but whatsoever he shall hear, that shall he speak: and he will shew you things to come. - John 16:13

> [15] <u>Study to shew thyself approved unto God</u>, a workman that needeth not to be ashamed, <u>rightly dividing the word of truth</u>. - 2 Timothy 2:15

As this is a collaborative effort by Bill and Karen, it was primarily penned and researched by Karen while Bill was on the road driving a tractor trailer. While Karen did most of the writing, Bill cross-examined and confirmed, offering editorial assistance and significant insights throughout the book. We each seek Truth in both Spirit and Word through our prayers and studies, individually and together. This book is our best effort to communicate our collective perceptions.

This book has merely evolved from a great deal of mutual Scriptural examination, scrutiny, and analysis, (putting line upon line and precept upon precept, here a little and there a little).

Two Trees, Two Kingdoms, Two Kings

> [10] For precept must be upon precept, precept upon precept;
> line upon line, line upon line; here a little, and there a little: -
> Isaiah 28:10

Hopefully this book will be a springboard to inspire further study on the part of you, the reader, and even dialogue between you and us so that we might all glean from the process. It is not our attempt in this book to step on toes, but as views do vary within the body of Christ, some will surely think we are doing so. That being the case, we will try to tread lightly. We simply desire to search out various matters and present our findings for the reader's consideration.

> [2] It is the glory of God to conceal a thing: but the honour of kings
> is to search out a matter. - Proverbs 25:2

Our views may change over time, and we reserve the right to revise this book accordingly.

Extra-Biblical references are occasionally used in addition to the Bible, only as long as they do not appear to contradict the actual Biblical text. Please check our book against the Scriptures to be sure we do not conflict in any way – even as those of Berea did in the days of Paul, per Acts 17:10-11. Should you find that any such conflict arises, please advise us of your thoughts for our evaluation. You will find contact information in the Epilogue. Your comments are welcome.

May our studies challenge and enrich the reader as we work through God's Word together.

Regarding our Choice of Biblical Text and Style of Writing:

Biblical quotations are from the authorized King James Version (KJV). Within these Biblical references we have frequently utilized the bolding and under-lining features, and (on occasion) capital letters in order to highlight pertinent areas, so these features are our added emphasis. Scriptural quotations will not contain either italicized or red lettering notations (as might be found in some Bibles) unless we designate that we have included it for a specific purpose. We often include Lexical definitions to bring clarity to the text. These defini-tions will be in italicized print for ease of identification.

Regarding Our Choice of Names for the Father and the Son:

Our Bible is the sacred Word of the Almighty being presented to mankind for our spiritual nourishment. When making use of this great gift it is important to realize that the Bible is <u>not an American document</u> and was <u>not written by English-speaking people</u>. The Almighty inspired men from other ages to record its wealth of information. <u>It is a Middle Eastern document</u> <u>written by Middle Eastern men</u> <u>who are primarily Jewish</u> <u>with a Jewish perspective</u>. Accordingly, we intensely favor the use of the language from which our English Bibles were derived, when referring to the Father and the Son by their proper names.

Our English Bibles typically substitute the words "the LORD" (using all upper case) for the proper name of the Father, and the Son is referenced as Jesus. While we will leave the KJV quotations of Scriptural text unchanged, we will otherwise use what we see as the proper Hebrew names for the Father and the Son in our writing. We hope this will not offend the reader, but our reasons for this will become clear as the book progresses.

Accordingly, we will refer to **Yahweh** (instead of "the LORD") and **Y'shua** (instead of Jesus) when we address the Father and the Son respectively by their proper names.

DISCLAIMER:

It is critical for the reader to understand that this book is <u>not</u> a teaching. While there are some personal conjectures in the text, this book is largely composed in the nature of a doctrinal thesis with what is simply <u>our opinion</u> relative to Biblical exposition being portrayed as factual. This is <u>merely stylistic</u> so we do not have to repeat the references to "we believe", "maybe", "potentially", etc. throughout the entirety of the text. As our thoughts have developed over the years, it became desirable to formulate them in a manner that would be somewhat conducive to our own continuing study. We share them now with others in the form of a book, knowing that they will stir a wide range of sentiments. Although we are reluctant to make waves, sometimes such stirring is healthy. Though our convictions are founded upon a great deal of research and study, they are still simply our <u>opinions</u>. **<u>Please do NOT view this writing as a "teaching"</u>**, but merely as a springboard for your own study. May it inspire questions and elicit research that will prompt your own conjectures, whether or not they match ours. All we desire to do is to motivate our readers to evaluate the validity of the message they have taken to heart over the years from a purely Biblical perspective with the Holy Spirit overseeing the process. We anticipate for each of you a challenging but rewarding ride!

Acknowledgments

I (Karen) would like to acknowledge the roles my parents have played in my life to bring me to the point where I am now. Rearing me in the church, my mother and father provided a backdrop of a loving Christian atmosphere where I could be nurtured in the faith. Our home always provided strong Christian values and upstanding moral ethics. When my step-father came into the picture later in life, he too espoused these principles, and has been instrumental in my provision and care, offering considerable moral substance to my walk. As my views have changed over time, my parents have not always grasped my new insights, but they have always understood that my walk was totally dedicated to the One Whom I serve. They have always encouraged me to follow my path without hesitation, knowing that I am firmly in God's hands.

We (Bill and Karen) have shared mutual friends and acquaintances over the years who have provided wonderful inspiration to our spiritual walks. Each of us likewise have some companions from our past whom the other was not privileged to know, but all have played a part. They have provided the insights and contrasts which have enabled us to come to the understandings we now hold. Changes in locale have brought new friends into our lives who have become near and dear to us in the present, and continue to offer much loving encouragement, spiritual insight and integrity as we share our thoughts and desires together. While we all disagree periodically, the times we share and the discussions which ensue are always immensely meaningful and rich. While they deserve individual recognition, the list would be too lengthy. We would also like to mention the young upcoming adults and children of these wonderful people. They stand apart in the world today as being exemplary beyond measure. The strength of their families and their carefully honed parenting skills have brought about a quality of character in these young ones that is far above the norm. Each of them is special to us. Being young and yet so ethically sound, they have been a great encouragement, that the moral fabric within mankind today can surmount the corruptions of our society, if given the right upbringing.

A special thanks goes to all our dear friends who have assisted us in this endeavor. Father brings the right people at the right times!

Finally, our thanks goes to Father. It is He who has provided the strength and the provision to bring this to fruition.

Introduction

The book you are about to read is a treatise which has been compiled after years of research, using many varied sources coupled with diligent study of the Word. It is a discourse which probes some common tenets of our faith, and exposes some troubling tendencies which can serve to usurp the designed harmony of the Biblical text - the harmony which God intends for His children to find, to understand and to uphold in their walk of faith.

> [3] Endeavouring to keep the unity of the Spirit in the bond of peace.
>
> [4] There is one body, and one Spirit, even as ye are called in one hope of your calling;
>
> [5] One Lord, one faith, one baptism,
>
> [6] One God and Father of all, who is above all, and through all, and in you all. - Ephesians 4:3-6

This underlying harmony is designed to lend impetus to the construct of a unity of faith - that singularity of thought, word, and deed which is instrumental to our growth in Christ.

This is not a book to be read for pleasure, but should be viewed as an undertaking which can open doors for understanding that may have been previously unavailable. If you are one who likes to remain in the comfort zone, you might want to stop reading here. It is important to understand that some discomfort is often initially felt when God deals with the heart in a new and awesome way. When we begin to glimpse the depths of God's love AND His displeasure with misconceptions about His Word, we will begin to see how we are to align more completely to His truth and grow more abundantly within His grace.

It is a book which may jolt the innermost emotions from disbelief to anger, but when the reader persists through these rough spots, it will begin to stir the utmost deep-seated ambitions of the heart and soul to grasp the truth at all cost and walk within it to please our Father above. How will it happen? What will be the cost?

> [27] And whosoever doth not bear his cross, and come after me, cannot be my disciple.
>
> [28] For which of you, intending to build a tower, sitteth not down first, and counteth the cost, whether he have sufficient to finish it?
> - Luke 14:27-28

It is a challenge to all Believers to come to grips with the hard and fast truth of the Word. This is not a book for the faint of heart, or the one who does not care about his spiritual journey. It is for the one who desires a committed walk with the One who created him – a more intimate communion with the One who cares about every move we make and every thought we think. It is a book to draw the reader into a deeper relationship with the One who loves us and wants to be our Abba (Daddy).

It is a book that brings out both the judgment and the mercy with which He oversees His children, and the manner in which it is meted out to His own. It promotes a healthy understanding of the iniquity in the life of the Believer and how to relinquish it, drawing us into the righteousness Father intends for us to maintain, and the spotless bride the Son desires.

It is, it is, it is... It is what it is, and that is not going to be the same for everyone who reads it. Let the reader experience what it is to him. Our desire is that it will prompt new commitment to God and His ways, but may it be one thing if nothing else – a blessing to all who take up the challenge to read it!

PART 1
TWO TREES

CHAPTER 1

PERCEPTIONS

We (Bill and Karen) now agree on the concepts we have expressed in this book, though there was a time when our views differed significantly. We have come a long way down our individual bumpy roads to get to this point of convergence and integrate our thoughts into the picture we present. We grew up with vastly different backgrounds. Our views of life and truth (both in and apart from the church) began at the cradle and continued to form throughout our childhood, and into our adult years. We have come to realize that our parents, our spiritual encounters, and even our surroundings have influenced our belief systems. Furthermore these imprints (coupled with cultural influences) have largely dictated our methods of deduction and analysis. Coming from different directions, we formed preconceptions which were quite divergent from one another. It took a heart-felt desire for Biblical Truth to draw us onto the same path of understanding. Recognizing these preconceptions, we were each shown to re-evaluate our perspective and find God's Truth on the matter. We took to heart 1 John where we were told:

> [27] But the anointing which ye have received of him abideth in you, and ye need not that any man teach you: but as the same anointing teacheth you of all things, and is truth, and is no lie, and even as it hath taught you, ye shall abide in him. - 1 John 2:27

Therefore, we made the decision to study God's Word apart from the outside instruction of man's theology, simply relying on the Holy Spirit to draw us into the fullness of God's Biblical Truth. Neither of us has looked back or in any way regretted this step of faith, as it has paved the way for some fantastic spiritual growth.

The multifaceted nature of the Holy Bible has presented challenges through-out the entire New Testament era. We had to confront such challenges and meet some questions head-on as we worked together: Did a breach or change of truth occur during the chasm of time which separates the pages of our Old and New Testaments? How does this spiritually ordained division in time relate to our beliefs today? How are we to deal with the New Testament text in contrast to that which came before it? What impact does our <u>method</u> of deduction and modern analysis have on our proper understanding of God's Word?

Patterns of Thought

There is definitely a shift in the manner in which God's Word is brought forth to us in our New Testament text, but how does this shift in style affect the continuity of the message which comes forward as we progress from Genesis to Revelation? There are predominantly two schools of thought, and it is important to understand what they are and where each is rooted. This is the impetus behind this book, as we are convinced that obtaining the proper perspective is crucial to our spiritual walk and our relationship with God. What seems to be an overwhelming subject is actually remarkably simple at its root level. Once we come to see this, it opens up the Word in a way that many say they have never seen or experienced before. It establishes a new journey in faith and spiritual growth that is very rewarding in both this age and the next.

In order to begin this journey, we must get to the root of a controversy which centers around the means of Biblical interpretation one uses. Which of the two schools of thought we use to substantiate our Biblical interpretations dramatically impacts the core of our belief system. In order to determine the correct approach, we must look closely at the origin of our Biblical text. It is important to realize that Americans did not write God's Word to man. It was written by people of Middle Eastern descent, and worded from their own perspective. The culture of the authors of the Biblical text was decidedly Hebraic, and the thought pattern was emphatically different from that of our western culture. Even the New Testament writers, such as Paul, were raised under the Hebraic pattern of thought, and this thought pattern permeated their teachings. Paul readily acknowledged his Hebraic roots:

> [22] Are they <u>Hebrews</u>? <u>so am I</u>. Are they Israelites? so am I. Are they the seed of Abraham? so am I. - 2 Corinthians 11:22

He spoke fluently in the Hebrew tongue:

> [2] (And when they heard that <u>he spake in the Hebrew tongue to them</u>, they kept the more silence: and he saith,) - Acts 22:2

It was likewise in the Hebrew tongue that Paul heard from Y'shua (the Hebrew name for Jesus):

[14] And when we were all fallen to the earth, <u>I heard a voice speaking unto me, and saying in the Hebrew tongue</u>, Saul, Saul, why persecutest thou me? It is hard for thee to kick against the pricks. - Acts 26:14

The Hebraic thought patterns vs. those of our western culture are decidedly different. Therefore, we must remember that those who wrote all the books of our Bible (including the New Testament) were of Hebrew origin, and the writings themselves reflect Hebraic thought patterns. They did not pattern their writings to accommodate the western way of thought, so to apply western thinking to their writings can easily lead to errant understanding.

Mankind (particularly in our western world) has become adept at thinking of time in a linear fashion. When someone mentions one event relative to a second event, we picture a time LINE. This straight line extends from the past (on the left) through the present and into the future (on the right). It is like a railroad track which runs from the west coast to the east coast in one linear horizontal level line.

We have come to understand that Father's patterns are actually spiraling in nature. Rather than being a flat horizontal measure of time, Father's view can be better understood as a circular version with a spiraling upward trend. If we picture that railroad running from the ground up into the air in a continuous spiraling motion, we see what might be a more appropriate view of time from Father's perspective. Each 360 degree rotation of the spiral begins a new cycle, yet the spiral continues onward and upward. In our human existence, we repeat these cycles over and again, and we age as this repetition occurs. This aging is represented by the upward motion. No two cycles will be exactly the same. They will, however, maintain an integrity of essence as they progress upward with each new cycle. The word "integrity" here means: *a steadfast adherence to a strict moral or ethical code*. The "essence" is this *code*. Essence is: the intrinsic, indispensable quality which characterizes and identifies something. This integrity of essence then is a steadfast adherence to God's moral code - His imposed character and identity within the cyclical layering. It cannot deviate. It must maintain its character throughout the cyclical advancement. It is uniform throughout. This repetitive upward spiral motion is the basis of the Hebraic thought pattern.

After seven days elapse, a new week begins and the seven days are repeated yet again. Though they may be similar, they will not be identical to the seven days which just transpired, and time will have intervened between the two. In the spiraling motion, day one of the new week would be over day one of the previous week. Likewise our months, seasons, and years progress as well. It is a type of wheels within wheels, except that the wheels would be spiraling. It would bear a slight resemblance to Ezekiel's vision:

> ... and their appearance and their work was as it were a wheel in the middle of a wheel – Ezekiel 1:16

As time marches on, the cycles continue ever round and around, spiraling upward as they go. The pattern was orchestrated in the week of creation by our sovereign God, and it carries through with each weekly Sabbath, new month, annual Sabbath Festival celebration, and new year - as well as in seven and fifty year cycles.

The spiraling cyclical patterning is not just relative to calendar cycles, but the same repetitive thought pattern relates to the Biblical text as well. So it is that Torah (the first five books of the Bible) was given to man first in written form (via Father) through Moses:

> [105] Thy word is a lamp unto my feet, and a light unto my path. - Psalms 119:105

Then it was given to man again in the human form (via Y'shua):

> [14] And the Word was made flesh, and dwelt among us, (and we beheld his glory, the glory as of the only begotten of the Father,) full of grace and truth. - John 1:14

Finally, it was given yet again to man in Spirit form (via the Holy Spirit):

> [3] Forasmuch as ye are manifestly declared to be the epistle of Christ ministered by us, written not with ink, but with the Spirit of the living God; not in tables of stone, but in fleshy tables of the heart. - 2 Corinthians 3:3

Each progressive administration of this sacred Word spirals ever upward over that which preceded it, bringing fresh insight as it merges earth to Heaven. As time advances, God's Torah teaching cycles into new heights, increasing man's understanding to greater spiritual levels.

Unfortunately, man's linear thinking predominates in much of the church today. This linear sequencing starts and stops, with abrupt changes. The standard theological orientation establishes a time line and designates the far left as the past and the far right as the future. It then puts a dividing line at the timing of the cross of Calvary and teaches that everything to the left of that divide is rendered virtually obsolete by Y'shua's victory. According to this view, everything which preceded the cross is severed from that which follows it. The relevance of anything to the left then simply vanishes. As a result, much of our modern theology is built almost exclusively around the gospels and the epistles of Paul which fall to the right of that line. This, in effect, totally re-orchestrates the Divine moral code.

By its very nature the spiraling pattern uses repetition as the mechanism of instruction. Each revolution of a cycle repeats the one which preceded it, bringing new enlightenment and maturity as the pure essence of the cycle is repeated. This pure essence is static. It will not change, because its very substance is derived from each subset or previous revolution. The substance of the underlying circuits cannot be altered or deleted when the successive circuits advance. Such alteration would destroy the sacred essence. This very essence is prerequisite and fundamental to the structural basis of the whole. As a result, each successive circuit always retain its relevance.

Using the linear format, lines can be drawn to create new beginnings with new thought processes, and such deviation is totally acceptable. With this linear format, there is no subset with which to contend. Any correlation to the past (or left side) is obscured, and man can simply disregard that which came before.

Such correlation is only evident through the repetition of the spiral model. Therefore, the introduction of the linear timeline by man's western mindset has altered the sacred flow of instruction. Its use breaks the continuity which God ordained in His instructional patterning. This in turn leads to some grievous misunderstandings which corrupt current theological views.

The cyclical rotation of the spiral model develops an ideology of unity and singularity as revealed in the entirety of God's Word. The subset which underlies this cyclical motion is the seed of the plant that will grow. The seed of an apple will not produce an orange. Neither will that which grows from the seed of the original subset produce a result that is estranged from the original seed.

Conversely, the cessation of the old and the total remodeling of the new leads to a replacement ideology. This ideology is dual in nature (old and new), so it is divisive at its core. God's seed of His patterning subset is spliced and compromised through the linear thought process. The end result then is a GMO (genetically modified organism) - a GMO version of theology. The plant of the GMO seed is simply not equipped to provide the same nutrition which the plant of the undefiled seed would provide. While the GMO version of physical fruit typically does not seem to be destructive right away, over the long haul it can be devastating. Unfortunately, this holds true theologically as well. The spiritual GMO fruit can appear to be nutritious, but it can ultimately damage our spiritual state tremendously.

We see then that the cyclical spiraling concept is front and center to God's patterning. The flat horizontal linear concept is typically central to man's perception. Only with this linear theoretical construct can splicing occur. The inherent repetition of the cyclical model does not allow for it. Accordingly, much of the gospel message being taught in our western churches has a structural flaw which tarnishes the gospel message being presented. Divisions in the linear construct result in divisions of the Biblical text. Rather than the New Testament being built on the Old, the New is now viewed as being separated from and in opposition to the Old. The Old, being on the left of the line, is seen as obsolete. This then precipitates a GMO gospel message that is causing a great deal of harm in the body of Messiah.

We have come to see that Paul's intellect was formed and shaped around Father's Hebraic construct, and his teachings were written from this perspective. The Old Testament was the only Scripture they had at that time. Paul understood that his teachings must be a spiraling outgrowth of their subset, the Old Testament. They must then maintain the same essence, and simply could not be separated from that subset. He understood that to do so would be to sabotage the continuity and integrity of the original seed. When he presented his teachings, he expected his audience to view them from the perspective of their Old Testament subset. Likewise, those who received his teachings in that time would have had no reason to view them in any other way. It was a mutual understanding. If we read the words of Paul with this cyclical mindset, we will preserve the pure essence of the Hebraic subset which underlies Paul's teachings. This Hebraic subset is essential to properly understand his message, as his epistles were built on it. Only by considering it can we have an unobstructed view of Paul's instruction. Without this perspective, we will almost certainly misunderstand his message to us and come up with oranges from his apple seeds.

This is the reason we believe theological interpretations today tend toward the divisive teachings that the New Testament nullifies the Old. Our linear western thinking divides the New from the Old, and the Old is discarded as being out of date. In reality, God's patterning demands that the Old must underlie and provide the pure essence for the New, as the New is progressively revealed in cyclical perfection.

Levels of Biblical Interpretation

It is commonly accepted that there are four layers of understanding which relate to the Biblical text. These are addressed by Biblical scholars as PRDS (Pardes). The concept of Pardes is often correlated to our word "Paradise" (composed of the same four sounds – PRDS). We believe that the fullness of Pardes is found in the Tree of Life, and will ultimately provide us with the complete understanding we are intended to have. When all is one day restored, our minds will almost certainly be able to comprehend the fullness of this synchronized relativity. In the meantime, this integration process is a slow one. Sadly, man was destined to see through a glass darkly for a time after his fall (1 Corinthians 13:12). Therefore, it is necessary at this time to toil in order to derive these various levels of understanding from our Biblical text. We will not be totally aware of its fullness until restoration is completed. We must adjust our eyes to the Pardes view. Then we begin to see evidence of this patterning, this upward spiraling, in the Biblical text itself. It is yet another aspect of the majesty of God in His presentation of His Word to His children.

There are four levels of understanding in the spiritual food of Pardes. In God's cyclical patterning, each level of understanding builds on that which is beneath it. The four levels of understanding spiral upward, each one encircling that which lies beneath it. At times they will overlap a bit, but this simply relates to their continuity.

First we will present a brief description of each level, then we will show how they interlock to provide the nutrition we need as Believers today.

Pashat (pah-shat) is a Hebrew word meaning: *plain meaning*. It is the simplest, most elementary level – a literal or surface meaning of the text, the basic primary meaning of the words in context. It provides the overall flow of thought when using the customary meaning of the words in the text. The Pashat is to be a prerequisite to all students of the Scriptures before they look to any other meaning for the text. Therefore, a historical passage such as the story of Joseph should be discerned first at its simplest literal understanding before trying to apply typology or other inferred meaning to its words.

Remez (rah-mehz) is a Hebrew word meaning: *indication; sign; hint; allusion; suggestion*. It is the hint level - a more implied meaning to which the text alludes - a somewhat allegorical and philosophical level. It transcends our elementary knowledge with wisdom. It is the more practical application of Scripture – the means by which we assimilate knowledge and learn to live by it.

Drash (drahsh) is a Hebrew word meaning: *homiletical interpretation.* Homiletical is a form of homily which means: *a sermon, especially one intended to edify a congregation on a practical matter and not intended to be a theological discourse; a moralizing lecture or admonition; an inspirational saying or platitude.* It is the regal level - a far more sophisticated level of interpretation that deals with parables or riddles. It is sometimes derived by using multiple Scriptural references, putting "line upon line" and "precept upon precept". The moral principles (aggadah) found in Drash are more expansive than the simple literal rules of Law (halacha). These Drash principles then are built on the literal rules of Law, but expand on them to form a more spiritual application for our lives.

Sod (sohd) is a Hebrew word meaning: *secret.* It is considered to be a more Divine level. It is a secretive level, containing a more mystical meaning that is somewhat hidden from the reader. This level supersedes our earthly realm of existence. It elevates us to the Heavenly to view higher aspects of God's Glory within the Scriptures from a spiritual perspective. Sod is not of this world. It originates in the Heavenly realm and comes down to man from above. Sod includes various methods of addressing the underlying Scriptural text from a completely non-literal position. Its subjective nature therefore necessitates a great deal of discernment.

This discernment is needed when advancing through any of the Pardes levels, but ignoring it at the sod level can easily lead to vast misunderstandings. What we might simply term the "rule of advancement" will be critical to this discernment process. This "rule of advancement" checks the validity of the higher levels. It is a simple rule: <u>Each progressive level MUST interlock with the essence of all preceding levels</u>. In our example of Joseph, the understanding of how Joseph is a type of Christ (Remez) must be built on the literal meaning of that passage (Pashat). It cannot be separated from that Pashat layering. Implications that Joseph is a type and shadow of the Messiah to come can be formed as the text is studied in depth. Extensive lists have been compiled which itemize the amazing similarities between the attributes and roles of Joseph and Y'shua. This is an example of Pardes as it is applied to particular Biblical passages. Some Biblical passages might exhibit all four Pardes aspects as the text is studied in depth. Not every detail will match as the typology unfolds, but the general essence must remain intact.

Progression through the four levels of Pardes necessitates that they all be joined together as a single comprehensive unit. Each level must adhere to those beneath it, and not be viewed independently of them. Choosing to disregard this "rule of advancement" when trying to piece together deeper levels is not a viable option. To do so results in losing the congruent integrity of the Biblical text. The essence (seed) of the lower meanings must be maintained (per God's patterning) as the escalation (growth of the seed) proceeds upward. This process is the nucleus of the validation process for interpretations of a deeper level. If the interpretation cannot advance from that which preceded it without conflict or contradiction of the primary essence, it is an invalid interpretation.

God's handiwork, known as our Bible, is a living book that repeatedly shows His glorious design. Biblical scholars have actually found that Scriptural Pardes is evidenced in a second way as well. The second type of Scriptural Pardes is not relative merely to a single passage, but rather to the entire Biblical text. The same "rule of advancement" applies here as well. Scholars have found a Pardes progression of thought as the Biblical text advances in complexity and purpose. It builds on the basis of Scriptural foundation in Genesis to an advanced spiritual culmination in Revelation. Obviously, the complex symbolism in the book of Revelation (a Sod aspect) is far from the more simplistic literal writing style found in Genesis (a Pashat level). It is primarily this second manner of progression (the unfolding Pardes as the Bible proceeds) that we will reference in this book.

We believe the basic Torah instructions are on the level of Pashat. The superficial meaning of these instructions is pretty basic and straight forward, such as:

[15] Thou shalt not steal. - Exodus 20:15

Then we believe the prophets brought forth the Remez level of understanding, building on the Torah to project practical application to the initial instructions. An example in Ezekiel might be:

[44] Behold, every one that useth proverbs shall use this <u>proverb</u> against thee, saying, As is the mother, so is her daughter. - Ezekiel 16:44

The reference to the word "proverb" in this verse is actually a prime example of this application. It is Strong's #H4911 ("mashal") - *to represent, liken, be like similar; to compare*. Indeed the entire book of Proverbs is also primarily composed from a Remez perspective. It is built on (to be superimposed over) the primary level of Torah Pashat, and must never be removed from it. All understanding gleaned from it must be in consort with the original understanding of the Pashat layer of Torah.

Two Trees, Two Kingdoms, Two Kings

Y'shua points to the Pashat level of initial Torah instructions and the Remez level of the teachings of the Prophets in Matthew:

> [17] Think not that I am come to destroy **the law, <u>or the prophets</u>**:
> I am <u>not</u> come <u>to destroy</u>, <u>but to **fulfil**</u>. - Matthew 5:17

"The Law" indicates the Pashat and "the prophets" indicates the Remez. He clarified here that He did not come to delete either of them with His instruction. Rather He came to "fulfill" them. The word "fulfil" brings in Drash. "Fulfill" here is Strong's #G4137 ("plēroō") - *to make full, to <u>fill to the full</u>; to cause to abound, to furnish or supply liberally; to fill to the top: so that nothing shall be wanting to full measure; to make complete in every particular, to render perfect; <u>to carry through to the end</u>, to accomplish, carry out, (some undertaking); in matters of duty: to perform, execute of sayings, promises, prophecies, to bring to pass, ratify, accomplish; to cause God's will (as made known in the Law) to be obeyed as it should be, and God's promises (given through the prophets) to receive fulfillment.*

Y'shua brings in the Drash layer of understanding. He inspires us to obey God's Will (as made known in the Pashat layer of Torah Law), and allows God's promises (given through the Remez teachings of the prophets) to receive their Drash fulfillment of understanding. Rather than disregarding the Pashat and Remez layers which preceded His teachings, He came to "fulfill" them (carry them through to more advanced understanding which is derived from them):

> [35] That it might be fulfilled which was spoken by the prophet,
> saying, I will open my mouth in parables; I will utter things
> which have been kept secret from the foundation of the world. -
> Matthew 13:35

This Drash layering brought forward by Y'shua serves to "fill to the full" that which we are to understand relative to the physical realm. Likewise Y'shua also pointed to the Heavenly and made provision for the Sod fulfillment as well. We will address this level momentarily.

Y'shua often spoke in parables, Drash teachings. The parables of Y'shua are also rooted in Pashat. However, His presentation of them on a Drash level of comprehension was designed to force man to think on more than a superficial level. Therefore, the understanding we are to glean from His teachings must reach back to the Torah roots from which His teachings were extracted:

> [27] Ye have heard that it was said by them of old time, Thou shalt
> not commit adultery:

[28] But I say unto you, That whosoever looketh on a woman to
lust after her hath committed adultery with her already in his heart.
- Matthew 5:27-28

Y'shua referenced first the Torah instruction that we are not to physically
commit adultery, then He expounded a more spiritual Drash application of
this initial Pashat teaching. A preliminary study of Torah on a Pashat level is
so very important! It is important to understand what Y'shua is building on,
even when it is not otherwise stated.

When asked why He spoke in parables, Y'shua had a very interesting answer:

[10] And the disciples came, and said unto him, <u>Why speakest
thou unto them in parables</u>?

[11] He answered and said unto them, Because <u>it is given unto
you to know the mysteries of the kingdom of heaven, but to them it
is not given</u>.

[12] For whosoever hath, to him shall be given, and he shall have
more abundance: but whosoever hath not, from him shall be taken
away even that he hath.

[13] Therefore speak I to them in parables: because they seeing
see not; and hearing they hear not, neither do they understand.

[14] And in them is fulfilled the prophecy of Esaias, which saith,
<u>By hearing ye shall hear, and shall not understand; and seeing ye
shall see, and shall not perceive</u>:

[15] For this people's heart is waxed gross, and their ears are dull
of hearing, and their eyes they have closed; lest at any time they
should see with their eyes, and hear with their ears, and should
understand with their heart, and should be converted, and I should
heal them.

[16] But <u>blessed are your eyes, for they see: and your ears, for
they hear</u>.

[17] For verily I say unto you, That **many prophets and righteous
men have desired to see those things which ye see, and have
not seen them; and to hear those things which ye hear, and
have not heard them**. - Matthew 13:10-17

What did Y'shua mean in verse 17 when He said: "many prophets and righteous men have desired to see those things which ye see, and have not seen

them; and to hear those things which ye hear, and have not heard them"? He might well have been indicating that the prophets (though they had advanced above the primary Pashat level of Torah instruction) were still bound to the Remez level. They had not yet advanced to the Drash level which Y'shua was opening up to man. They were more advanced than the simplest understanding of Torah, but had not yet seen what Y'shua was bringing forth. Drash understanding is one level higher than Remez, and it would come with Y'shua after the conclusion of their ministry.

Some are troubled by Y'shua's words of explanation: "Because it is given unto you to know the mysteries of the kingdom of heaven, but to them it is not given." This appears to imply that there is an intentional design from God to obscure the understanding for some. Even many theologians struggle with this concept. Why are some unable to understand Y'shua's teachings?

There may be a simple explanation for this. They may be trying to perceive Y'shua's Drash words merely on a Pashat level, which is simply ineffective. To stop with the Pashat level is valid, but falls far short of the intent of the parable on the Drash level. The hearer must apply more depth to the words using the "rule of advancement". By doing so he will allow his eyes and ears to be opened to the more spiritual understanding that is intended. Then the fullness of Y'shua's teachings can come into view. We see that some are told: "it is given unto you to know the mysteries of the kingdom of heaven". It is likely that He realizes that these select ones not only understand the Pardes principle, but are devoted to applying it.

Applying this principle takes some effort and determination. Not all are willing to do so. Some want to be fed only pablum. They desire their instruction to be in simplified form. They may also desire to hear only those things that will satisfy their itching ears. Y'shua's words are rather candid regarding such folks: "For this people's heart is waxed gross, and their ears are dull of hearing, and their eyes they have closed; lest at any time they should see with their eyes, and hear with their ears, and should understand with their heart...." He indicates here that the failure to see, hear, and understand is a personal choice, and this "choice" has caused their heart to be "waxed gross". This term "waxed gross" is Strong's #G3975 ("pachynō") - *to make thick, to make fat, fatten; to make stupid (to render the soul dull or callous).*

Some will fail to advance from the Pashat level, while others will jump to conclusions regarding advanced levels without carefully considering the levels beneath their conclusions. Either way is to fall short of proper understanding

- ears dull of hearing and eyes being closed. The former results in conclusions which are merely incomplete, but the latter is far more dangerous. Being built on improper foundations, these erroneous conclusions can cause spiritual harm. Only those who are faithful and committed to build on the proper foundation established by Father in Torah would be given eyes to see and ears to hear His expanding Truth as these levels of understanding unfold.

Y'shua actually explains what a few of the more simplistic parables mean in order to give us the flavor of that which will follow. By doing so He illustrates how spiritual teachings are to be put in the Pardes perspective! As the teachings of the Word get deeper still, we must be careful to apply the Pardes "rule of advancement" by layering appropriately. Relating things on the Drash level enabled Y'shua to lay the groundwork for the mysteries of the Kingdom of Heaven (verse 11). That will actually be the thrust of Paul's teachings in the days that follow.

The Father put forth the literal instructions of Torah on a basic Pashat level. The prophets expounded further with the Remez perspective to expand our understanding. Y'shua then amplified with the Drash frame of reference to culminate the earthly knowledge and point to the Heavenly. Paul will deal with the Sod.

This final level of Sod is referenced in Proverbs chapter 3 relative to the righteous:

> [32] For the froward is abomination to the LORD: but his **secret** is with the righteous. - Proverbs 3:32

The word "secret" is Strong's #H5475 ("cowd") - *secret counsel; intimacy (with God)*. Sod then is the level of secret counsel, intimacy with God which correlates to inspiration or revelation which comes through the Holy Spirit. The word "righteous" here is Strong's #H3477 ("yashar") - *straight, upright, correct, level, right, pleasing, straightforward, just, fitting, proper*. There is a prequalification then to receiving the proper "sod" perception. This prequalification is to be walking in righteousness - a straightforward and correct manner. This is accomplished through applying the Pardes "rule of advancement" of retaining the former while applying the latter. They will retain Torah Truth at all levels and walk justly in it, which enables them to be righteous - pleasing to God.

Y'shua's death and resurrection opened the way for those who would believe on Him to receive the indwelling Holy Spirit. God's Spirit now ministers to the Believer from within to provide him with God's counsel. This counsel can be through <u>guidance</u> to think through things from God's perspective or even through <u>direct revelation</u>, but it will not <u>force</u> one to think properly.

Paul had a profound Pashat knowledge of Torah, but he was misapplying it because he had yet to grasp what Y'shua had taught. When Y'shua enlightened him on the road to Damascus, Paul began to walk properly and in a straightforward and righteous way, pleasing to Father. He was then given supernatural revelation. He says in Galatians:

> [11] But I certify you, brethren, that <u>the gospel which was preached of me is not after man</u>.
>
> [12] For I neither received it of man, neither was I taught it, **but by the revelation of Jesus Christ**. - Galatians 1:11-12

Since Paul was opposed to the teachings of Y'shua until his conversion (which was after Y'shua's resurrection), this revelation was not from Y'shua in His physical state. It is obvious that the revelation of Y'shua which Paul references was brought to him via the Holy Spirit (sent by Y'shua from the Father) after Y'shua's resurrection:

> [26] But when the Comforter is come, whom <u>I will send unto you from the Father</u>, even <u>the Spirit of truth</u>, which proceedeth from the Father, he shall testify of me: - John 15:26

Paul's revelation was "not after man", but was rather by the Holy Spirit from Father above. This was an earmark of Sod, which is of Divine rather than earthly origin. The Holy Spirit brings us Sod understanding, on both a corporate and individual basis. Y'shua brought the fullness of understanding (Drash) for the physical realm and began to cross over into the spiritual aspect of teaching. The Holy Spirit then brings us more depth of understanding relative to the Heavenly or spiritual realm - the Sod aspect. It is for that reason that much of Paul's writing is on the Sod level. That makes his writings very subjective in nature and easily misunderstood, as the Truth of the Sod level can be very elusive:

> [12] For now **we see through a glass, darkly**; but then face to face: **<u>now I know in part</u>**; but then shall I know even as also I am known. - 1 Corinthians 13:12

He speaks of his revelation as being in association with mysteries:

> [25] Now to him that is of power to stablish you according to my

> gospel, and the preaching of Jesus Christ, according to the <u>revelation of the mystery</u>, which was kept secret since the world began,
> - Romans 16:25

> [7] But we speak the wisdom of God in a <u>mystery</u>, even the <u>hidden wisdom</u>, which God ordained before the world unto our glory:
> - 1 Corinthians 2:7

He also indicates that such mysteries have been revealed to him, and that he is a steward of the mysteries of God:

> [1] Let a man so account of us, as of the ministers of Christ, and <u>stewards of the mysteries of God</u>. - 1 Corinthians 4:1

> [3] How that by revelation he made known unto me the <u>mystery</u>; (as I wrote afore in few words,

> [4] Whereby, when ye read, ye may understand my knowledge in the <u>mystery</u> of Christ) – Ephesians 3:3-4

> [32] This is <u>a great mystery</u>: but I speak concerning Christ and the church. - Ephesians 5:32

Every time the word "mystery" or "mysteries" is used by Paul, it is the same Greek word. It is always Strong's #G3466 ("mystērion") - *hidden thing, <u>secret, mystery</u>; generally mysteries, religious secrets, confided only to the initiated and not to ordinary mortals; hidden or secret thing, not obvious to the understanding; a hidden purpose or counsel; the secret will of men or God: the <u>secret counsels which govern God in dealing with the righteous</u>, which are hidden from ungodly and wicked men but plain to the godly.*

This Greek word then concurs totally with the Hebrew word "sod" (secret) used in our Old Testament writings, as being a counsel of God's secret things which is revealed to the righteous:

> [32] For the froward is abomination to the LORD: but his **secret** is with the righteous. - Proverbs 3:32

Paul's writings are replete with these Sod mysteries. Therefore, we must <u>consistently</u> start with Pashat in order to accurately work through them and get to the proper spiritual perspective. Man must now work to gain the understanding he once had but lost in the fall. This loss of Truth was a major consequence of the fall, but it is God's plan that man regain that which was lost. In these last days He has provided for us the full range of Pardes Truth so we could construct our understanding from the Pashat of Genesis to the Sod of

Two Trees, Two Kingdoms, Two Kings

Revelation. To recover what we lost in the fall, man must work together with God's Spirit, and must till the soil of the Word He gave us:

> [9] Whom shall he teach knowledge? and whom shall he make to understand doctrine? them that are weaned from the milk, and drawn from the breasts.

> [10] For precept must be upon precept, precept upon precept; line upon line, line upon line; here a little, and there a little: - Isaiah 28:9-10

Short of Divine revelation such as Paul was given, the Sod level is not easily perceived, and is frequently derived through intensive study:

> [2] It is the glory of God to conceal a thing: but the honour of kings is to search out a matter. - Proverbs 25:2

The Art of Assimilation

The Pardes application of the Word is the design of God for man to regain his lost understanding after the fall. This understanding would not fall into place after a single reading of His Word. Nor would it be available to man by extracting portions of His Word from the context of the whole book. It must be carefully assimilated - putting "line upon line", and "precept upon precept" (Pashat through Sod). This seems to be intentional on God's part - to see who would care enough – who would love His Truth enough - to "search out" His matters as He expects us to do.

The parable of the sower illustrates the way Y'shua wanted us to understand this process. It is a Drash teaching:

> [3] And he spake many things unto them in parables, saying, Behold, a sower went forth to sow;

> [4] And when he sowed, some seeds fell by the way side, and the fowls came and devoured them up:

> [5] Some fell upon stony places, where they had not much earth: and forthwith they sprung up, because they had no deepness of earth:

> [6] And when the sun was up, they were scorched; and because they had no root, they withered away.

> [7] And some fell among thorns; and the thorns sprung up, and choked them:

[8] But other fell into good ground, and brought forth fruit, some an hundredfold, some sixtyfold, some thirtyfold.

[9] Who hath ears to hear, let him hear. - Matthew 13:3-9

A few verses later, He explained the meaning of this teaching:

[18] Hear ye therefore the parable of the sower.

[19] When any one heareth the word of the kingdom, and **understandeth** it not, then cometh the wicked one, and catcheth away that which was sown in his heart. This is he which received seed by the way side.

[20] But he that received the seed into stony places, the same is he that heareth the word, and anon with joy receiveth it;

[21] Yet hath he not root in himself, but dureth for a while: for when tribulation or persecution ariseth because of the word, by and by he is offended.

[22] He also that received seed among the thorns is he that heareth the word; and the care of this world, and the deceitfulness of riches, choke the word, and he becometh unfruitful.

[23] But he that received seed into the good ground is he that heareth the word, and understandeth it; which also beareth fruit, and bringeth forth, some an hundredfold, some sixty, some thirty. - Matthew 13:18-23

We see here that "understanding" is key, and application of Pardes enables that "understanding". Then we must be faithful to stand firm in that "understanding", not allowing persecution or cares of the world to deter our growth. The mind then is the ground into which the seed for understanding is sown. It must be properly prepared to receive the seed. Perhaps that which tills and fertilizes the ground is the heart. We believe that when the love of the Father abounds in the heart, the ground is tilled, and when the heart embraces the fullness of His Truth, it is fertilized. It is then ready to receive the "engrafted" seed, and spiritual fruit will abound:

[21] Wherefore lay apart all filthiness and superfluity of naughtiness, and **receive** with meekness the **engrafted word**, which is able to save your souls. - James 1:21

The word "engrafted" in verse 21 is Strong's #G1721 ("emphytos") - *implanted*. It is derived from Strong's #G5453 ("phyō") - *to beget, bring forth, produce; to be born, to spring up, to grow*. It is by engrafting God's Word into our tilled and fertilized minds that we produce and bring forth the nutritional nourishment we need to thrive in our spiritual walk.

All of the seeds for this food must be "heirloom" seeds (pure seeds) from Torah (the first five books of our Biblical text). As we read Torah and implant these seeds in the prepared soil of the human mind and heart, the seeds take root and grow into an abundance of spiritual food. This perfect food then supplies our spiritual understanding and meets our spiritual nutritional needs. The Pashat seed is to produce the plant. The plant must start with the Pashat seed and grow from there into the Remez, the Drash, and ultimately the Sod level. Then the fruit of the Spirit will proliferate:

> [23] But he that received seed into the good ground is he that heareth the word, and <u>understandeth</u> it; which also beareth fruit, and bringeth forth, some an hundredfold, some sixty, some thirty. - Matthew 13:23

> [9] (For the fruit of the Spirit is in all goodness and righteousness and truth;) - Ephesians 5:9

For that reason, all which is found in later portions of the Biblical text must always be properly applied to its Torah base in order to develop valid interpretation. Failure to do so brings errant analysis which leads to flawed belief systems. When we form our belief systems based on teachings which are drawn from primarily New Testament text, it is rather like starting a garden with plants which are partially grown and not knowing the seed from which they came. If the interpretation of these teachings was from seeds other than Torah (due to failure to apply the proper Pashat subset), the plant could be a dangerous - if not toxic - source of spiritual food. We do not want to eat from spiritual GMO food!

Paul writes of the olive tree in Romans:

> [16] For if the <u>firstfruit be holy</u>, the lump is also holy: and if the root be holy, so are the branches.

> [17] And if some of the branches be broken off, and thou, being a <u>wild olive tree</u>, wert graffed in among them, and with them partakest of the <u>root and fatness of the olive tree</u>; - Romans 11:16-17

We believe the original olive tree was cultivated by God in the Heavenly garden of Eden – that it was the Tree of Life. That would be why its "firstfruit" (the element of this tree which was brought forth in the initial Torah teachings) is linked here with holiness. It is this holiness which provides the seeds of Torah Truth that are to grow our spiritual fruit of goodness, righteousness and truth. This is why Paul relates the Hebrew people to branches of this good (cultivated) olive tree. They have and understand the foundational truths of Pashat Torah Truth that came down from Heaven.

On the other hand, the wild olive tree would be the Tree of Knowledge of Good and Evil. Those of us who came to Y'shua from being outside of Judaism are equated to being branches from this wild olive tree. Our initial belief is formed around and based on the Drash teachings of Y'shua and the Sod teachings of Paul. However if our instruction base does not teach us to apply Pardes, the fruit we produce will be "wild" and invalid, subverting our spiritual growth. Paul says here that we must be grafted from the wild olive tree into this cultivated tree <u>so we can receive of its root and fatness</u>. The root and fatness of this cultivated tree (Tree of Life) would be the initial Pashat Torah instruction followed by the Remez teachings of the prophets. Having this background enables us to build our New Testament understanding from the heirloom seed up. It is only then that our root and branches will be holy, and the fruit we bear will be good fruit.

Most Christians come from a Gentile background of the wild olive tree, and we are grafted into the Hebrew seed line of the cultivated olive tree through Abraham:

> [29] And if ye be Christ's, then are ye Abraham's seed, and heirs according to the promise. - Galatians 3:29

As Believers we are to be Abraham's seed. It is essential then to partake of the root and fatness of this seed of Abraham. It comes from the tree whose "firstfruit" is holy. It is a seed which was engendered in Heaven and sown here on earth as our written Torah. Only when we start from this foundation, can we mature properly, advancing from the Pashat and Remez of the Old Testament text into the Drash and Sod of the New. Only then will we be able to comprehend the fullness of the message the New Testament brings to us.

This Pardes perspective should be the underpinning of the Christian faith. Unfortunately the Christian faith has largely digressed from the sacred roots of Pashat, and consequently the underpinning of the faith has been greatly compromised. Without application of Pardes to New Testament teachings, it is very easy to produce wild olive tree (Tree of Knowledge) fruit.

These first five books of the Bible are the base of the Pashat level from which

Two Trees, Two Kingdoms, Two Kings

our Biblical knowledge is to be built. This construction begins in Genesis and progresses through the entire Bible. The Pashat of Torah is the level on which all other levels must be overlain; it is the foundation for all which comes after it. The balance of the Biblical text simply provides the deeper understandings of these first five books. The New Testament is in the Old concealed, and the Old Testament is in the New revealed. They are not to be isolated from one another.

The definitions of the words "overlie" and "overlay" are quite different. The word "overlay" means: *to <u>cover</u> the surface of with a <u>decorative</u> layer or design*. The word "overlie" means: *to lie or <u>rest upon</u> as a <u>stratum</u> (a layer having approximately <u>the same composition throughout</u>)*. We see that properly building on Torah's Pashat layer is to <u>"overlie" it with progressive strata which are cohesive in integrity of essence</u>. Each layer then rests on that which precedes it. We also see that much of that which is concluded from current theology does not properly <u>"overlie"</u> Torah's Pashat <u>with like composition</u>. Instead it <u>"overlays" it with a decorative layering of man's design</u>. The two words overlie and overlay look very similar. However, just as their meanings are quite different in nature, the gospel message which springs forth from the roots of the proper tree is quite different from the one which does not.

We fully acknowledge that the saving grace of Y'shua can be found in the first four books of the New Testament without going back to Torah. This in itself is an act of grace to provide a measure of understanding. However this grace is merely a jump-start to initiate the journey for the Gentile who was not reared with a background of Old Testament instruction. It is not an end product in itself. When we come to understand Paul's writings properly, we will see the obligation to begin at Torah to build a proper foundation for our spiritual understanding and our walk of faith. Without making an effort to partake of the roots and fatness of the cultivated olive tree after our initial belief, we set ourselves up for deception to follow.

God <u>declares</u> that which is at <u>the end</u> <u>from the</u> very <u>beginning</u>:

> [9] **Remember the former things of old**: for I am God, and there is none else; I am God, and there is none like me,

> [10] <u>**Declaring the end**</u> <u>**from the beginning**</u>, and **from ancient times the things that are not yet done**, saying, <u>My counsel shall stand</u>, and I will do all my pleasure: - Isaiah 46:9-10

To come to proper conclusions about the end, the beginning must be understood! We must "remember the things of old" and perceive God's counsel about them in order to understand the present and the future. This reference in Isaiah explicitly shows us that the end was **declared** from the very beginning. We are obliged to refer to the beginning in order to comprehend God's counsel and properly understand that which comes toward the end of our Biblical text.

The new Believer is often told to begin his walk by reading the book of John. Even John tried to point man in the right direction, but that is often overlooked. His book begins with these express words:

[1] In the beginning was the Word, and the Word was with God, and the Word was God.

[2] The same was in the beginning with God. - John 1:1-2

The next few verses then relate back to the creation story in Genesis. John wanted to direct the reader to the Pardes so he could build on the proper foundation as he embraced the Savior.

Ecclesiastes correlates by showing us that there is nothing new under the sun:

[9] The thing that hath been, it is that which shall be; and that which is done is that which shall be done: and **there is no new thing under the sun**. - Ecclesiastes 1:9

Until we see the need to understand the first and most primary of these levels, we are not equipped to advance to the deeper levels. To build a theological belief structure around perceptions drawn in the deeper waters of the Biblical text without relating them properly to the earlier levels of literal Torah will almost certainly yield erroneous doctrine. It is crucial that the Believer obtain a root structure for his belief system by going back to the beginning and establishing the steps to correct understanding. Virtually any theological structuring which ignores these roots will produce errant fruit. Therefore, it is essential that we (especially those who instruct others) come to grips with the basis of Torah instruction before advancing in our theological constructs.

Again (and this can NEVER be stressed sufficiently enough), the key to understanding Sod level writings such as Paul's, is that any interpretation of them must interlock with all of the layers which underlie them. This then is the key to validating the proper Sod understanding, and it is the means to validating the proper interpretation of Paul's writings. If the interpretation cannot advance from that which preceded it without conflict or contradiction of the primary essence, it is an invalid interpretation.

Later layers will never deviate from the <u>essence</u> of the previous layers. A Sod understanding of spiritual Law (as in Paul's writings) will overlie without contradiction the Pashat layer of the Law of written Torah which under girds it as well as any relative Remez and Drash layers. This is the mark of the Tree of Life essence being brought forth in its various and faceted layers.

We are awed at the majestic complexity of the Hebrew language! One day a pure language will be restored to humanity:

> [9] For then will I turn to the people a pure language, that they may all call upon the name of the LORD, to serve him with one consent. - Zephaniah 3:9

We believe this pure language will be a version of the Hebrew tongue. Becoming familiar with the various aspects of this language is certainly a plus when we begin to devour the Biblical text. God's orchestration of it is beyond human comprehension. He has created a scope and magnitude within His Biblical text that is not easily conceived from a human perspective. Any attempt to translate our Bibles from Hebrew (and even from the Greek) to English is somewhat like trying to explain a college course in kindergarten terms. There simply was no way to preserve and maintain the full intent of the Biblical wording in its ancient tongue when putting it into English. So very much was lost – even in our best English translations. Even the inspiration that went into the KJV English translation as far back as 1611 was not intended to stand alone. It was drawn from Semitic languages which were a great deal fuller than what could be expressed in the limited wording of our English text. The layering within individual words and the Hebrew language itself is multifaceted to accommodate Pardes interpretations. The underlying design of the Greek is similar in nature. Our English discourse, on the other hand, simply does not share this capacity.

For instance, a single Hebrew word can have a diversity of meanings. This provides great flexibility when discerning the various levels of understanding in a single passage. Only God could compose His language with such a degree of adaptability. In this way He is able to formulate the multiple layers which are buried in the depths of His Word. This flexibility for Pardes likewise carries through in the Greek language, which our omniscient God could foresee as the language to be used as the basis for our English New Testament text.

Exercising this Divinely orchestrated linguistic flexibility allows us to relate to the various Pardes layers in single verses or passages. Again, no upper level is independent of the ones which under gird it. In spiraling cyclical fashion, each layer overlies the one beneath it to complete the picture. Because these four levels interlock, one cannot be viewed in opposition to another without destroying the integrity of the Scriptural text.

Messages which are established without this structure are based on a faulty premise. When such messages are entertained, the mind becomes cluttered with the thorns of false interpretations. The design of man is revered rather than looking to the valid Scriptural underpinning. The end result is no production of any true and lasting spiritual fruit:

> [15] Beware of false prophets, which come to you in sheep's clothing, but inwardly they are ravening wolves.
>
> [16] Ye shall know them by their fruits. Do men gather grapes of thorns, or figs of thistles?
>
> [17] Even so every good tree bringeth forth good fruit; but a corrupt tree bringeth forth evil fruit. - Matthew 7:15-17

When Paul's epistles were given to the churches, he was not trying to bring forth a new message with no roots from that which had come before. Rather he knew that the churches to whom he wrote would apply his teaching and instruction to these underlying roots of the Torah seed. He knew that those who received his letters had been constantly and continually saturated with Torah precepts and that they would understand the subset on which his instruction was based. Therefore, much of what he wrote to them was not continually prefaced with the subset knowledge which he presumed they knew already - Torah Truth. He understood that the Son of the Father did not come to separate our perceptions from that which the Father had taught, but to build on the foundation which Father had established:

> [17] Think not that I am come to destroy the law, or the prophets: I am not come to destroy, but to fulfil. - Matthew 5:17

Adam's Curse

When Adam fell from grace in Eden, he was chastised by God:

> [17] And unto Adam he said, Because thou hast hearkened unto the voice of thy wife, and hast eaten of the tree, of which I commanded thee, saying, Thou shalt not eat of it: <u>cursed is the ground for thy sake; in sorrow shalt thou eat of it all the days of thy life;</u>

> [18] **Thorns also and thistles shall it bring forth to thee**; and thou shalt eat the herb of the field;
>
> [19] In the sweat of thy face shalt thou eat bread, till thou return unto the ground; for out of it wast thou taken: for dust thou art, and unto dust shalt thou return. - Genesis 3:17-19

The ground became cursed and obtaining his food (which apparently had been pretty easy before the fall) would now be much more work intensive. He would have to combat thorns to get it.

On a very basic level we can take this at face value and say that the consequence of the fall was that mankind would now struggle with physical thorns and thistles in the physical realm to supply his physical food. However, on a much more important and deeper layer, we must realize that a spiritual component was involved in the curse of the ground. The food Adam was to consume was not just physical in nature. In a very real secondary application, the ground can also be seen as the spiritual venue which produces the food for our spiritual nourishment. The spiritual fruit in the Garden was also readily available prior to the fall. After the fall, man's spiritual food would not be accessed as easily either:

> [9] For we know in part, and we prophesy in part.
>
> [10] But when that which is perfect is come, then that which is in part shall be done away.
>
> [11] When I was a child, I spake as a child, I understood as a child, I thought as a child: but when I became a man, I put away childish things.
>
> [12] For now **we see through a glass, darkly**; but then face to face: **now I know in part**; but then shall I know even as also I am known. - 1 Corinthians 13:9-12

When the perfect (Y'shua) comes again (verse 10), we will see Him face to face and will be able to grasp a greater understanding of that which is now so elusive to us. In the meantime, the spiritual food we need in order to thrive in our spiritual growth is somewhat difficult to obtain. We must fight through the thorns of misinterpretation to get to the good fruit. It requires a great deal of effort to grow the right food from the right seed, reap its spiritual fruit and obtain our spiritual nourishment:

> [9] Whom shall he teach knowledge? and whom shall he make

<u>to understand doctrine</u>? them that are weaned from the milk, and drawn from the breasts.

[10] For precept must be upon precept, precept upon precept; line upon line, line upon line; here a little, and there a little: - Isaiah 28:9-10

As a consequence of the fall, God designed the Bible in such a way that it was not laid out in a simple straight-forward manner. Determining our course of life in conjunction with the Will of God could be drawn from its text, but it is not as simple as 1-2-3. The book He gave us as our reference manual is filled with mysteries which must be unlocked to reveal God's deeper Truth within its pages, and this is not a job for the casual disciple. The word "mystery" or forms of the word are used 27 times throughout the Scriptures, and it takes spiritual kings to unlock the elements that are hidden:

[2] It is the glory of God to conceal a thing: but the honour of kings is to search out a matter. - Proverbs 25:2

It requires some effort to extract the valid and undefiled message of the Tree of Life Truth that is tucked away in the precious pages of our Biblical text. We have to work in order to uncover Scriptural Truth by uprooting the thorns and thistles (the mix of worldly interpretation) from the spiritual ground in order to cultivate the proper spiritual food.

As a consequence of the fall, it is necessary to WORK at proper discernment so we do NOT fall prey to deception. The manner in which our Bible is written necessitates a great deal of study in order to avoid the pitfalls of misinterpretation that can result from linear thinking. The job at hand is to discern accurately what the messages on these pages mean. Sadly, far too often man does not want to labor for his spiritual food any more than he wants to exert any effort for his physical nutrition:

[15] Study to shew thyself approved unto God, a workman that needeth not to be ashamed, rightly dividing the word of truth. - 2 Timothy 2:15

When one fails to recognize the various Pardes levels or neglects the necessity of integrating them in order to check the validity of an interpretation, the spiritual thorns and thistles of the mind take over, and deception reigns.

Some portions of the Biblical text (particularly Paul's writings) are worded in such a way that thorny fruit can easily be <u>derived</u> from the text. This is not the fault of the text, as the words of the Bible are pure. This thorny fruit results from neglecting the obligation to check the validity of such an interpretation through the Pardes validation process. We will soon work with some of Paul's passages which have been routinely misinterpreted through this type of negligence, producing thorny fruit.

If we maintain a love for Torah and build on its principles, Paul's words will be properly understood. If such love of God's Torah Truth is fleeting, Paul's words can easily be misused to bring forth thorny fruit. Through this application of Pardes, God will prove the student of the Word. Will we use western style linear logic to produce our fruit? Or will we use the Hebraic spiraling cyclical thought pattern, being faithful to put "line upon line" and "precept upon precept" in order to interlock Paul's words to that which under girds them?

It is only by doing so that we fight through the thorns and thistles to get to the good fruit which we are to consume. If we will only listen, the Holy Spirit will guide us to properly discern the levels of Pardes. The current default is to put the teachings of man on the throne.

Through the progression of Torah to Revelation, God's Divine Glory becomes evident as Pardes is applied. As we eat of the good fruit it produces, this Glory fills our being, and it will be manifested when we receive our new bodies in the day of redemption:

> [18] But we all, with open face beholding as in a glass the glory of the Lord, are changed into the same image from glory to glory, even as by the Spirit of the Lord. - 2 Corinthians 3:18

God's Test

Once we come to understand the need to discern the true intent of Paul's words, we should be faithful to do so. We must come to see how important it is to God that we love His Truth in its fullness. We must also come to understand that the fullness of His Truth is based on Torah Truth and the moral precepts of it. Only when we have this understanding will we be diligent to seek God's expanding Truth throughout the written Word of New and Old Testaments alike.

We know of many instances where Believers are judged in the New Testament. One such passage is found in 2 Thessalonians:

> [10] And with all deceivableness of unrighteousness in them that perish; **because they received not the love of the truth**, that they might be saved.

> [11] And for this cause <u>God shall send them strong delusion, that</u>
> <u>they should believe a lie</u>:
>
> [12] That they all might be damned who believed not the truth, but
> had pleasure in unrighteousness. - 2 Thessalonians 2:10-12

These words come after the prophesied "falling away" - Strong's #G646 ("apostasia") - a few verses earlier:

> [3] Let no man deceive you by any means: for that day shall not
> come, <u>except there come a falling away first</u>, and that man of sin
> be revealed, the son of perdition; - 2 Thessalonians 2:3

It seems that this falling away then means: *departing from an important aspect of the fundamental faith*. This aspect is apparently tied here to God's Truth. Such Believers are then in jeopardy of falling under God's judgment for <u>failing to love His Truth</u>. This judgment would be a strong delusion to believe the lie they want to embrace rather than the Truth He has for His people. We fear that modern theology is precipitating such departure from this Truth in much of the body of Messiah today.

Common sense would suggest that there is likely some criteria of testing in order for Father to determine if we have departed from His Truth. He would have some method to try the reins of the heart before abandoning a man's mind to this strong delusion:

> [2] <u>Examine me, O LORD</u>, and <u>prove me</u>; <u>**try** my reins and my</u>
> <u>heart</u>. - Psalms 26:2

We believe that the inspiration which prompted the wording of Paul's epistles was carefully designed to be specific and yet ambiguous. This may sound somewhat confusing, but it is not, if we see that the actual wording may be designed as just such a test. The words of his writing can be construed in two different ways. If his epistles were not so specifically worded by inspiration, the ambiguity which allows for these two differing views would not be possible. One of these two manners of interpretation is to see the intent of Paul's epistles as a linear projection which provides justification to walk away from the God's Law. The other is to apply Pardes interaction through cyclical Hebraic construction which maintains coherent association with this Law.

The choice of how to discern Paul's intent is determined by the interpretation we use as we read Paul's epistles. Will we accept the superficial meaning of his words to develop a linear concept and walk away from God's expressed

Two Trees, Two Kingdoms, Two Kings

Law? Or will we hold tightly to His Law in total Truth by using the Hebraic cyclical patterning? One who loves God's Truth and understands its cumulative singularity will not be swayed from its consistency. Conversely, one who uses linear logic may choose to leave God's Law behind. Paul warns us to heed his message without perversion:

> [8] But though we, or an angel from heaven, preach any other gospel unto you than that which we have preached unto you, let him be accursed.
>
> [9] As we said before, so say I now again, If any man preach any other gospel unto you than that ye have received, let him be accursed. - Galatians 1:8-9

As we proceed we will begin to see that the gospel message which Paul intended for his audience to understand is not the same gospel message which is often attributed to Paul's words today. It is entirely possible that the accursed version may be the linear interpretation of Paul's gospel message which brings it into conflict with God's Torah.

Indeed we will see as we continue, how many of Paul's words can be taken either of two ways throughout his epistles. To choose the "freedom from God's Law" interpretation means that one has to discard a huge portion of the Biblical text which addresses this error. Such interpretation is a distinct departure from the entirety of God's Truth as it is revealed in the complete Word. We are to understand Scripture from the mindset by which it was composed, the spiraling cyclical mindset which allows the New to overlie the Old (building on its foundation) rather than to replace it.

We will begin to understand how BOTH the true Divine Gospel message AND the faulty interpretation of this message can both be drawn from the same words penned by Paul. Which one will we (as Believers) embrace? When God "proves" (tests) us with Paul's words, what will He find? A passage from Deuteronomy might relate to this:

> [1] If there arise among you <u>a prophet</u>, or a dreamer of dreams, and giveth thee a sign or a wonder,
>
> [2] And the sign or the wonder come to pass, whereof he <u>spake unto thee, saying, Let us go after other gods</u>, <u>which thou hast not known</u>, and let us serve them;
>
> [3] Thou shalt not hearken unto the words of that prophet, or that dreamer of dreams: <u>for the LORD **your God proveth you**</u>, to

> know whether ye **love the LORD your God with all your heart and with all your soul**. - Deuteronomy 13:1-3

"Your God proveth you". To <u>love God with all of your heart and soul</u> is to love His Law and His Truth which embodies it, then to refrain from putting anything else before Him. The church does concur that anything we put <u>before God</u> becomes an idol (another god) and a snare to us. Putting our own ways OR the ways of man before God's ways would fit this category as well:

> [14] And <u>thou shalt not go aside from any of the words which I command thee</u> this day, to the right hand, or to the left, to go after <u>other gods</u> to serve them. - Deuteronomy 28:14

Continuing this thought to its rightful conclusion, however, we would need to understand what "before God" is. God's Law is Truth, and God's Truth is His heart. When we begin to understand how important God's Law is to Him, we begin to see that whatever we put before God's Law, we are putting before His Truth, before His heart, and before God Himself. Therefore, it becomes an idol (another god) to us.

Considering this concept, the word "prophet" in verse 1 of our Deuteronomy text above is Strong's #H5030 ("nabiy'"), and can simply mean: *spokesman* or *speaker*. Any pastor or instructor can fall into this category. If a teaching or message does not align with God's Law, then it is not of His Truth, or His heart, and it can lead to iniquity. It can be the snare to seduce us to "another god" whom we are not to know – the contra god of this world. Even if such a one uses signs or wonders like healings or miraculous feats, these miracles do not validate an errant message. We are still to discern a message according to the entirety of God's Word. Then we can detect error and reject it for the potential deception it poses. If we accept an errant message which leads us to disregard God's Law, we soon find that we are justifying iniquity without thinking twice about it. We are putting our pleasure before God's Will – indulging in self as an idol or other god. Per Deuteronomy 13:3 above, we are being shown that God is <u>proving us to see if we love Him fully</u>. John further illustrates in our New Testament text how Father will know if we love Him as we should:

> [3] For this is the love of God, that we keep his commandments: and <u>his commandments are not grievous</u>. - 1 John 5:3

How will we fare in this test? Do we love His Truth? If we say we do, we must integrate His Truth from Genesis through Revelation as a cohesive unit. In terms of His Law, "his commandments are not grievous" as some would say.

Two Trees, Two Kingdoms, Two Kings

Who will we believe? The complex wording of Paul's writing can easily lead one to conclusions that are in conflict with the Father's Word as it is outlined in the original Scriptural text of the Old Testament. Paul's writing produces a serious obligation on the part of the disciple to discern his messages within the framework of Torah. As we commit to love God and His Truth, we will be shown the Torah connection to our New Testament text.

In doing so, we must learn to identify the influences of the Tree of Life as well as the influences of its counterpart, the Tree of Knowledge of Good and Evil. We are about to see how they enter the picture.

CHAPTER 2

DISCERNMENT

It had been puzzling to me (Karen) how the Armenians and the Calvinists could draw such opposing views from the same Bible. If they were both taken from the book of Truth, then why were some of their teachings diametrically opposed to one another? If there was but one Truth, why were they not in total agreement? Gradually, it became apparent that both theological constructs were based on only partial truth. Neither could convey the entire truth, because each was formulated around only select portions of Biblical text while disregarding other key clarifying passages. Through prayer the Holy Spirit had me suspend everything I had learned from man's teachings to see a more complete picture. Father wanted to reveal it to me using the full scope of His Word. Being prompted to return to the very beginning of Genesis, I was brought to the two trees in the garden, and shown that they represented much more than a couple of trunks with leaves and fruit! These two trees and the character of them were at the core of the entire Biblical message.

Identifying with the dichotomy of the two trees in the Garden of Eden, I (Bill) began to understand the Holy Spirit in a whole new way. I began to realize that my soul understood and had an affection toward the "good" of the Tree of Knowledge. I also began to realize there was a greater living essence of God with the Holy Spirit that my soul did not always want to embrace. Yet Scripture became more alive to me and started to intrigue my mind with a thirst for more.

Together we (Bill and Karen) have built on the concepts of these two trees as we have been led to develop them. The balance of the book will bring out what we have been shown so far about these two trees and the paramount importance of understanding them as it relates to Christians today. Once we grasp the importance of this understanding, the Bible opens up entirely new vistas. We had to ask and answer this question: How are the two trees diametrically opposed and how are they actually similar in nature?

Two Trees, Two Kingdoms, Two Kings

Tree of Life

Two trees were pointed out by God to Adam in the garden:

> [9] And out of the ground made the LORD God to grow every tree that is pleasant to the sight, and good for food; the **Tree of Life** also in the midst of the garden, and the **Tree of Knowledge of Good and Evil**. - Genesis 2:9

The depth of cryptic symbolism that was inherent within these two trees would shape the destiny of man and God's plan for him. The fall of man and his redemption from that fall all stemmed from their constitution. As we mentioned previously, we must build on that which came first to understand that which follows, so returning to Genesis and studying these two trees provides quite an interesting journey:

> [9] **Remember the former things of old**: for I am God, and there is none else; I am God, and there is none like me,
>
> [10] **Declaring** the **end from the beginning**, and **from ancient times the things that are not yet done**, saying, My counsel shall stand, and I will do all my pleasure: - Isaiah 46:9-10

There were many trees that were pleasant to the sight and good for food in the garden. However, the Tree of Life and the Tree of Knowledge of Good and Evil were specified with obvious contrast. The understanding of these two trees is an integral component to understanding everything else in the Word of God. We will be working with these two trees throughout the duration of this book, but we want to introduce them to you one at a time.

The Tree of Life is the first of these two trees referenced by God. We will call it the true tree. (Reasons for this will become more evident momentarily when the two trees are contrasted.)

It is worthy of note that the Tree of Life had a <u>singular</u> notable vibrant characteristic – that being "Life". This word "life" is Strong's #H2416 ("chay"). It is the same word as the "life" from the breath of God which was breathed into Adam in Genesis 2:7. In every respect it would have provided the needed nourishment and sustenance for the life-force that was given to him. The word "chay" does not always pertain to the physical. This Tree of Life was designed to provide spiritual as well as physical nourishment.

This is the same "chay" (life) that we find as the phrase "living thing" in Job's observation of chapter 12:

[7] But ask now the beasts, and they shall teach thee; and the
fowls of the air, and they shall tell thee:

[8] Or speak to the earth, and it shall teach thee: and the fishes of
the sea shall declare unto thee.

[9] Who knoweth not in all these that the hand of the LORD hath
wrought this?

[10] In whose hand is the soul of every **living thing**, and the
breath of all mankind. - Job 12:7-10

Here it reflects the creative hand of God in bestowing the Tree of Life "chay"
to His creation. We find it again a few chapters later in Job in the word "liveth"
in a prophecy of Messiah:

[25] For I know that my redeemer **liveth**, and that he shall stand at
the latter day upon the earth: - Job 19:25

This word "chay" is derived from the Hebrew root word, Strong's #H2421
("chayah") - to *live; to remain alive; to revive from sickness or death; to be
quickened; to preserve alive; to give life; to refresh; to cause to grow; to restore; to revive; to restore to health or life*. This relates to spiritual quickening
as found in the references below from Psalms 119:

[25] My soul cleaveth unto the dust: **quicken** thou me <u>according to
thy word</u>. - Psalms 119:25

[88] **Quicken** me <u>after thy lovingkindness</u>; so shall I <u>keep the testimony of thy mouth</u>. - Psalms 119:88

In each of these verses, the word "quicken" is a related word, "chayah". This
quickening of the soul is the refreshing of Life from the Tree of Life. We see
here that this quickening is associated with the development of God's loving
kindness and obedience to His instructions.

The true tree embodies the Heavenly realm, and Life comes from this realm.

[33] For the bread of God is he which cometh down <u>from heaven</u>,
and giveth **life** unto the world. - John 6:33

When mankind was expelled from the garden after eating the forbidden
fruit, he lost his access to this realm and his access to the Tree of Life itself.
This tree was then guarded with a flaming sword so he could no longer eat
from it:

> [24] So he drove out the man; and he placed at the east of the gar-
> den of Eden Cherubims, and a flaming sword which turned every
> way, to keep the way of the Tree of Life. - Genesis 3:24

This presented somewhat of a conundrum: Only eating of the tree could heal man's corrupted condition, but due to this condition, he was prevented from eating of this tree. Consequently, God designed another means by which man could be granted an incorruptible status and be restored once again to a condition that is fit for Eternal Life:

> [53] For this corruptible must put on incorruption, and this mortal
> must put on immortality.

> [54] So when **this corruptible shall have put on incorruption**,
> and **this mortal shall have put on immortality**, then shall be
> brought to pass the saying that is written, **Death is swallowed up
> in victory**. - 1 Corinthians 15:53-54

Mankind had stepped into the modality of death through eating the forbidden fruit, and only through repentance, healing and restoration could life once again reign in victory over death.

Thus it was that Father began to unfold His plan for restoration by bringing forth from this Tree of Life carefully measured and monitored morsels of nutrition so those who would have a desire toward righteousness might begin to be drawn by Father. In our fallen state, we must be fed Life a tiny bit at a time. Being given too much too quickly would overwhelm us. Those who develop a desire for obedience to God's ways then begin to align to Father's will for mankind. This begins the restoration process back to Him. Eventually they will become equipped to enter into redemption which will once again allow for immortality. This carefully measured nutrition from the Tree of Life is Torah Truth in its various aspects. It is the message of this tree, which is unveiled gradually at the Father's discretion. This message is "the Word" itself, which embodies ALL TRUTH, and is the means by which the sanctification process begins:

> [17] **<u>Sanctify</u> them through thy truth: thy <u>word</u> is <u>truth</u>**. - John 17:17

> [1] **In the beginning was the <u>Word</u>, and the Word was with
> God, and the Word was God**. - John 1:1

As we open our hearts and minds to Father, the Spirit of this tree will draw us into the fullness of its Truth:

[34] For **he whom God hath sent speaketh the <u>words</u> of God**: for God giveth not the Spirit by measure unto him. - John 3:34

[13] Howbeit when he, **the Spirit of <u>truth</u>**, is come, he **will guide you into all <u>truth</u>**: for he shall not speak of himself; but whatsoever he shall hear, that shall he speak: and he will shew you things to come. - John 16:13

Torah is the first five books of the written Word (our Bibles). Within these pages the guidelines for living can be found – the heart and will of the Father, given by Him to mankind (via Moses) from the Tree of Life in His Heavenly realm:

[46] And he said unto them, **Set your hearts unto all the words which I testify among you** this day, which ye shall command your children to **observe to do, all the words of this law**.

[47] For <u>it is not a vain thing for you</u>; because **it is your life**: and through this thing ye shall **prolong your days** in the land, whither ye go over Jordan to possess it. - Deuteronomy 32:46-47

The word "life" in verse 47 is "chay". We are shown here that observing Father's instructions is not only essential, it is our "chay" - our very life-force. Father wants us to set our hearts to that which He instructs so we can share His heart which is being poured out to us.

When we say that Torah is the heart of the Father, it may not be merely a whimsical analogy. The Hebrew language is intricate, and Father's patterning is often exact. It is of interest therefore that the Hebrew word for "heart" is Strong's #H3820 ("leb") and is composed of only two Hebrew letters: "lamed", "beit". Ironically, the first letter of Genesis is a "beit", and the last letter of Deuteronomy is a "lamed". Hebrew is read from the right to the left, so to see the word for "leb" in Hebrew lettering, the "lamed" would be to the right of the "beit". Therefore, the "lamed" being at the end of Torah, and the "beit" at the beginning is the correct ordering for God to show us that this five book package is the gift of His heart to mankind. Oftentimes both Yahweh and Y'shua are said to be the "aleph and tahv" (the first and last letters of the Hebrew alphabet) or the "alpha and omega" (the first and last letters of the Greek alphabet). The actual implication of this phrase in either the Hebrew or the Greek is: the full scope - the beginning and the end, as well as all that is between. Likewise, the final letter and the initial letter of Torah and all that is in between is then the "heart" of Father Who dictated its words. We should not treat His heart lightly!

Two Trees, Two Kingdoms, Two Kings

Though "the Word" as used Biblically can indicate the entire Biblical text, in many references, it simply means: *Torah*. Often the use of this term is even prior to the existence of the New Testament text. The first five books (Torah) were written by Moses, and there is overwhelming evidence of the supernatural patterning of God within it to validate that it was given to Moses by God Himself. The Word is sacred from the beginning of time:

> [140] <u>Thy word is very pure</u>: therefore thy servant loveth it. - Psalms 119:140

> [160] Thy <u>word is true from the beginning</u>: and every one of thy righteous judgments endureth for ever. - Psalms 119:160

> [89] <u>For ever, O LORD, thy word is settled in heaven</u>. - Psalms 119:89

When speaking to Father in His famous prayer, Y'shua acknowledges that Father's Word is Truth and that embracing the Truth of the Word is integral to our sanctification:

> [17] Sanctify them through thy truth: **thy word is truth**. - John 17:17

Father's Truth was amplified by Y'shua as the living Torah many years after it was initially given:

> [14] And **the Word was made flesh**, and dwelt among us, (and we beheld his glory, the glory as of the only begotten of the Father,) full of grace and **truth**. - John 1:14

Then it was directed later still by the Holy Spirit as the indwelling Torah:

> [34] For **he whom God hath sent speaketh the words of God**: for God giveth not the Spirit by measure unto him. - John 3:34

> [13] Howbeit when he, the **Spirit of truth**, is come, he **will guide you into all truth**: for he shall not speak of himself; but whatsoever he shall hear, that shall he speak: and he will shew you things to come. - John 16:13

Thus the nutrition of the Tree of Life was brought to mankind in three different manners: Father, Son, and Spirit. Throughout this transition the congruency of essence is not only essential, but amazingly obvious as the entire Biblical text is harmonized. As the book proceeds we will strive to clarify how this congruency impacts the lives of Believers today.

At the conclusion of time, many will overcome and be allowed once again to eat of the Tree of Life. This overcoming is linked by the second reference below to obedience:

> [7] He that hath an ear, let him hear what the Spirit saith unto the churches; <u>To him that overcometh</u> will <u>I give to eat of the Tree of Life</u>, which is in the midst of the paradise of God. - Revelation 2:7

> [14] Blessed are <u>they that do his commandments</u>, that they may <u>have right to the Tree of Life</u>, and may enter in through the gates into the city. - Revelation 22:14

The Tree of Life is singular in essence, being nothing but good. Likewise all which emanates from this tree is purely good. This good in fact is so much higher than the good we know of today, that there really is no comparison. It is perfect in its goodness. It is holy. When our Bible uses the term "holy" we can relate it back to the singular pure essence of this tree. When we see "holy" in the Old Testament, it typically comes from one of two Hebrew words which are closely related and mean virtually the same thing. It will usually be either Strong's #H6918 ("qadowsh") - *sacred, holy, Holy One, saint, set apart* – OR - Strong's #H6944 ("qodesh") - *apartness, holiness, sacredness, separateness*. In the New Testament it is nearly always Strong's #G40 ("hagios") - *most holy thing, a saint, consecrated; reverend, worthy of veneration*. "Hagios" is derived from Strong's #G53 ("hagnos") - *venerable, sacred, pure*. Thus the New Testament carries through the same connotation.

The essence of this tree permeates all that come from it. The Father is holy. All that He gives us as fruit from this tree is holy. It is perfect. The Son is holy and perfect as well. The message He brings is pure and holy, agreeing totally with the message given by the Father. There is only one state of holiness, and it is shared by all that comes from this tree. This tree provides a singular essence. Its fruit is the Truth, the whole Truth, and nothing but the Truth – not shades of Truth or partial Truth, but pure Truth. The Holy Spirit unites us with the Father through the Son. The word "him" in the following verse is Y'shua:

> [18] For through him we both have access by one Spirit unto the Father. - Ephesians 2:18

The Spirit of God is called the Spirit of Truth because through the Spirit we will be led to all Truth. Y'shua is speaking in the following passage from the Gospel of John:

> [13] Howbeit when he, <u>the **Spirit of truth**</u>, is come, he **will guide you into all truth**: <u>for he shall not speak of himself; but whatsoever he shall hear, that shall he speak</u>: and he will shew you things to come.

> [14] He shall glorify me: for **he shall receive of mine**, and shall shew it unto you.

> [15] **All things that the Father hath are mine**: therefore said I, that <u>he shall</u> take of mine, and shall <u>shew it unto you</u>.
> - John 16:13-15

It is evident here that the Truth relative to the Spirit, the Son, and the Father is singular in essence. Verse 15 indicates that the Son has the things of the Father. Verse 14 says the Spirit receives these things, and verse 13 indicates that the Spirit will impart these things to us. This progression shows us Father to Son, Son to Spirit, and Spirit to man. These things which go from the Father to the Son, from the Son to the Spirit, then from the Spirit to us remain consistent. They do not start out as apples and end up as oranges. This singular Truth runs throughout this tree.

This Truth is from Father:

> [17] Sanctify them through thy <u>truth</u>: thy word is truth. - John 17:17

This Truth is from the Son:

> [6] Jesus saith unto him, I am the way, the <u>truth</u>, and the life: no man cometh unto the Father, but by me. - John 14:6

This Truth is from the Spirit:

> [13] Howbeit when he, the Spirit of truth, is come, he will guide you into all <u>truth</u>: for he shall not speak of himself; but whatsoever he shall hear, that shall he speak: and he will shew you things to come. - John 16:13

The path of Truth and holiness is cohesive, and what we receive through the Spirit will be consistent with that which originated in the Tree of Life and advanced through this line of progression from Father to Son to Spirit to man. It will bring us "chay" (life). There is but one Truth and one essence of this "chay" throughout this progression:

> [26] For as the **Father** hath **life** in himself; so hath he given to the **Son** to have **life** in himself; - John 5:26

[11] And after three days and an half <u>the **Spirit** of **life** from</u>
<u>God</u> entered into them, and they stood upon their feet; ...
- Revelation 11:11

Thus we see that the Father, the Son, and the Spirit embody the Life from the Tree of Life.

The Light of this tree is brought down to us as well through this same progression of Truth. The message (Word) of the Tree of Life provided by the Father is Light for us:

[105] **Thy word is** a lamp unto my feet, and **a light unto my path**.
- Psalms 119:105

Y'shua is a Light for us:

[12] Then spake Jesus again unto them, saying, **I am the light**
of the world: he that followeth me shall not walk in darkness, but
shall have the **light of life**. - John 8:12

We are to walk in God's Light <u>and</u> in the Spirit, making them congruent to one another and illustrating that the Spirit provides a type of this Light to us as well:

[7] But if we **walk in the light**, as he is in the light, we have fellowship one with another, and the blood of Jesus Christ his Son
cleanseth us from all sin. - 1 John 1:7

16] This I say then, **Walk in the Spirit**, and ye shall not fulfill the
lust of the flesh. - Galatians 5:16

As we understand it, the Tree of Life is the tree of Truth, Light and Life. Therefore, all which is derived from this tree maintains the singularity of essence that this tree emanates. The authority of this tree is the Spirit which governs it. It is the Spirit of the Almighty, the Spirit of Truth in our John 16 passage:

[13] Howbeit when he, the <u>Spirit of truth</u>, is come, he will guide
you into all truth: for he shall not speak of himself; but whatsoever
he shall hear, that shall he speak: and he will shew you things to
come. - John 16:13

[17] Now the Lord is that Spirit: and where the Spirit of the Lord is,
there is liberty. - 2 Corinthians 3:17

Likewise there is also but one holiness, and it is carried forth by all who come from this tree. Peter addresses the seriousness of continually striving toward the holiness of Father while we are here:

> [13] Wherefore <u>gird up the loins of your mind</u>, <u>be sober</u>, and <u>hope to the end</u> for the grace that is to be brought unto you at the revelation of Jesus Christ;
>
> [14] <u>As obedient children</u>, not fashioning yourselves according to the former lusts in your ignorance:
>
> [15] But **as he which hath called you is holy, so be ye holy** in all manner of conversation;
>
> [16] Because it is written, **Be ye holy; for I am holy**.
>
> [17] And if ye call on **the <u>Father,</u>** who without respect of persons **<u>judgeth according to every man's work</u>**, **<u>pass the time of your sojourning here in fear</u>**: - 1 Peter 1:13-17

Obedience brings holiness, and holiness is fed by God's living water. The Father is our initial source of this living water:

> [13] O LORD, the hope of Israel, all that forsake thee shall be ashamed, and <u>they that depart from me</u> shall be written in the earth, because they have forsaken <u>the LORD</u>, <u>the fountain of living waters</u>. - Jeremiah 17:13

If we depart from obedience to God's ways and the holiness it brings, we turn our backs on the fountain of living water He provides. Another source of living water is the Son:

> [17] For <u>the Lamb</u> which is in the midst of the throne shall feed them, and shall lead them unto <u>living fountains of waters</u>: and God shall wipe away all tears from their eyes. - Revelation 7:17

Then we see also the Holy Spirit as a source of living water:

> [37] In the last day, that great day of the feast, Jesus stood and cried, saying, If any man thirst, let him come unto me, and drink.
>
> [38] He that believeth on me, as the scripture hath said, out of his belly shall flow <u>rivers of living water</u>.
>
> [39] (But <u>this spake he of the Spirit</u>, which they that believe on him should receive: for the Holy Ghost was not yet given; because that Jesus was not yet glorified.) - John 7:37-39

Thus we see the living water also being provided through the three sources which stem from the Tree of Life itself. In conjunction with this third source of the Holy Spirit we find a rather obscure verse in Acts, but one which may warrant our attention. It provides an inference that the Holy Spirit will instruct those who obey, but that this instruction may be impeded in those who disobey:

> [32] And we are his witnesses of these things; and so is also <u>the Holy Ghost</u>, <u>whom God hath given</u> **to them that obey him**. - Acts 5:32

Thus disobedience to Father's precepts may have bearing on our ability to hear the Holy Spirit:

> [9] He that turneth away his ear from hearing the law, even his prayer shall be abomination. - Proverbs 28:9

This brings us full circle around again to that which we found in Jeremiah 17:13 above, that obedience is linked to receiving the living water.

This then is the simple message of the Spirit of the Tree of Life as we see it: Obedience to God's ways brings support and nurturing by God, and generates holiness before God. He wants us to be One with Him in Spirit, in Truth and in Life. Holiness is a prerequisite to this unity. It is only through separation from the world and alignment to Him that we can achieve the unity with Him which He desires. All that is derived from this tree maintains the singular essence of this tree. When properly viewed, there is no variance in its directives. The theme of holiness prevails throughout the Old and New Testaments, and the means by which we are to attain to this holiness will be the subject of this book.

The Holy Spirit will encourage the Believer to align to the ways of Father, walking in obedience and emulating His holiness. This state of being (holiness) can only be achieved when one strives to comply with the expressed will of Father as found in His Word. While the church would teach that we can rest in our positional purity through belief in Y'shua, we understand that our relationship is to be more than positional. We see that our obligation is to manifest that purity by living as He lived - to pass the time of our sojourning here in a reverent fear of the holiness of the Father and striving to be obedient to His ways. His will is expressed throughout the ENTIRETY of the Biblical text.

Likewise the message of the true Spirit of this tree is a singular unified Gospel message of holiness. Every aspect of this tree emits this essence of singularity through unity. This true Gospel message shows how the ENTIRETY of the Biblical text works together in this essence to provide harmony and structure for the Believer. Through its message we can be led to the holiness we are meant to find, so the Almighty can be our God, and we can be His people:

> [3] And I heard a great voice out of heaven saying, Behold, the tabernacle of God is with men, and he will dwell with them, and they shall be his people, and God himself shall be with them, and be their God. - Revelation 21:3

By the entirety of the Biblical text, we mean that every shred of text is important and cohesive with the rest of Scripture. There is no lack of relevance from one passage to the next. We will cover this more in depth as the book progresses to show how the Law of the Old Testament is being fulfilled by Y'shua, by the Holy Spirit and even by our own lives. The ongoing revelation of Truth from the front cover to the back follows the same line of progression we have witnessed above. It proceeds from the Father down through the Son, then on through the Spirit, and into man. The singularity of this coherent Truth runs throughout the Biblical text. No portion or portions of it are worthy of our exclusion. EVERY piece of the Biblical text from Genesis through Revelation has a place in the puzzle. If any pieces are ignored or left out of the puzzle, the picture is incomplete, and it can veer us off God's intended course for restoration back into the Tree of Life.

In our personal walks with Messiah (as Believers), we (Bill and Karen) are being shown to embrace the Tree of Life in the fullness of its emanation. It has made a profound and significant change of course in our lives. Of course we desire this change for you as well, as you are prompted by the Spirit, and we hope this book will find a place in your hearts.

In summary, our lives have been changed as we were shown to receive the richness of the Tree of Life essence which we followed throughout the Biblical text from Genesis to Revelation. We have come to embrace this singular unified package in all of its aspects. We have reaped from the Truth, Light, and Life of this tree in all three of its different manifestations: 1) the written Word of Torah dictated by the Father and recorded by Moses in our Old Testament text, 2) the living amplified Word of Torah as manifested by Y'shua and chronicled in the four Gospels of our New Testament text, and 3) the revealed Word of spiritual Torah as presented to our hearts and minds by the indwelling Spirit of God and through the reading of the remaining New Testament writings which were Holy Spirit inspired.

We have come to understand the necessity of the concept of singularity through unity - a unified Divine Truth which builds on itself. It is this unity in

Truth that emanates from the Tree of Life. We find great peace through resting in the certainty that these three branches of Torah given to us are united in the essence of the Truth, Light and Life from this one tree. This insures that as we filter any theological instruction through the filter of the <u>entire</u> Bible, we will be able to see whether it aligns with this singular unified Truth. We can then discern between Truth and error, and that allows for us to walk in uncompromised Truth. Then we can begin to align to the holiness which Father desires for us to know intimately. We see Truth then as being the foundation that will mature us as Believers and make us whole.

Tree of Knowledge of Good and Evil

Then we have the Tree of Knowledge of Good and Evil. It is the second of the two trees referenced by God to Adam – the tree from which they were forbidden to eat:

> [16] And the LORD God commanded the man, saying, <u>Of every tree of the garden thou mayest freely eat</u>:
>
> [17] But <u>**of the tree of the knowledge of good and evil**</u>, <u>thou shalt not eat of it</u>: for in the day that thou eatest thereof thou shalt surely die. - Genesis 2:16-17

We will call this tree the contra tree. The term "contra" (as we intend it to be understood) simply means: *against, in opposition to, contrary to*. The path and way which is initiated and propagated by this tree is contra to (against, in opposition to, and contrary to) the path and way intended by the Tree of Life. The spirit of authority for this tree is likewise contra to the true Spirit of the true tree, so we will call it the contra spirit. It is still very active today and is the spirit which has influenced all who have opposed God's ways throughout time. There are various names given to the adversary. Just a few of the myriad of wicked entities of our past, present, or future would be: the serpent, the devil, Satan, Lucifer, the red dragon, the two beasts of Revelation, and the <u>feigned</u> messianic figure to come – the antichrist. Regardless of which of these entities is being referenced, we can be certain that the same contra spirit rules within all of them. It is the spirit of the Tree of Knowledge which embodies the earthly realm and promotes the ways of the world.

This spirit is not benign, and its effects are all-encompassing and lethal. There is a message associated with this spirit which permeates the fallen world in which we live. It is this fallen world which became the designated habitation for mankind after eating of the deadly fruit from this tree. This contra message is imparted at every turn in the fallen realm. The thrust of this contra message evokes departure from God's Tree of Life holiness rather than drawing us into it. The Tree of Knowledge offers its own version of holiness which does not meet with God's standards. We will cover this more as we proceed.

Verse 17 tells us that Adam and Eve were not to eat from the Tree of Knowledge of Good and Evil. God understood that it would bring opposition, reversal and distortion to the ways of the Tree of Life, and deliver in its fruit the promise of death. There was a sacred Truth buried within the physical reality which Father understood. The physical eating of this tree carried with it a metaphysical consequence which would result in spiritual death. Though the bodies of Adam and Eve lived on for many years rather than dying that very day, verse 17 designates that a death would occur that day. God does not lie, and indeed there was a death that day – a spiritual death which would plague Adam and Eve and their descendants throughout time. Not only did they experience a spiritual death that very day, but their bodies also began to deteriorate through the aging process. They were now mortal, and their lives would culminate in physical death. The consequence of death associated with this tree was very real in both a physical and a spiritual sense.

The contra tree is <u>dual</u> in nature, offering a knowledge of both good and evil. More is not always good, and that is certainly the case with this tree, as the duality of this tree is definitely inferior to the singularity of the Tree of Life. The duality of this tree would be a curse on mankind throughout time.

This tree offers the duality of opposing forces (both good and evil) and it abounds in death. The word for "knowledge" in the Tree of Knowledge of verse 17 above is Strong's H1847 ("da`ath") - *knowledge; perception, skill; discernment, understanding, wisdom*. While it sounds wholesome, this knowledge and discernment is to determine good from evil, and they should never have had to taste of evil. It is the tree that embodies the world, and its wisdom is of this world:

> [19] For <u>the wisdom of this world is foolishness with God</u>.
> For it is written, He taketh the wise in their own craftiness. -
> 1 Corinthians 3:19

Just as we correlated Light to Life in the Tree of Life, the same correlation holds true for this tree in the inverse condition: It is the tree of darkness and death. (Death in the spiritual sense is a state of separation from God.) When one fails to be <u>separated TO God</u>, that one ends up being <u>separated FROM God</u>. Straddling the fence is not an option in God's eyes. **<u>Within God</u> one**

abides in <u>Life</u>; <u>without God</u> one abides in <u>death</u>. The importance of this concept cannot be overstated. This Life or death determination lies with God. So, does He see us as being within Him or without Him? To answer this we need to see how we relate to His expectations.

What appears to be good when viewing the "good" of this tree is actually the good of this world, and it simply does not suffice for God's approval. Even the good of this tree is of a drastically inferior grade, as this good is simply a worldly version of good. The spirit of this tree aligns with the world, and the good of this tree simply capitalizes on the good intent of man's human nature. The fruit of man's intent <u>always</u> falls short of the standards of the Almighty. Man in and of himself is not equipped in his fallen state to produce good works which are pleasing to God. Trying to do good while being separated from God is to perform works of self rather than Holy Spirit-driven works. Such works are a practice of futility. When we (separate from the Holy Spirit) try to accomplish what we view as good, it is putting ourselves in the place of God. Only when we are producing works <u>through the Holy Spirit within</u>, are those works acceptable to God. We must realize that it is not our view that matters, but God's view! When we are "without God" we are as an unclean thing to Him and all of the righteousness which we believe we are accomplishing is as filthy rags in Father's sight:

> [6] But we are all as an unclean thing, and all our righteousnesses are as filthy rags; and we all do fade as a leaf; and our iniquities, like the wind, have taken us away. - Isaiah 64:6

Our observations suggest to us that many people are trying to be good. However, they are perhaps doing so without a full commitment to God because they do not want to contend with His standards. By abiding outside of this commitment, they may be mistakenly clinging to the "goodness" of this tree, attempting to secure an avenue of restoration back to the paradise existence which man once knew. Obviously doing the "good" of a worldly nature which benefits man and self is much more preferable than doing "evil" which is designed to harm and destroy man and self. When the good of this tree is contrasted to its evil, it is natural for man to view this good as being "of God". This is not the case though, and man often fails to see that this way or means to achieve restoration is fatally flawed. He fails to understand that it is actually intensely destructive. It brings false assurance of being right with God, while he is still abiding within the tree of death:

> [12] There is a way which seemeth right unto a man, but the end thereof are the ways of death. - Proverbs 14:12

Two Trees, Two Kingdoms, Two Kings

There is a "way" which is designed to bring reconciliation, and we will cover it at length shortly. However, because the "good" of the contra "way" can never produce works which meet with God's approval, the restoration sought by those who are on this venture is only a mirage:

> [8] For by grace are ye saved through faith; and that not of your-selves: it is the gift of God:
>
> [9] **Not of works**, lest any man should boast. - Ephesians 2:8-9

The "works" of verse 9 are works derived by man's flesh (good works of the contra tree), and such works do not lead to Life:

> [8] So then they that are in the flesh cannot please God. - Romans 8:8

This will be illustrated more fully as we proceed. For now though, we will simply say that eating of the forbidden fruit brought man down into the physical mortal realm of the Tree of Knowledge of Good and Evil. As a result, he has had to contend with an evil he should never have known. In this realm he is intimately exposed to the abhorrent effects of evil throughout the entire struggle of his now mortal human experience. The only good he is shown by the spirit who rules this fallen realm is a good which falls exceedingly short of the standards of holiness which God desires for His people.

Not only is the contra tree a tree of duality, the message it brings forth is of a dual nature as well. This characteristic of duality is consistent through all aspects of the knowledge base of the contra spirit. This gospel message arises from the dark and puts forth a "new light" which is not true Light, but appeals to the one who has fallen into error as though it is the true. The name Lucifer means: *light bearer*, and the Bible clearly advises us that the adversary can appear as an angel of light:

> [14] And no marvel; for Satan himself is transformed into an angel of light. - 2 Corinthians 11:14

The contra spirit has no originality; it can only counterfeit or mimic the true. This is due to the Tree of Knowledge having no light of its own, but being reflective in nature. Just as the moon has no light of its own but reflects a considerable amount of light from the sun, likewise the Tree of Knowledge and the spirit that rules it can only reflect the real. It is actually a reflective composite of the garden with its two trees. The good of this tree represents the Tree of Life, and the evil represents the Tree of Knowledge. A very important key to understanding this realm is to realize that <u>everything derived from this contra tree is a counterfeit of the real</u>. Within the contra tree itself we see the picture of the two trees in the garden. However, this contra picture is one step removed from the garden, and the good of this tree is one step removed from the good of the Tree of Life in the garden. The confusion we find in today's world is often derived from viewing the good of this tree AS the Heavenly, when it is simply the reflection of it.

The reflected light that shows forth in the gospel message of the Tree of Knowledge is merely the reflected light of the true Gospel message. Per the laws of physics of our physical realm, <u>reflected light must obey the laws of refraction; therefore, there is always a bending of the rays of light being reflected. This bending produces a degree of distortion</u>. This is true in the spiritual message of this tree as well. The reflected light which composes the contra gospel message is likewise bent through refraction, producing distortion in the message. It is critical that we understand that the distortion of the contra message can be corrosive to the Believer, and can derail his spiritual life.

Once we understand the reflective nature of the contra tree AND that everything of this tree is derived from and mimics the true, Scripture comes alive and discernment increases by leaps and bounds:

> [6] I marvel that ye are so soon removed from him that called you into the grace of Christ <u>unto another gospel</u>:
>
> [7] Which is <u>not another</u>; but there be some that trouble you, and <u>would pervert the gospel</u> of Christ. - Galatians 1:6-7

The contra gospel is not another gospel, it is a perversion of the true, by which the contra spirit defiles the pure and simple message of Y'shua:

> [3] But I fear, lest by any means, as the serpent beguiled Eve through his subtilty, so your minds should be corrupted from the simplicity that is in Christ.
>
> [4] For if he that cometh preacheth **another Jesus**, whom we have not preached, or if ye **receive another spirit**, which ye have not received, or **another gospel**, which ye have not accepted, ye might well bear with him. - 2 Corinthians 11:3-4

Thus it accomplishes the mission of opposing God by distorting His Scriptural intent and drawing His children to follow the wrong spirit into a contaminated theological view and a compromised spiritual walk. The simplicity of Y'shua's Divine singularity with Father has been corrupted, and a version of

Jesus who is not seen to promote the Father's ways has emerged. Developing discernment for the contra message reveals its seductiveness and exposes its danger:

> [12] That they all might be damned <u>who believed not the truth</u>, but had pleasure in unrighteousness. - 2 Thessalonians 2:12

The fallen tree which rules our earthly realm is a tree of duality and opposition. Everything within the knowledge base of this contra spiritual tree and its gospel message is based on something of validity within the Truth of the Tree of Life. However, it invariably comes through the contra tree with a slight twist or distortion which turns it from a message of Life to one of death. All of the basic values, concepts, and deeds which relate to both the good AND the evil of the fallen realm are derived from the true Light of the Tree of Life. It is reflecting something from the Tree of Life in an attempt either to **imitate** it to produce the "**good**" **OR** to **reverse** it to produce the "**evil**". Going back to our definition of contra, we see again that it means: *against, in opposition to, contrary to.* One can come against and oppose by merely derailing that which is on the right track, OR by turning it upside down. Both means are apparent in this contra tree. The good of the tree mimics (but with fatal twists) the good of the true. This derails the true, accomplishing the former. On the other hand, the evil of this tree will turn the good of the true upside down and accomplish the latter. Satanic rituals are often total reversals of Scriptural instruction, and the satanic bible teaches the total opposite for all of God's ways. The opposing forces within this tree attack from both sides those who abide within the Tree of Life:

> [12] Yea, and all that will live godly in Christ Jesus shall suffer persecution.
>
> [13] But evil men and seducers shall wax worse and worse, deceiving, and being deceived.
>
> [14] But continue thou in the things which thou hast learned and hast been assured of, knowing of whom thou hast learned them; - 2 Timothy 3:12-14

The contra gospel message attempts to draw man into the good of this tree. Believers ARE NOT exempt from such attempts, and many have unwittingly fallen prey to this gospel message already. It will be exposed in great detail as we proceed so we can identify it for what it is. As Believers it is vital that we understand what is happening during such times of seduction. The refracted light of the gospel message which emanates from the contra tree contains

<u>aspects</u> of truth, which make it very believable. However, because it is missing major portions of truth, it becomes extremely dangerous to the spiritual state of man.

Being a counterfeit of the real, the gospel message of the contra tree is of necessity based on the same Biblical text as the true Gospel message of the Tree of Life. The spirit of the contra tree appeals to the carnality of the human nature. This part of our being desires to be unaccountable to God, and the nature of this gospel message accommodates that desire. That makes it very easily received in today's society. It is invariably presented in such a manner that its distortion is well concealed. It appears to mankind to <u>be</u> Truth and is absorbed by the mind and heart <u>as</u> Truth. Again, Proverbs comes to mind:

> [12] There is a way which seemeth right unto a man, but the end thereof are the ways of death. - Proverbs 14:12

> [2] Every way of a man is right in his own eyes: but the LORD pondereth the hearts. - Proverbs 21:2

> [8] For my thoughts are not your thoughts, neither are your ways my ways, saith the LORD.

> [9] For <u>as the heavens are higher than the earth</u>, **<u>so are my ways higher than your ways, and my thoughts than your thoughts</u>**.
> - Isaiah 55:8-9

Consequently the contra-based theological structuring is tarnished and defiled. However, once the Believer falls prey to it, internalizes it, and begins to walk in it, the voice of the contra quickly takes charge and the Believer thinks it is the Holy Spirit. This makes it exceedingly difficult for the one who has been derailed to see the error and return to the true understanding of the Word of the Tree of Life.

The one vital bit of understanding we need to retain, is that the message this tree brings forth will look very valid to our natural minds. We must be able to discern its error and the danger it poses for us through our spiritual understanding. The Holy Spirit within will provide the wisdom or the discernment, as well as insight, to harmonize the <u>entire</u> Biblical text.

Many are being seduced into the contra gospel today and are not yet aware that this is happening. This book is dedicated to shedding what we believe to be the Light of the true tree on our Biblical text, so the contra can be discerned for what it is. We pray that any fruit it might bear will spare a great deal of heartache for each of us when we stand before our Maker.

Two Trees, Two Kingdoms, Two Kings

Trees and Fruit

By way of review, there are two trees which provide the backbone for all that Scripture rests on. The contra tree (the Tree of Knowledge) is against, in opposition to, and contrary to the true tree (the Tree of Life). Each tree represents a kingdom, each has a spiritual authority, and each spiritual authority presents a spiritual message. The Tree of Life has the Holy Spirit of God (the Spirit of Truth), and the Tree of Knowledge has the contra spirit of the fallen realm (the spirit of error):

> [6] We are of God: he that knoweth God heareth us; he that is not of God heareth not us. Hereby know we <u>the spirit of truth</u>, and <u>the spirit of error</u>. - 1 John 4:6

Each spirit brings forth the fruit of its tree as a gospel message to the people. The true Spirit brings forth a message of Truth, so this Spirit is called by John the Spirit of Truth. The contra spirit (being a counterfeit which can only reflect the Truth) brings forth a refracted truth which distorts the true, and John calls this spirit the spirit of error. While the Tree of Life is the Truth, the whole Truth, and nothing but the Truth, the contra is merely shades of Truth, partial Truth and Truth with some distortion thrown into the mix.

We can learn to identify these two gospel messages by identifying the fundamentals for which each spirit stands.

The Tree of Life message is one of singularity and harmony. It is operative throughout the entire canon of Scripture when one seeks to find the integrity of Truth throughout its pages:

> [140] <u>Thy word is very pure</u>: therefore thy servant loveth it. - Psalms 119:140

> [160] Thy <u>word is true from the beginning</u>: and every one of thy righteous judgments endureth for ever. - Psalms 119:160

> [89] <u>For ever, O LORD, thy word is settled in heaven</u>. - Psalms 119:89

The contra gospel message is earmarked by and riddled with duality. This duality begins by dividing the Biblical text into opposing segments, which results in **perversion and corruption of** the <u>singularity of intent</u> of the Truth of God's Word.

Jeremiah may have been warning of this contra message with his prophetic message from God:

[13] For my people have committed two evils; they have <u>forsaken me the fountain of **living** waters</u>, and **hewed them out cisterns, broken cisterns, that can hold no water**. - Jeremiah 2:13

The fountain is a singular source which provides the water where the cistern simply holds it. Cisterns that can hold no water would be contra doctrines which depart from the Tree of Life message of living water. The duality of the contra is divisive, breaking the cistern into segments so that it can no longer hold this living water.

If we picture God's Word as a gigantic puzzle, we would say that the perversion of the contra message endeavors to divide the singular puzzle into two portions, leaving neither with a defining edge. There is one puzzle - not two - comprised by the Biblical text. The appealing distortions of this perverted dual message have been responsible for leading many into the deception of the contra. This will become abundantly clear as we continue.

In order to properly discern the interpretation of any portion of text, context is key. The meaning of context is: _text that surrounds a particular word or passage and determines its meaning_. We have been trained to consider a few verses around a statement to establish its context. The Hebraic understanding, which is the basis of the Biblical text, sees context as being the <u>entirety</u> of that Biblical text. At the time the New Testament was being penned, the "entirety" of the Biblical text was basically just the Old Testament Scriptures, as the New had not yet come into being. Now we view both together as being the entirety of the Biblical text:

[16] **All scripture** is given by inspiration of God, and <u>is profitable for doctrine</u>, for reproof, for correction, for instruction in righteousness: - 2 Timothy 3:16

No portion of our Bible is intended to stand alone. Indeed the Bible was sublimely laid out in just such a manner – designed for its fullness to provide the context for interpreting its passages.

To isolate any portion of Biblical text from the balance of Scripture makes it easy prey for the contra message. Paul understood this concept. That is why he praised the Bereans for referencing the Scriptures (simply the Old Testament in Paul's day) to see if what he had said was true:

[10] And the brethren immediately sent away Paul and Silas by night unto <u>Berea</u>: who coming thither went into the synagogue of the Jews.

> [11] These were more noble than those in Thessalonica, in that <u>they received the word with all readiness of mind, and searched the scriptures daily, whether those things were so</u>. - Acts 17:10-11

The context imposed by the contra to verify an interpretation is merely a verse or two on either side of the verse or passage being interpreted. This makes it possible to misinterpret the verse or passage with ease. We must always understand that the context for true interpretation must be substantiated by the entire Biblical text. This is to apply the Pardes "rule of advancement". The subset of Old Testament Truth must be applied to New Testament teaching to validate any New Testament interpretation.

An improper contra interpretation can be determined as error only by using the entirety of the Biblical text as a filter of Truth. Any message we hear should be sifted through this filter. If it conflicts with the Truth of another portion of the Word, then it is not coherent Truth. It is only a partial truth at best - a fundamental characteristic of the contra gospel. When other passages seem to conflict with an interpretation, these other passages are not to be tossed aside. They are red flags to indicate that there is some misunderstanding in the interpretation. When proper understanding is accomplished, there will no longer be conflict. There will be harmony of text from one end of the Bible to the other.

The two gospel messages and their effects are contrasted by Paul in 2 Corinthians:

> [15] For we are unto God a sweet savour of Christ, in <u>them that are saved</u>, and in <u>them that perish</u>:
>
> [16] To the one we are <u>the savour of death unto death</u>; and to the other <u>the savour of life unto life</u>. And who is sufficient for these things?
>
> [17] For we are not as <u>many</u>, which **corrupt the word of God**: <u>but as of **sincerity**, but as of God, in the sight of God speak we in Christ</u>. - 2 Corinthians 2:15-17

The word "sincerity" in verse 17 is Strong's #G1505 ("eilikrineia") - *purity*. The purity of the Word is of the Tree of Life, while the corruption of the Word emanates from the Tree of Knowledge. The savor of "death unto death" signifies the contra tree, while the savor of "life unto life" signifies the true.

We would note here an interesting clue about Truth vs. death that God orchestrated into the very words of His Hebrew language. The Hebrew language is extraordinary – a Divine orchestration. Each individual Hebrew letter has meaning and association with a concept. When Hebrew words are broken down into the letters which form them, more detailed depictions of the words often emerge. The typical Hebrew word that is translated "truth" is Strong's #H571 ("'emeth"). It is spelled with just three Hebrew letters: aleph, mem, and tahv. Aleph is the letter associated with Father. Mem is associated with water, and tahv (being the last letter of the alphabet) is associated with the conclusion. The breaking down of this word then signifies: the Father's water yields the conclusion: Truth. The Hebrew word for the word which is translated "death" is Strong's #H4191 ("muwth"). It too is spelled with only three Hebrew letters: mem, waw, tahv. Two of the three letters are the same in both words. The aleph is not there. Instead we have a waw which is associated with man. The breaking down of this word then signifies: the waters of man yields the conclusion: death. Ephesians 5:26 links water to the Word (teaching). Thus if man tries to interject his own interpretation of the Word to replace the original intent of Father's Word to us (Truth), this departure of man from the Truth of Father's realm of Life leads to the contra realm of death.

The Bible often gives us the contrast between these two realms. It uses opposites to show us the Heavenly spiritual realm (with the singularity of the Holy Spirit, the true) in its opposition to the earthly physical realm (with the duality of the the contra spirit, the counterfeit). However, it is not always as easy to spot as total opposites are, such as black and white. Father sees the gray areas as being black as well. He wants the pure white of holiness, which is what His tree is about. For that reason what Father sees as opposites may not appear as opposites to us because (still being in the fallen state) our minds are not yet purified:

> [5] This then is the message which we have heard of him, and declare unto you, that <u>God is light, and **in him is no darkness at all**</u>. - 1 John 1:5

The contra message appeals to the carnality of our being and actually looks very good and even noble because it DOES contain truth. It cannot reflect the good of the Tree of Life without presenting a convincing portrait of God's good. It cannot reflect the Truth of the Tree of Life without maintaining a veneer of that truth. It is the distortion of the Tree of Life Truth that makes it so dangerous. It is of supreme importance to remember that though the contra gospel message is hopelessly flawed and perverted, <u>the truth it DOES exhibit and the good it DOES set forth is what makes it a good counterfeit</u>. Without those features it would not be believable. It is the way that seems right to the world but leads to death (Proverbs 14:12).

Two Trees, Two Kingdoms, Two Kings

The contra is extremely subtle, so the contra message presented to man throughout time is subtle as well:

> [1] Now <u>the serpent was more **subtil** than any beast of the field which the LORD God had made</u>. And he said unto the woman, Yea, hath God said, Ye shall not eat of every tree of the garden? - Genesis 3:1

John uses the word "anti" in his epistles. He uses it only four times, and always in the term antichrist. It is the first of two words that form the word "antichrist". This word "anti" is Strong's #G473 ("anti") and can mean: *opposed to*. However we must remember that the serpent was the first manifestation of this spirit to man. He was endowed with the distinction of being very "subtle" - tricky in an underhanded and almost undetectable way. While the mission of the contra spirit is to oppose all that is of the Tree of Life, this mission is accomplished through stealth – posing as the true. The contra message with its reflective nature of defiled refraction is presented as the true. Thus he opposes God by subverting and undermining the true message with subtle perversion.

His temptation to have Eve eat of the wrong tree was subtle then, and the fruit of the contra message is waved before us with the same subtle skillfulness today. Father wants us (as Believers) to be cleansed by the washing of His Word. If we do so, we will be able to identify the contra gospel and avoid its pitfalls:

> [25] ... even as <u>Christ also loved the church, and gave himself for it</u>;

> [26] That he might <u>sanctify and cleanse it</u> with the **washing of water by the word**, - Ephesians 5:25-26

When we fail to do so we can fall prey to the contra message, BECAUSE it looks so right. Y'shua warned us that the one who presents the false would look like Believers, but that the danger he posed would be tremendous:

> [15] Beware of false prophets, which come to you <u>in sheep's clothing</u>, but inwardly they are ravening wolves. - Matthew 7:15

> [16] Behold, I send you forth as sheep in the midst of wolves: be ye therefore wise as serpents, and harmless as doves. - Matthew 10:16

<u>**THE SINGULARITY OF THE REAL AND THE DUALITY OF THE COUNTERFEIT IS THE KEY.**</u> <u>It is a key that should never be forgotten.</u>

It is played out in every turn of the pages in our Bibles. To understand this is paramount.

A passage in Matthew addresses this:

> [22] The light of the body is the eye: <u>if therefore thine eye be **single**, thy whole body shall be full of light</u>.
>
> [23] <u>But if thine eye be evil, thy whole body shall be full of darkness</u>. If therefore the light that is in thee be darkness, <u>how great is that darkness</u>!
>
> [24] <u>No man can serve two masters</u>: for either he will hate the one, and love the other; or else he will hold to the one, and despise the other. Ye cannot serve God and mammon. - Matthew 6:22-24

We find the <u>singularity</u> as being the Light of the <u>single eye</u>, and the duality as being the light of the evil eye. The word "evil" here is Strong's #G4190 ("ponēros") - *of a bad nature or condition*. This corrupted condition comes from defiling the singularity of the true Gospel message. This will be discussed in more detail later. Then Y'shua points again to these two gospel messages in chapter 7:

> [13] Enter ye in at the <u>strait gate</u>: for <u>wide</u> is the <u>gate</u>, and broad is the way, that leadeth to destruction, and many there be which go in thereat:
>
> [14] Because strait is the gate, and narrow is the way, which leadeth unto life, and few there be that find it. - Matthew 7:13-14

Again, this will be discussed later, but we want you to have some foretaste as to how this all fits together before we proceed.

Some examples of these types of opposites (many of which can be found in the Word) are: life and death; light and darkness; good and evil; sweet and bitter; spiritual and carnal; spiritual and natural; spirit and flesh; obedience and disobedience; peace and confusion; righteousness and unrighteousness; truth and error; pure and filthiness; pure and defiled; holy and unholy; clean and unclean; etc. When we find any of these (as well as other) opposites listed together as contrasts, we can be virtually certain the reference is about the spiritual Heavenly realm with the true Spirit in contrast to the physical earthly realm with the contra spirit. The contra spirit side of the equation will range somewhere between the good and the evil, but it is crucial to remember that even the good of the contra is wickedness when compared to God's holy standards.

Two Trees, Two Kingdoms, Two Kings

When man is under the influence of the contra spirit rather than the Holy Spirit, he is seen as being unclean and his righteousness is always inadequate (being as filthy rags, per Isaiah 64:6 referenced earlier). Going back to Ephesians 5:25-26 above, it is when we (as Believers) agree to let the Holy Spirit take charge and immerse ourselves in the entirety of the Word, that we can be viewed as properly cleansed and spotless in the sight of the Father.

In Matthew we find the parable of the fruit and the fruit trees. It shows the difference between the fruit of the Tree of Life, and that of the Tree of Knowledge:

> [15] Beware of **false prophets**, which come to you in sheep's clothing, but inwardly they are ravening wolves.
>
> [16] **Ye shall know them by their fruits**. Do men gather grapes of thorns, or figs of **thistles**?
>
> [17] Even so every good tree bringeth forth good fruit; but **a corrupt tree** bringeth forth **evil fruit**.
>
> [18] A good tree cannot bring forth evil fruit, neither can a corrupt tree bring forth good fruit.
>
> [19] Every tree that bringeth not forth good fruit is hewn down, and cast into the fire.
>
> [20] Wherefore **by their fruits ye shall know them**. - Matthew 7:15-20

Again the word "evil" which pertains to the contra fruit is the same word "ponēros" that we found in Matthew 6:23 above, which means: *of a bad nature or condition*. Ministers of the Word are seen here as either good prophets or false prophets. They both wear sheep's clothing. The trees seen here would correlate to the Tree of Life (the good tree) and the Tree of Knowledge of Good and Evil (the corrupt tree). The prophets bring forth the messages of the two trees (the good prophet bringing forth the true, and the false prophet bringing forth the contra). We must not fail to see that the contra (evil or corrupted) fruit message is being served up by those who dress in sheep's clothing, leaders in our religious system. We also must realize that it must be a deceptively and seductively close match to the true, or the parishioners would not receive it.

Some believe that the fruit of a person is the "works" he produces. This is true in other references of the Biblical text. It also has application here to a degree. However, it is evident that verse 20 is telling us that the fruit is readily discernible. We should not have to sit under a pastor at length and follow him around to see his works in order to know if he is a true or a false "prophet". The message he preaches is the fruit. We can immediately validate or reject this fruit by filtering the message through the entirety of the Biblical text. We are warned here that the message from the pulpits of our church in these days may be errant (from the corrupt tree), yet this warning is typically just brushed aside.

When the minister (usually inadvertently) accepts his nourishment from the contra spirit of the corrupt tree, he brings forth teachings which are (again inadvertently) evil per God's standards - fruits of thorns and thistles. These are spiritual thorns and thistles. The fruit goes down smoothly, then the thorns and thistles ensnare the mind of those who consume them, and they never even know it. Even though the false prophet may not at all INTEND to teach falsehood, he fulfills this role. He becomes a "false prophet" simply due to the nourishment that he received to grow the fruit of the message he presents. Going one step further, a majority of our pastors received their instruction from seminaries, and many of these instructional institutions have inadvertently fed our pastors the thorny fruit to pass along to the flock:

> [8] But that which beareth thorns and briers is rejected, and is nigh
> unto cursing; whose end is to be burned. - Hebrews 6:8

The enemy within the contra tree has been at work since the garden of Eden, and is deceiving even the highest of the religious echelons in order to ultimately feed the populace the thorny fruit of the contra message. We emphasize again that it is probably unintentional. The desire is to edify mankind, but this edification is simply of the wrong fruit. The adversary has done its job very well, and the subtlety of the counterfeit is amazing. This should cause any reader of the pastoral vocation to take notice. The balance of the book should be carefully evaluated to see how it aligns to the teachings from any individual pulpit. A pastor is highly accountable for what he teaches:

> [1] My brethren, be not many masters, knowing that we shall re-
> ceive the greater condemnation. - James 3:1

If a pastor has been taught errant theology, he may himself be teaching it to others, and he needs to recognize and correct that immediately. It is our hopeful prayer that any pastors who are bristling at our words would please consider our prospect openly, put their preconceptions on the shelf and allow the Holy Spirit to speak to their hearts. We realize through our own past experience with our own preconceptions that all this may be very difficult to digest. It is not our intent to point fingers at any individual or judge any one person, rather to judge only the fruit that is offered up for consumption. We flinch to even address this passage, yet we feel we must. Even as we present it, we are praying for spiritual eyes to be opened and for the contra gospel to be seen for what it is.

It is far too easy to accept that which is taught, because it is what we are used to hearing – both on the part of the pastor in the seminary and the parishioner who sits in the congregation. It should not be so. There is an obligation to study to show ourselves approved, which means not just taking for granted that the understanding we grew up with and/or what we have been taught is correct:

> [15] Study to shew thyself approved unto God, a workman that needeth not to be ashamed, rightly <u>dividing</u> the word of truth. -
> 2 Timothy 2:15

The word "dividing" in this verse is Strong's #G3718 ("orthotomeō"). Though it means: *to divide*, it is not division in the sense of cutting apart the text into opposing segments. It actually means: *to discern properly; equivalent to doing right; without perversion; to proceed on straight paths; hold a straight course; to teach the truth directly and correctly.*

It is simply to cut away error and derive the straight course of the pure intent of the Word.

Since Scriptural references which have been extracted from the context of the entirety of the Word can be misinterpreted, we cannot validate a message simply because it uses a few isolated passages from our Biblical text. Even when entire books of the Bible are taught, there can be misinterpretation, because the view of the seminary of choice is presented and the contrasting passages from Torah are not presented.

Parishioners often depend almost exclusively on their pastors for their spiritual food, as many are too absorbed in their daily grinds to give the Bible the attention it deserves. That too is in need of adjustment, but nonetheless, the state of the world is what it is, and pastors have a <u>very</u> high calling which comes with a great deal of responsibility.

Please understand that this book is not written to bring any accusation, denunciation, or reproof to anyone (including pastors), but rather to prompt individual introspection for pastor and parishioner alike. We wish to reach out in God's love with what is a very delicate subject, in order that the end result might lead to correction as needed and potentially save souls:

> [19] **Brethren**, <u>if any of you do **err from the truth**, and one con-</u><u>vert him</u>;

> [20] Let him know, that he which converteth the sinner from the error of his way shall **save a soul from death**, and shall hide a multitude of sins. - James 5:19-20

Twice in the previous Matthew 7 passage regarding false prophets we are cautioned to evaluate the fruit of the teachings we hear! "Ye shall know them by their fruits." This fruit can only be identified by studying the entirety of the Biblical text to show ourselves approved. The entirety of the Word upholds the singularity of the Tree of Life Gospel message from cover to cover. If <u>an</u> <u>interpretation</u> of any portion of Scripture comes into conflict with other portions of Scripture, it is an invalid interpretation of thorny fruit and should be rejected. The integrity of the entire Bible as a congruent message is foundational to the Truth of the Tree of Life.

If we do not have time to read, study, and evaluate Scripture for ourselves, perhaps we are too busy. <u>Most of us</u> can find time to do this, if we adjust our priorities just a bit, and the Bible indicates that it needs to be a priority of very high order. It is likely we will be shown how to make a segment of our day available for this, if we make it a matter of prayer to Father. A "through the Bible in a year" version of the Bible breaks the text into small portions, and is ideal for the one who has little time. Time in the Word is so very important though, and it is worthy to be put it at the top of our priority list. It is the means by which we are to discern truth.

The importance of discernment relative to instruction is so important that Y'shua presented it in yet another parable application:

> [24] Another parable put he forth unto them, saying, The kingdom of heaven is likened unto a man which sowed good seed in his field:

> [25] But **while men slept**, <u>his enemy came and sowed tares</u> <u>among the wheat</u>, and went his way.

> [26] But when the blade was sprung up, and brought forth fruit, then appeared the tares also.

[27] So the servants of the householder came and said unto him, Sir, didst not thou sow good seed in thy field? from whence then hath it tares?

[28] He said unto them, An enemy hath done this. The servants said unto him, Wilt thou then that we go and gather them up?

[29] But he said, Nay; lest while ye gather up the tares, ye root up also the wheat with them.

[30] Let both grow together until the harvest: and in the time of harvest I will say to the reapers, Gather ye together first the tares, and bind them in bundles to burn them: but gather the wheat into my barn. - Matthew 13:24-30

Wheat and tares look very much alike. There is a notable difference though that becomes apparent when the breeze blows. The wheat will bend with the breeze, and the tares remain stiff and upright. In spiritual application the breeze is the voice of God's Spirit. The tares do not respond to this voice, but heed only the voice of the contra. They look like the real thing, but their failure to bend to the voice of the true shows them for what they are.

The wheat seed is the correct teaching of the true Gospel message. Its ultimate end is to produce holiness in the life of the Believer. This holiness in the Believer is as wheat. Wheat is the main ingredient of most bread. Y'shua is THE Bread of Life:

[48] I am that bread of life. - John 6:48

As wheat, we are to follow in the footsteps of Y'shua, and become a type of Bread of Life as well – Life as produced through our alignment to the ways of the Tree of Life.

The seed of the tares is the errant teaching of the contra gospel message through misapplication of the words of our Bible. Its ultimate end is to produce unholiness in the life of the Believer – tares. The tares look very similar to wheat, and they believe themselves to be wheat. However, the wheat is flexible – yielding to the <u>fullness</u> of the true Gospel message, and the tare yields only to the distorted version, being stiff (stiff-necked and stubborn) toward the fullness of the true message. The future of the wheat and the tares is drastically different. Per verse 30, it is as different as Life and death. The Tree of Life produces Life, and the Tree of Knowledge produces death; so too do their seeds.

The true wheat seed message that produces wheat instills compliance to the Father's will which engenders obedience and effects holiness:

> [8] I delight to do **thy will**, O my God: yea, **thy law** is within my
> heart. - Psalms 40:8

This indicates that the Law is indelibly linked to the Will of the Father. Law (when properly discerned) and grace complement one another and work together in singularity to bring about holiness. (We will see this in detail as we proceed.) Holiness produces the wheat which yields to the <u>fullness</u> of the true Gospel message.

The harmony of Scripture provides the interpretation which supports the singularity of essence throughout both Testaments. Conversely, the distorted interpretation of the duality of the tare seed message pits certain Scriptures against others. This message virtually always serves to project the Law as being evil and grace as being good – the Old Testament as being evil, and the New as being good. It removes the obligation of Pardes from the validation process. The end result is tragic. Acceptance of this teaching effectively removes expressed moral precepts of God's Law from this present dispensation. The resulting effect of this message almost always engenders rebellion or disobedience to portions of God's moral precepts, culminating in unholiness (iniquity). It produces the tare which yields only to the distorted gospel message. It is stiff (stiff-necked and stubborn) toward obedience to Father's ways, as expressed by the entirety of the Word and the voice of the true Spirit:

> [27] For I know thy **rebellion**, and thy **stiff neck**: behold, while
> I am yet alive with you this day, ye have been **rebellious**
> **against the LORD**; and how much more after my death? -
> Deuteronomy 31:27

> [23] For **rebellion** is as the sin of witchcraft, and **stubbornness**
> is as **iniquity** and idolatry. Because thou hast **rejected the**
> **word of the LORD**, he hath also rejected thee from being king.
> - 1 Samuel 15:23

Being stiff-necked and stubborn is linked here with rebellion to Father (the LORD) and His Word. This rebellion is seen as iniquity, and even idolatry, because we have put something before the Word of instruction He gave us. <u>We have ALL done this, but we are to recognize what we have done and repent of it.</u> The contra gospel throws out the guidelines Father gave us in the Word, so we do not recognize transgression, which prevents repentance from occurring:

Two Trees, Two Kingdoms, Two Kings

> [158] I beheld the transgressors, and was grieved; because they kept not thy word. - Psalms 119:158

Old Testament Torah is often called the Law. While it contains the Law, it is first and foremost Father's teaching and instruction, which is designed to keep us in alignment with Him and His ways. If we abide in His ways, we have great blessings in store. It is vital that we come to realize that Father loves us tremendously, and His patience is beyond understanding:

> [6] Seek ye the LORD while he may be found, call ye upon him while he is near:
>
> [7] Let the wicked forsake his way, and the unrighteous man his thoughts: and let him return unto the LORD, and he will have mercy upon him; and to our God, for he will abundantly pardon. - Isaiah 55:6-7

However, we adamantly believe that His view of what is right and wrong does not equate with what is commonly taught today. Nor is His view of what constitutes iniquity in alignment with most of today's teachings.

The sowing of the tares message among the brethren happens when we are asleep – not fully focused on the fullness of Father's Truth. The enemy lures us to sleep, then plants the seed. He is no fool. Once we eat, fully digest, and integrate the seed (gospel message) of the tares, we become one with it! The seed of a tare will not produce wheat! We must uproot the seed of the tare and plant the seed of wheat in its place.

The contra spirit desires to stealthily draw us from the true Gospel message to its own, and there is implication that its false prophets (if we allowed them to do so) will draw away even the elect:

> [24] For there shall arise false Christs, and **false prophets**, and shall shew great signs and wonders; insomuch that, **if** *it were* **possible, they shall deceive the very elect**. - Matthew 24:24

We should note that the words "it were" are in italics which indicates that they are not in the original manuscripts, but were added for a more fluid flow of our English text. If we take out the added words, we get: "if possible, they shall deceive the very elect". We are warned repeatedly in the Word how seductive and insidious the contra can be!

If the elect (who desire to do as Father wills) are to be drawn away, it can hardly be accomplished by the contra spirit revealing itself as the adversary.

The elect would not budge. It has to be through subtlety that is very intense and insidious. We have to be convinced that the distortion is the real:

[14] I will ascend above the heights of the clouds; I will be like the most High. - Isaiah 14:14

Therefore the most important thing to understand relative to contrasting the true Gospel message to that of the contra is that the contrast is not stark. We will be contrasting the bright Light of the true to the somewhat dimmer, or less bright reflective light of the contra. The total darkness of the contra can be the end result of abiding within the "evil" side of this fallen tree, but typically (at least at first) it is merely the dimmer light of the "good" side which entraps the elect, and it will appear to be the real thing! That makes it hard to spot, and many Believers will not recognize it:

[6] If we say that we have fellowship with him, and walk in darkness, we lie, and do not the truth: - 1 John 1:6

Every underlined phrase in this verse is crucial to understand. We would break it down as follows: We can very often think we are walking with God, and yet be in what He sees as darkness. It is so easy to inadvertently lie to ourselves about our walk, because we do not know we are under the contra's influence. We do not abide in God's Truth, because the contra prevents us from recognizing it.

As we proceed, we will look at the contra gospel message in exquisite detail and compare it to the true. In the meantime we will state generally that the knowledge which abounds within the contra tree is far from that of the knowledge of the unified vibrant Life of the true tree. Rather than the unity which abides in Life, the contra's form of knowledge offers the duality of opposing forces (both good and evil) and it abounds in death. The unity of Life comes forth through the Spirit:

[2] And the spirit of the LORD shall rest upon him, the spirit of wisdom and understanding, the spirit of counsel and might, the spirit of knowledge and of the fear of the LORD;

[3] And shall make him of quick understanding in the fear of the LORD: and he shall not judge after the sight of his eyes, neither reprove after the hearing of his ears: - Isaiah 11:2-3

We realize that Isaiah is speaking of the Spirit of God which would come to rest on Y'shua, but that same Spirit is available to each of us today who come to belief in Y'shua, and it can do the same for us.

Two Trees, Two Kingdoms, Two Kings

Then Paul paints the contrast of this contra wisdom of the world to that of the true message of the Heavenly:

> [19] For <u>the wisdom of this world is foolishness with God</u>. For it is written, He taketh the wise in their own craftiness. - 1 Corinthians 3:19

> [6] Howbeit we speak wisdom among them that are perfect: yet <u>not the wisdom of this world</u>, nor of the princes of this world, that come to nought:

> [7] But we speak <u>the wisdom of God in a mystery, even the hidden wisdom, which God ordained before the world unto our glory</u>:
> - 1 Corinthians 2:6-7

There is no comparison to the depth of knowledge, wisdom, and understanding offered by our Father through His Spirit of the Tree of Life to that which is offered by the spirit of the contra tree. Likewise, <u>even the good side of the tree of duality is far removed from the good of the Tree of Life, falling profoundly short of God's holy standards</u>. To operate within the contra gospel message is to cling to death rather than to be transformed to the Life of the Tree of Life.

Life is found only in the Tree of Life message, which is identified by its singularity of essence throughout the Biblical text. Death is hinged to the contra message which is identified by the duality and divisiveness it emits, through splintering the true essence of singularity. The filter of the entirety of the Word (<u>the filter of Life</u>) must be utilized in order to project accurate meaning to the passages of our Bible. Death will not fit through this filter, in that it mangles God's Truth and is characterized by its opposing dualities. It is so very important to use this filter to spot the impostor!

CHAPTER 3

CONGRUENCY

After getting a grip on these two trees, we (Bill and Karen) were better able to understand that there is a singular thread of integrity that runs through the essence of the Tree of Life and that this thread winds throughout the pages of the Biblical text as well. Consequently, we began to realize that God's precepts as expressed in Torah actually could not be in opposition to the God's precepts as expressed in our New Testament text. We were beginning to understand Paul's writings from a slightly different perspective. This is when the excitement began to build. Validating it would prove to be a tedious process, but yet the end result would be ever so freeing. Could the whole Bible really work together as a single harmonious unit?

Biblical Harmony

[16] **All scripture** is given by inspiration of God, and is profitable for doctrine, for reproof, for correction, for instruction in righteousness: – 2 Timothy 3:16

Note that this does not say "Our doctrinal choice of Scripture", nor does it say our New Testament Scripture; it says, "ALL Scripture". To use the ENTIRETY of the Word as the filter for doctrinal belief is to be Berean, which Paul praised, even in reference to his own teachings:

[11] These were more noble than those in Thessalonica, in that they received the word with all readiness of mind, and **searched the scriptures** daily, whether those things were so. - Acts:17:11

The "Scriptures" referenced by Paul which the Bereans searched did not merely INCLUDE the Old Testament; these Scriptures WERE ENTIRELY of the Old Testament. The New had not yet been written. It is critical to understand that Paul knew his teachings would align with the precepts found in the

Two Trees, Two Kingdoms, Two Kings

<u>Old Testament</u>. He praised the Bereans for confirming his words by comparing them to the Old Testament precepts. This would validate the true meaning of his message and assure that his words would NOT be misunderstood. If we are to properly understand Paul's writings today, this must be front and center of our foundation of study as well. Many pastors of the churches in our New Testament era have chosen to largely ignore the Old Testament and its Torah instruction in the formation of their theology. Remember that such reference to the Old Testament is what Paul stated as being the noble way to address his writings. Even churches which feature "Berean" as a part of their church name rarely live up to the intent behind this reference. To do so they would have to faithfully align the Old Testament precepts with their New Testament instruction. Paul's words were always spoken in correlation to the Torah text. The failure to align Paul's words to the Old Testament is where confusion regarding the messages within his epistles begins, and where the contra gospel message appears to get its foothold and momentum.

Various seminaries espouse differing versions of denominational instruction, based on their particular perspectives of the Biblical text. These diversified views have developed over the centuries. One doctrinal stance will contrast with another because of the divisive nature of the contra message structure. If they were teaching the true unified Tree of Life message, there would be little if any disharmony of theological belief:

> [3] Endeavouring to keep **the unity of the Spirit** in the bond of peace.

> [4] There is **one** body, and **one** Spirit, even as ye are called in **one** hope of your calling;

> [5] **One** Lord, **one** faith, **one** baptism,

> [6] **One** God and Father of all, who is above all, and through all, and in you all. - Ephesians 4:3-6

Divide and conquer has taken a toll on the Christian belief system. Such divisiveness is the earmark of the contra gospel. We readily acknowledge that virtually each and every pastor in our churches today has a deep desire to draw the people entrusted to him into a closer relationship with God. It is a vocation of intense commitment. His inspiration and desire almost always stems from the relationship he has found through his upbringing in the church, and his experience is built around the particular understanding of the denomination he attended. He typically then attends a seminary which further expounded on those beliefs and entrenches them in his heart and mind. The subtle contra gospel is available in a lot of flavors. Each seminary has its favorite. The serving of this thorny fruit by a pastor to his congregation is then the byproduct of a devoted heart that has simply been fed the wrong diet.

For this reason we believe pastors are often totally unaware that they have come into jeopardy and have put their congregations into jeopardy with them. By not properly uniting all of Scripture as a congruent whole, they lose the coherence, balance and harmony between the physical application of written Torah to the spiritual amplification of it. Paul actually contrasts the New with the Old in order to help people understand the spiritual transition to the New; not to replace the Old with the New.

The Old and New were not meant to stand in opposition to one another. They are both in God's Word, and are meant to be integrated and work together as one. The two do not work against one another, but are designed to work together in sovereign unity to bring us to the singularity of the Tree of Life essence. Many segments of the Hebrew Roots movement are now dedicated to finding this harmony – committed to merging the Old with the New to find the total picture. Only when the two are seen in tandem can the Tree of Life speak to the heart of the Believer properly.

Unity Rather than Strife

In the fullness of Tree of Life Truth, our Old Testament and New Testament versions of God's Word are unified in singular essence to bring the Believer's entire being (physical and spiritual) into the <u>sanctified state of holiness:</u>

> [17] **Sanctify** them <u>through thy **truth**</u>: **<u>thy word is truth</u>**. - John 17:17

> [23] And the very God of peace **sanctify you <u>wholly</u>**; and I pray God your whole spirit and soul and body be preserved blameless unto the coming of our Lord Jesus Christ. - 1 Thessalonians 5:23

In chapter 4 of 1 Thessalonians we find that the sanctification in verse 3 leads to the holiness in verse 7:

> [3] For this is the will of God, **even your <u>sanctification</u>**, that ye should abstain from fornication:

> [4] That every one of you should know how to <u>possess his vessel in sanctification and honour;</u>

> [5] Not in the lust of concupiscence, even as the Gentiles which know not God:

[6] That no man go beyond and defraud his brother in any matter: because that the Lord is the avenger of all such, as we also have forewarned you and testified.

[7] For <u>God hath not called us unto uncleanness</u>, but **unto <u>holiness</u>**. - 1 Thessalonians 4:3-7

The unity of the Old entwined with the New brings spiritual Life, beginning with Torah and emanating throughout the balance of the Biblical text. Conversely, the duality of the contra message estranges the Old from the New which causes discordance and eventually leads to spiritual death. Our thoughts and our walk as Believers today must exhibit God's unified essence.

The sanctification process to put uncleanness away and enter into holiness involves both the physical Law of Torah and the spiritual Law of our New Testament text:

[12] Wherefore **the law is holy**, and **the commandment holy, and just, and good**. - Romans 7:12

[14] For we know that **the law is spiritual**: but I am carnal, sold under sin.

[15] For that which I do I allow not: for what I would, that do I not; but what I hate, that do I.

[16] If then I do that which I would not, I consent unto <u>the law that it is good</u>. - Romans 7:14-16

[2] For the **law of the Spirit** of life in Christ Jesus hath made me free from the law of sin and death. - Romans 8:2

No more would death result from failure to properly adhere to the totality of Torah Law. The Law of the Spirit emanates from the Law of Torah, bringing Life to the Believer. It will never refute or countermand that which came before it, but will overlie it to bring Life:

[31] Do we then make void the law through faith? God forbid: yea, we establish the law. - Romans 3:31

The Old Testament Torah Law seems to have more relativity to our physical bodies, while the "Law of the Spirit" in the Romans 8 passage above would relate more to the spiritual portion of our being. A passage in Hebrews seems to allude to both, referring to the Torah Law as "carnal commandment", and the "Law of the Spirit" as being "after the power of endless Life":

[16] Who is made, not after **the law of a carnal commandment**,
but <u>after the power of an endless life</u>. - Hebrews 7:16

This does not mean however, that the physical Law should be left standing
in the dust. It too has a purpose since the carnal part of our being must be
brought under subjection in the walk of sanctification. Otherwise, we could
not be wholly sanctified. Both aspects are needed in order to bring about the
full sanctification of body, soul, and spirit indicated in the 1 Thessalonians
chapter 5 passage above. They need to work together in unity to lead one into
holiness. In this manner we properly possess our vessels and complete this
sanctification process of 1 Thessalonians 4:

[4] That every one of you should know how to <u>possess his vessel
in sanctification and honour</u>; - 1 Thessalonians 4:4

[7] For <u>God hath not called us unto uncleanness</u>, but **unto holiness**. - 1 Thessalonians 4:7

Neither the physical or the spiritual aspects should be neglected.

The light of the body should be the singular Light which brings harmony to
the total Truth of God as found in the entirety of His Word to us. If we divide
the Word into the opposing camps of Old and New Testaments and we ignore
the Old, then the eye is no longer single (unified), and the body does not have
the Light it needs for total sanctification. It is only when the unified singular
shines within, that the WHOLE shall be full of Light:

[36] If thy whole body therefore be full of light, having no part dark,
the <u>whole</u> shall be full of light, as when the bright shining of a
candle doth give thee light. - Luke 11:36

The Believer can then become WHOLLY sanctified in body, soul, and spirit.

Most Christian theology now construes the "freedom from bondage" mentioned by Paul as being "freedom from the Old Testament Law". We will soon
show what we believe Paul actually meant. The serpent helped Adam and Eve
find that same kind of "freedom" from God's instruction, and look at the cost.
In those days God had only one rule of Law – that they were to abstain from
the fruit of the contra tree, yet Eve believed the contra spirit, that it would
be alright to step out in "freedom" and depart from that Law. Consequently,
Y'shua had to suffer unbelievable humiliation and physical anguish, then suc-
cumb to death, which He should never have had to endure. It was the only
way to breach the chasm that man's new found "freedom" caused between
man and Father.

Two Trees, Two Kingdoms, Two Kings

The freedom that we (as Believers) are granted today is a fragile commodity. It is wrapped around the intent of Father and contingent on the keeping of His precepts. We are warned in Hebrews that there is no more sacrifice if we choose to depart from God's ways after receiving Y'shua:

> [26] For if we sin wilfully after that we have received the knowledge of the truth, there remaineth no more sacrifice for sins, - Hebrews 10:26

God's gift of grace through Y'shua offers propitiation (expiation, appeasement, placation) for remission of sins which are <u>past</u> (prior to our initial belief):

> [25] Whom God hath set forth to be a propitiation through faith in his blood, to declare his righteousness for the **remission of sins that are <u>past</u>**, through the forbearance of God; - Romans 3:25

Peter refers to our sins that are "past" as being "old sins". He indicates that we cannot afford to forget that we have been purged from our "old sins", and fail to conform to the image of Y'shua after being purged of them. It could endanger our election!:

> [3] <u>According as his divine power hath given unto us all things that pertain unto life and godliness,</u> **<u>through the knowledge of him that hath called us</u>** <u>to glory and virtue</u>:

> [4] Whereby are given unto us exceeding great and precious promises: <u>that by these ye might be partakers of the divine nature, having escaped the corruption that is in the world through lust</u>.

> [5] And beside this, **giving all diligence**, add to your faith virtue; and to virtue knowledge;

> [6] And to knowledge temperance; and to temperance patience; and to patience godliness;

> [7] And to godliness brotherly kindness; and to brotherly kindness charity.

> [8] For if these things be in you, and abound, they make you that ye shall neither be barren nor unfruitful in the knowledge of our Lord Jesus Christ.

> [9] But he that lacketh these things is blind, and cannot see afar off, and <u>hath forgotten that he was purged from his **old sins**</u>.

[10] Wherefore the rather, brethren, **give diligence to make your calling and election sure**: for if ye do these things, ye shall never fall:

[11] <u>For so an entrance shall be ministered unto you abundantly into the everlasting kingdom of our Lord and Saviour Jesus Christ</u>. - 2 Peter 1:3-11

The sins committed after our belief are to be acknowledged and confessed in order to find forgiveness for them:

[9] If we confess our sins, he is faithful and just to forgive us our sins, and to cleanse us from all unrighteousness. - 1 John 1:9

Confession is the acknowledging of our sin, then we are to repent of it and walk away from it:

[8] Bring forth therefore fruits meet for repentance: - Matthew 3:8

[19] As many as I love, I rebuke and chasten: be zealous therefore, and repent. - Revelation 3:19

Henceforth, we are to remain in God's Truth, abstaining from sin:

[26] For if we sin wilfully after that we have received the knowledge of the truth, there remaineth no more sacrifice for sins, - Hebrews 10:26

Willful departure from God's ways without going through the process of repentance shows a disregard for the sacrifice of Y'shua that is intended to provide our redemption. Such deviant behavior is viewed by God as "doing <u>despite</u> to" (treating with spite or malice, contempt, defiance, or disregard) the Spirit of Truth that we were given by God's grace:

[29] Of how much sorer punishment, suppose ye, shall he be thought worthy, who hath <u>trodden under foot the Son of God</u>, and hath <u>counted the blood of the covenant, wherewith he was sanctified, an unholy thing</u>, and hath <u>done **despite** unto the Spirit of grace</u>? - Hebrews 10:29

[4] For it is impossible for those who were <u>once enlightened</u>, and have tasted of the heavenly gift, and were made partakers of the Holy Ghost,

[5] And have tasted the good word of God, and the powers of the world to come,

> [6] <u>If they shall fall away</u>, to <u>renew them again unto repentance</u>;
> seeing <u>they crucify to themselves the Son of God afresh, and put</u>
> <u>him to an open shame</u>. - Hebrews 6:4-6

The grace provided by the atoning blood of Y'shua does not afford one the license to murder. The Torah commandment of "thou shalt not kill" is still in effect. Yet when the soul is truly repentant, even the one who has murdered is able to find forgiveness now by this grace. His sin is then blotted out as though it never happened in the eyes of God. We are not to sin just because we are under grace, but when we do sin, we are able (by confession and repentance) to find atonement through grace:

> [1] My little children, these things write I unto you, that ye sin not.
> And if any man sin, we have an advocate with the Father, Jesus
> Christ the righteous: - 1 John 2:1

The question might be: What constitutes sin? It is very simply and explicitly defined in 1 John:

> [4] Whosoever committeth sin transgresseth also the law: for **sin**
> **is the transgression of the law**. - 1 John 3:4

The perceived "freedom" to disregard (and therefore walk in disobedience to) the moral fabric of Father's Law after coming to Y'shua is very dangerous ground. It is a feigned freedom which actually leads to the bondage of sin. The departure from Father's moral precepts is a breach of His singularity. This departure stems from the distortion of the contra message. It derails our walk toward holiness and leads to death:

> [2] For the **law of the Spirit** OF LIFE IN CHRIST JESUS <u>hath</u>
> <u>made me free from the</u> **law of sin and death**. - Romans 8:2

This law of sin and death is the law of sin nature that courses through man's veins and drives him to iniquity. Death is (at the very least) spiritual separation from God. It is the penalty that hangs over man's head due to sin, until he receives his pardon through Y'shua. It is from this law of sin (the sin nature) and death (the consequential penalty) that we are to be freed. We are given power over this desire to sin when we yield to the Holy Spirit within. It is through God's Truth (which leads to obedience) that we find real freedom — <u>freedom from the law of sin and death</u>:

> [32] And ye shall know the truth, and **the truth shall make you**
> **free**. - John 8:32

[36] If the Son therefore shall make you free, **ye shall be free indeed**. - John 8:36

God's **Truth** is what frees us. It is the total truth which is found by piecing together the entirety of the Biblical text. This truth frees us from the law of sin and brings us into conformity with Y'shua. It provides the perfect peace the Father intends for us to have – a peace that passes all understanding:

[165] **Great peace have they which love thy law**: and nothing shall offend them. - Psalms 119:165

[7] And the peace of God, which passeth all understanding, shall keep your hearts and minds through Christ Jesus. - Philippians 4:7

Y'shua modeled the obedient servant role (to which we are to conform) when He was here:

[13] Ye call me Master and Lord: and ye say well; for so I am.

[14] If I then, your Lord and Master, have washed your feet; ye also ought to wash one another's feet.

[15] For **I have given you an example**, that ye should do as I have done to you. - John 13:13-15

[29] For whom he did foreknow, he also did predestinate to be conformed to the image of his Son, that he might be the firstborn among many brethren. - Romans 8:29

If we are to be conformed to the image of Y'shua by following His example, we should remember at all times that Y'shua was obedient to the Father and His precepts, even to death on the cross:

[8] And being found in fashion as a man, he humbled himself, and became obedient unto death, even the death of the cross. - Philippians 2:8

We know He was obedient to Father's precepts throughout His life, as this is what qualified Him to be the Passover lamb without blemish. As we understand it, had He violated even one of the Father's precepts, it would have been sin (a spiritual blemish) for Him, and would have prevented Him from becoming the blemish-free sacrifice which would purchase our redemption.

To abandon the knowledge of the truth that we are to adhere to Father's precepts is to walk instead in the feigned truth and freedom that the contra offers.

Two Trees, Two Kingdoms, Two Kings

We actually step away from the conformity to Y'shua and fall under the bondage of sin once again. It is a frightening thought.

The reflected dimmer light from the spirit of the tree of duality is routinely <u>perceived</u> as new Light (Matthew 6:22-23) in today's world. Ironically, it actually <u>fills the vessel with spiritual darkness</u>. This reflected light promotes a perceived validation for the "freedom" which man's carnal nature desires – freedom from Father's Law. The carnal nature of the flesh is pleased with this new-found "freedom" and therefore resists any attempt to bring the true Light into focus:

> [12] There is **a way which seemeth right** unto a man, but the end thereof are **the ways of death**. - Proverbs 14:12

This "way" is when man enters the wide gate of deception and allows the contra spirit to begin to rule his walk. It is the broad path which leads to the death linked to the contra tree. It grieves us to consider that many well-intentioned Christians may be propelled in that direction because they have come to believe that departure from Torah is endorsed in our New Testament era:

> [13] Enter ye in at the strait gate: for wide is the gate, and **broad is the way**, **that leadeth to destruction**, and <u>**MANY** there be which go in thereat</u>: - Matthew 7:13

It will <u>seem SO right</u>! The wrong track is dangerous for a Believer who should know the whole truth! When a man who has received Y'shua begins to pull away from the fullness of God's Law, that man can easily fall into iniquitous actions and be seen by God as holding His Truth in unrighteousness:

> [17] For therein is <u>the righteousness of God revealed from faith to faith</u>: as it is written, <u>The just shall live by faith</u>.
>
> [18] For <u>the wrath of God is revealed from heaven against all ungodliness and unrighteousness of men</u>, <u>**who hold the truth in unrighteousness**</u>; - Romans 1:17-18

This indicates that eventually God's wrath can be stirred by this type of hypocritical behavior. The concept of "from faith to faith" in verse 17 would be from the beginning of faith through the initial belief of Y'shua's atoning blood to the end of faith where sanctification is fully realized. We'll cover this more fully shortly. If the Believer is derailed during this process, it can be devastating, unless he gets back on track.

The Holy Spirit (the Light of the <u>singular</u> eye) will attest to and bring one to find the <u>harmony</u> of <u>**ALL**</u> Scripture (keeping one aligned to Father's Law).

Conversely, the contra spirit will usurp the harmony any way it can (luring one away from Father's Law through seductive perversion). The contra is all about destruction! The Holy Spirit inhabits the unified patterning and structure of the Father, where the contra spirit inhabits the division, chaos and disorganization of the adversary:

> [1] In the beginning God created the heaven and the earth.
>
> [2] And the earth was without form, and void; and darkness was upon the face of the deep. And the Spirit of God moved upon the face of the waters.
>
> [3] And God said, Let there be light: and there was light. -
> Genesis 1:1-3

The words "without form" is a single Hebrew word, Strong's #H8414 ("to-huw"). Among its meanings are: *emptiness, wasteland, wilderness; place of chaos*. The word "void" also implies emptiness and waste. It was associated with darkness. The entire creative process was about bringing light to darkness and order to chaos. Thus it is for the Believer. We are to bring light to the darkness of our sin by overcoming it with the Light of Life. We are to bring order to chaos by yielding to God's ways in our lives.

Father is then about restoration and reuniting everything in purity under a single unified paradigm. On the other hand, in the duality of the contra Tree of Knowledge version, the diversification of light and dark inhabit the same area. This brings constant instability, uncertainty, separation and confusion. Unless God intervenes, things are all mixed up, and chaos reigns:

> [33] For **God is not the author of confusion**, **but of peace**, as in all churches of the saints. - 1 Corinthians 14:33

The word "saints" here is Strong's #G40 ("hagios") - *most holy; set apart; holy; sanctified; consecrated*. The churches of the saints then were those where God's Truth was taught in its fullness, where the parishioners walked in holiness. Peace abounds when the holiness of God's Truth prevails.

Conversely, everything is duality with the contra version. The Old Testament is viewed as the dark, and the New Testament as the light – the physical Law as the dark, and the spiritual Law as the light. The contra gospel causes division in the Kingdom of God's true Light, and when we splinter God's Light, we bring in confusion and transgress God. However, in the singular eye of His Light, all is Light and there is no conflict. All aspects work in harmony as a congruent whole.

Two Trees, Two Kingdoms, Two Kings

Confusion and peace are opposites. We are not to harbor division, chaos, and confusion, but embrace the unity of structure and harmony. Among other attributes, the singularity of the Tree of Life Gospel is depicted as being a gospel of peace in Ephesians. It is a part of our armor:

> [14] Stand therefore, <u>having your loins girt about with truth</u>, and having on the breastplate of righteousness;
>
> [15] And <u>your feet shod with the preparation of the **gospel of peace**</u>; - Ephesians 6:14-15

We would note that this gospel of peace follows having the loins girt about with God's Truth. Just as the voice of the Almighty brought order out of chaos in creation, He continues to do so through the Son. He brings peace with the abundant Life He offers. The enemy offers destruction which goes hand in hand with chaos and uncertainty:

> [10] The thief cometh not, but for to steal, and to kill, and **to destroy**: I am come that they might have life, and that they might have it more abundantly. - John 10:10

To "destroy" in this verse is Strong's #G622 ("apollymi") - *to render useless, to put out of the way, to put an end to, to ruin, to kill*. That is precisely what disharmony and chaos accomplishes. Disharmony of the Scripture renders the congruency of its substance as useless and effectively ruins its influence on the Believer. The Holy Spirit is about restoration - encouraging growth and transformation. Conversely, the contra spirit destroys it. The contra steals peace by drawing us away from Father's harmony of Truth, bringing death through destruction wrought by chaos.

The singularity of the Tree of Life message is secured through its repetition – being brought first by the Father, then through the Son, then by the Holy Spirit. The consistency brought forward from Genesis to Revelation reverberates the harmonic structure of order and continuity. The spiraling cyclical repetition found in the progressive narrative is the earmark of the Tree of Life essence. Likewise, embracing this patterning is integral to understanding the Tree of Life Gospel message.

The word "pattern" or "patterns" is used 16 times in the Word, and is an established trademark of the Almighty. It is in direct contrast to confusion:

> [40] And look that thou <u>make them after their pattern</u>, which was shewed thee in the mount. - Exodus 25:40

Likewise the word "order" is used some 100 times, and is in direct contrast to disorder:

[37] The pure candlestick, with the lamps thereof, even with the lamps <u>to be set in order</u>, and all the vessels thereof, and the oil for light, - Exodus 39:37

Pattern and order mark the ways of God. His spiraling cyclical patterning provides order and continuity. It is the means by which we find singularity of mind and will with Father. Conversely, the one who is trapped in the message of duality is double-minded and unstable.

James speaks of double-mindedness:

[8] A **double minded** man is **unstable** in all his ways. James 1:8

The duality of the contra message creates this type of thinking. There is peace in the uniformity and structure of the true, as contrasted to the instability of the duality of the contra:

[27] <u>Peace I leave with you</u>, my peace I give unto you: <u>not as the world giveth</u>, give I unto you. Let not your heart be troubled, neither let it be afraid. - John 14:27

There is implication here by Y'shua that there is a difference between the peace He provides and that which comes via the world (contra). Those who have the world's contra version will perceive that they have peace. This is because the carnal nature is content with the "freedom" of indulgence it has been granted by the fragmentation of the contra gospel message. However contentment with the carnal is no substitute for a true inner abiding peace. That is why the peace of the world's version cannot compare with that of Y'shua's version. The world's peace will fall far short of the deep-seated and full peace which permeates the mind and heart of the one who is staid on the true Gospel message – the deep-seated peace that is rooted in the stability and harmony of the singular true Light.

James had one more comment about the ones who were caught up in the double-mindedness of the tree of duality:

[8] <u>Draw nigh to God, and he will draw nigh to you</u>. Cleanse your hands, ye sinners; and <u>purify your hearts, ye double minded</u>. - James 4:8

Father has promised that He will draw near to us if we draw near to Him. We are to purify our hearts by leaving the double mindedness behind:

> [7] Sanctify yourselves therefore, and be ye holy: for I am the
> LORD your God.

> [8] And ye shall keep my statutes, and do them: I am the LORD
> which sanctify you. - Leviticus 20:7-8

We draw nigh to Him in the singularity of Truth that comes from the Light of the single eye, sanctifying the entire man in holiness, both physically and spiritually:

> [23] And the very God of peace <u>sanctify you wholly</u>; and I pray
> God your whole spirit and soul and body be preserved blameless
> unto the coming of our Lord Jesus Christ. - 1 Thessalonians 5:23

Shema

One of the most primary reasons the Jewish faith cannot accept the role Y'shua played for mankind is their steadfast belief that there is only one God. To them, Y'shua being God would be a second God, and in contradiction to their "one God only" stance. This one God is based on a passage in Deuteronomy which is known as Shema:

> [4] Hear, O Israel: **The LORD our God is <u>one</u> LORD**: -
> Deuteronomy 6:4

In all actuality the message of Shema is a bit more inclusive, presenting <u>the Godhead</u> as being of a singular essence. Paul states it as follows:

> [5] And there are <u>differences of administrations</u>, but **the same
> Lord**.

> [6] And there are <u>diversities of operations</u>, but it is **the same God**
> which worketh all in all. - 1 Corinthians 12:5-6

The word "God" in Deuteronomy 6:4 is Strong's #H430 ("'elohiym") which is usually written as "Elohim". It is the word which is translated "God" not only here but throughout the Old Testament text. Elohim is actually the plural form of Eloah. Though the word "Elohim" is plural in form, it is presented in this verse as though it is singular. That is because Elohim is a unified singularity of sorts which implies multiplicity in form yet singularity of essence. Our concept of a corporation indicates multiplicity in personnel but a unified singular enterprise of ambition. In a similar fashion, the title of Elohim indicates a multiplicity of manifestation with a unified singular essence of truth. In the Deuteronomy verse above, the very term Elohim carries with it the understanding of the unified singular essence of the Tree of Life. Then it verifies that indeed this unity is singular in essence with Yahweh (the LORD).

The word "one" in this same Deuteronomy verse is Strong's #H259 ("'echad"). It can simply mean: *one*. However, the use of this word "echad" is normally considered to be a type of "unity in diversity" which is actually in total harmony with the intent of this verse. The Hebrew word "yachid" means: *one and only one*. It was not used here. The use of the word "echad" here indicates the combining of multiple aspects into a singular whole. We find this in its other uses as well. It is the same word used in Ezekiel 37 when the two sticks come together as "one" (echad) stick:

> [19] Say unto them, Thus saith the Lord GOD; Behold, I will take the stick of Joseph, which is in the hand of Ephraim, and the tribes of Israel his fellows, and will put them with him, even with the stick of Judah, and make them <u>one</u> stick, and they shall be <u>one</u> in mine hand. - Ezekiel 37:19

Likewise, it is used in Genesis 2:24 when the husband and wife come together to become "one" (echad) flesh:

> [24] Therefore shall a man leave his father and his mother, and shall cleave unto his wife: and they shall be <u>one</u> flesh. - Genesis 2:24

When we understand the layering of the words in Shema we understand that it is communicating a unified singularity of Elohim (God) which brings our Tree of Life message. The singularity of essence is a singularity of purpose and truth in this message. The multiplicity is the means by which the message is disseminated. Likewise God's singular essence of Truth is disseminated in three different forms: our written Torah instructions (given by Father to Moses), amplified by the living Torah (Y'shua), and facilitated by the indwelling Torah (the Holy Spirit). These three forms of Torah Truth with singular essence work together as a type of unity in diversity - one (echad).

This Deuteronomy verse is known as "Shema" because that is the first Hebrew word of the verse. The word "hear" in this same verse is Strong's #H8085 ("shama`"). However, we should understand that to render this word as merely being "hear" is a rather incomplete definition. In reality the definition is much broader, meaning not only: *to hear*, but also: *to perceive, to understand, - to hear, to listen to, to give heed to, obey, to consent and agree to, to yield to and obey, and to sound the alarm and make proclamation.*

If we are to be true to this command, we must not only consider the full inference of it, but come to agree with it, walking in obedience to the fullness of God's Torah Truth. We must sound the alarm regarding the current devastating misunderstanding of its implications, and proclaim the fullness of the singularity which permeates it.

It is this concept that the contra spirit desires to rip out of the Word, but Y'shua confirms the importance of this multiplicity of the Godhead – this unity of singularity. In the New Testament He repeats its wording for those who have "ears to hear" (perceive and understand):

> [29] And Jesus answered him, **<u>The first of all the commandments</u> is**, **Hear, O Israel; The Lord our God is one Lord**: - Mark 12:29

In the New Testament the Greek word which is translated as "God" is Strong's #G2316 ("theos"). The Septuagint is the Greek version of the Old Testament. In it, the word "Theos" is used where the Hebrew uses Elohim, so we know Theos correlates to Elohim in the Biblical text. This tells us that the use of Elohim continues throughout the New Testament as well.

The importance of what we are saying now should not be overlooked! Please note carefully that Y'shua did NOT say the Shema of Old Testament Scripture was defunct. Instead He confirmed its validity and His words verify that the Old Testament and the New are forever indelibly linked. Not only is it valid, but it is THE SINGLE MOST IMPORTANT commandment, as explicitly stated by Y'shua. The two verses which follow this New Testament Shema are expressed in Matthew as well, and they are often thought of as the two great commandments, but Mark tells us that the foundation for these two greatest commandments is none other than the understanding of Shema:

> [29] And Jesus answered him, <u>The **first of all the commandments** is, Hear, O Israel; The Lord our God is one Lord</u>:
>
> [30] And thou shalt love the Lord thy God with all thy heart, and with all thy soul, and with all thy mind, and with all thy strength: this is the first commandment.
>
> [31] And the second is like, namely this, Thou shalt love thy neighbour as thyself. There is none other commandment greater than these. - Mark 12:29-31

Understanding Shema is the means by which we can properly express our love to Father and our fellow man. If we remove Shema from the picture, our understanding will be incomplete, and our expression of love to God and our fellow man will not be properly grounded in Torah Truth.

The Torah of the Old Testament was brought to us in living form through Y'shua:

> [14] And the Word was made flesh, and dwelt among us, (and we beheld his glory, the glory as of the only begotten of the Father,) full of grace and truth. - John 1:14

What Word became flesh? It was the Torah – the very Word of the Father which preceded the arrival of Y'shua into our earthly realm. Y'shua simply brought the Father's Word of Torah to us in living form so we could more fully identify with it. He WAS the living Torah.

Even before His birth, this identity of Tree of Life Torah Truth within Y'shua was made known to John the Baptist <u>through the Holy Ghost</u>. Elizabeth was still pregnant with John, and Mary still pregnant with Y'shua, when an extraordinary event occurred. So strong was the Torah presence within Y'shua, that the yet embryonic babe John jumped within Elizabeth's womb when the yet embryonic Y'shua came into his presence:

> [34] Then said Mary unto the angel, How shall this be, seeing I know not a man?
>
> [35] And the angel answered and said unto her, The Holy Ghost shall come upon thee, and the power of the Highest shall overshadow thee: therefore also that holy thing which shall be born of thee shall be called the Son of God.
>
> [36] And, behold, thy cousin Elisabeth, she hath also conceived a son in her old age: and this is the sixth month with her, who was called barren.
>
> [37] For with God nothing shall be impossible.
>
> [38] And Mary said, Behold the handmaid of the Lord; be it unto me according to thy word. And the angel departed from her.
>
> [39] And Mary arose in those days, and went into the hill country with haste, into a city of Juda;
>
> [40] And entered into the house of Zacharias, and saluted Elisabeth.
>
> [41] And it came to pass, that, when Elisabeth heard the salutation of Mary, the babe leaped in her womb; and Elisabeth was filled with the Holy Ghost: - Luke 1:34-41

Two Trees, Two Kingdoms, Two Kings

Indeed we are shown by Paul that the fullness of the Godhead was present in Y'shua:

> [8] Beware lest any man spoil you through philosophy and vain deceit, after the tradition of men, after the rudiments of the world, and not after **Christ**.
>
> [9] For in him dwelleth all the **fulness of the Godhead** bodily. - Colossians 2:8-9

Likewise is the Truth of the Tree of Life within Him, per Ephesians:

> [21] If so be that ye have heard him, and have been taught by him, as the **truth is in Jesus**:
>
> [22] That ye put off concerning the former conversation the old man, which is corrupt according to the deceitful lusts;
>
> [23] And be renewed in the spirit of your mind;
>
> [24] And that ye put on the new man, which after God is created in righteousness and true holiness. - Ephesians 4:21-24

This Truth directs us to be renewed in the spirit of our mind so we can put off the old man (of disobedience and sin) and put on the new (of righteousness and holiness). We are to walk in the singularity of Torah Truth through obedience to the fullness of the Law. We find this Law presented in the written Torah (first five books of our Old Testament text), then amplified by the living Torah (Y'shua), and finally directed by the indwelling Torah (the Holy Spirit).

However, when we choose to disregard Father's precepts in Torah Scripture, we align again with the contra spirit. This is seen as disobedience by Him, and as Believers it leads to a hobbling walk:

> [2] Wherein in time past ye walked according to the course of this world, according to the prince of the power of the air, the spirit that now worketh in the children of **disobedience**: - Ephesians 2:2

It is to return to our past state of corruption, rather than remaining in the present state of righteousness through Y'shua:

> [20] For if after they have escaped the pollutions of the world through the knowledge of the Lord and Saviour Jesus Christ, they are again entangled therein, and overcome, the latter end is worse with them than the beginning.

[21] For it had been better for them not to have known the way of righteousness, than, after they have known it, to <u>turn from the holy commandment delivered unto them</u>.

[22] But it is happened unto them according to the true proverb, The dog is turned to his own vomit again; and the sow that was washed to her wallowing in the mire. - 2 Peter 2:20-22

The carnal nature has quite an appetite, and with the guidance of the contra spirit and the newly perceived "freedom", the body will delight to walk after the flesh. It should not be so. We are to walk only in the true Spirit:

[16] This I say then, <u>Walk in the Spirit, and ye shall not fulfill the lust of the flesh</u>. - Galatians 5:16

[7] Be not deceived; God is not mocked: for <u>whatsoever a man soweth, that shall he also reap</u>.

[8] For <u>he that soweth to his flesh shall of the flesh reap corruption</u>; but <u>he that soweth to the Spirit shall of the Spirit reap life everlasting</u>. - Galatians 6:7-8

[6] That which is born of the flesh is flesh; and that which is born of the Spirit is spirit. - John 3:6

[63] It is the spirit that quickeneth; the flesh profiteth nothing: the words that I speak unto you, they are spirit, and they are life. - John 6:63

[8] So then <u>they that are in the flesh cannot please God</u>. - Romans 8:8

We must understand that some of what we have come to perceive as being acceptable practice in the Christian walk may be seen as fleshly by Father. That is because the common pulpit teachings have put a breach between our understanding and His. There are many today who (even inadvertently) indulge the flesh in opposition to Father's precepts. They do so while believing they are "living in the Spirit". They confuse a walk that is "in the flesh" <u>by God's standards</u> with a walk that is "in the Spirit" by man's standards. The contra message has caused this breach in our understanding of God's ways. By walking according to man's standards we may be walking under the power and authority of the contra spirit while thinking we are walking by God's Spirit. Such is the deceptive power of this false spirit. Paul himself says this should not be:

[16] This I say then, Walk in the Spirit, and ye shall not fulfill the lust of the flesh.

[17] For the flesh lusteth against the Spirit, and the Spirit against the flesh: and these are contrary the one to the other: so that ye cannot do the things that ye would. - Galatians 5:16-17

[25] <u>If we live in the Spirit</u>, **let us also walk in the Spirit**. - Galatians 5:25

To walk in the Spirit is to put the fullness of God's Light into perspective and abide within it. The entire Bible must harmonize or it becomes ineffective to produce the results God intends. To destroy the harmony of Scripture is to disavow the essence of its Tree of Life design. Again, the Holy Spirit will attest to and bring one to find the harmony of **ALL** Scripture, while the contra spirit will usurp the harmony any way it can. The Spirit of Truth will uphold the Word of Truth. There must be singularity of essence and unanimity in our Biblical comprehension of Truth.

Father's patterning is all about restoring peace through harmony, balance, and unity:

[22] And the glory which thou gavest me I have given them; that they may be one, even as we are one: - John 17:22

This is Truth. Shema is an enigma of multiplicity in a unified singularity of essence. Our God is ONE. This is Truth. A proper understanding of Shema is necessary in order to see that the precepts in written Torah are still needed in our lives today. John 14 relates the Truth of this unified essence when he explains how God's commandments relate to loving Him:

[17] Even the **Spirit of truth**; whom the world cannot receive, because it seeth him not, neither knoweth him: but ye know him; for he dwelleth with you, and shall be in you.

[18] I will not leave you comfortless: I will come to you.

[19] Yet a little while, and the world seeth me no more; but ye see me: because I live, ye shall live also.

[20] **At that day ye shall know that I am in my Father, and ye in me, and I in you.**

[21] **He that hath my commandments, and keepeth them, he it is that loveth me**: and he that loveth me shall be loved of my Father, and I will love him, and will manifest myself to him.

[22] Judas saith unto him, not Iscariot, Lord, how is it that thou wilt manifest thyself unto us, and not unto the world?

[23] Jesus answered and said unto him, **If a man love me, he will keep my words: and my Father will love him, and <u>WE</u> will come unto him, and make our abode with him**.

[24] **He that loveth me not keepeth not my sayings: and the word which ye hear is not mine, but the Father's which sent me**.

[25] These things have I spoken unto you, being yet present with you.

[26] <u>But the Comforter, which is the Holy Ghost, whom the Father will send in my name, he shall teach you all things, and</u> **<u>bring all things to your remembrance, whatsoever I have said unto you</u>**. - John 14:17-26

First he calls God's Spirit the Spirit of Truth. The Word which came from Father is Truth (John 17:17), Y'shua is Truth (John 14:6), and now the Spirit is Truth (John 14:17). How many Truths are there? If there are not three Truths, then they are one and the same Truth and essence. Y'shua is speaking in this passage, and says that we show Him we love Him by keeping that which He has spoken. He also clarifies that what He has spoken came from the Father. Will the Father contradict Himself? Then the Spirit will bring to our remembrance the things Y'shua said from the Father. They are SINGULAR in essence, all stemming back to the Father. We should look closely at the words **"If a man love me, he will keep my words: and my Father will love him, and <u>WE</u> will come unto him, and make our abode with him"**. The word "WE" here indicates that both the FATHER and the SON will take up residence within the one who adheres to God's ways. We know also that God's Spirit comes to abide within us per 1 Corinthians:

[16] Know ye not that ye are the temple of God, and that the Spirit of God dwelleth in you? - 1 Corinthians 3:16

Yet this John 14 passage says that the Father and the Son will BOTH come to abide within us as well. Does this happen THROUGH the indwelling presence of God's Spirit? We do not fully understand it all now, but it is full-blown proof that the essence of the Father AND the Son AND the Spirit are one and the same. They can not abide within man together in any form or manner without being one.

Two Trees, Two Kingdoms, Two Kings

The essence is the same now as it was from the beginning when Torah was originally penned. John reemphasizes this "from the beginning" eleven times in his epistles. One such time is:

> [24] **Let that therefore abide in you, which ye have heard <u>from the beginning</u>**. <u>If that which ye have heard from the beginning shall remain in you,</u> **ye also shall continue** in the Son, and **in the Father**. - 1 John 2:24

We are not to scrap that which we have heard from the beginning but we are to allow it to abide in us so that we can continue in **both the SON <u>and</u> the FATHER**.

The consistency of God's Truth is our promise, enabling us to avoid deception and learn to discern properly. Therefore, when the essence of one Scripture <u>appears</u> to contradict another, there must be a reconciliation:

> [16] **<u>All</u> scripture** is given by inspiration of God, and is profitable for doctrine, for reproof, for correction, for instruction in righteousness:
> - 2 Timothy 3:16

This indicates that no Scripture is to be exempted from the formation of doctrine, reproof or correction of our fellow man, or instruction in righteousness. In order for that to be the case, it must all agree. Thus Paul's words MUST be reconciled to the balance of Scripture, or they are heretical and should not be in the same book with the balance of Scripture. We can rest assured that the latter is not the case, so the former must apply. If an interpretation (analysis) of Paul's words does not align with the balance of Scripture, then it is not Paul's words that are wrong, but rather the interpretation of them. Paul's words can always be reconciled with the balance of Scripture, but the majority of church teachings today simply don't take this into account. Without a steadfast love and adherence to Old Testament principles which are rooted in Torah, the study of Paul's words can so easily be misunderstood.

Interpretation which results from such misunderstanding involves extracting Paul's words, segregating them from their relationship to Torah text, and viewing them via the contra linear perception. This then destroys the unity of essence within the balance of the Biblical text and divides God's Kingdom into vying factions. The concept that "walking in the Spirit" is somehow opposed to "the Law" effectively separates the Holy Spirit from the Father and sometimes even the Son, creating diversity in the essence of the Spirit's message from that of its originating source. When such diversity exists, it is evidence of being led by the wrong spirit.

The armor listed in Ephesians 6 is primarily defensive in nature except one piece, which is to be used offensively. God's Word is this single piece of offensive armor - the sword of the Spirit:

> [17] And <u>take</u> the helmet of salvation, and <u>the sword of the Spirit,</u> <u>which is the word of God</u>: - Ephesians 6:17

How can the sword of the Spirit be the Word of God if the essence of the Spirit is not aligned to that Word? The Word of God is equated with the sword again in Hebrews, where we see it is to serve as a guide in dividing and discerning:

> [12] For <u>the word of God</u> is quick, and powerful, and sharper than any <u>twoedged sword</u>, piercing even to the <u>dividing</u> asunder of soul and spirit, and of the joints and marrow, and is a <u>discerner</u> of the thoughts and intents of the heart. - Hebrews 4:12

This dividing is not to divide one portion of Scripture from another, it is to divide truth from error. Truth comes through the spirit, and error afflicts the soul. We will work with that more a bit later. If the Word of God (this sword) was not consistent, it would be useless to discern and separate truth from error in our thoughts and heart.

In order to differentiate between truth and error, we must study the entire Word of Truth so we can learn how to properly discern it. We study by comparing and contrasting various Scriptural passages until we find the harmony. This in turn brings a fuller and richer understanding of the Word and the nature of God, and builds our relationship with Him. This is an ongoing process for the dedicated disciple of God. This harmonious understanding then shows us how to divide truth from error:

> [15] Study to shew thyself approved unto God, a workman that needeth not to be ashamed, <u>rightly **dividing** the word of truth</u>. - 2 Timothy 2:15

As mentioned previously, the word "dividing" in this verse is Strong's #G3718 ("orthotomeō") - *to discern properly; equivalent to doing right; without perversion; to proceed on straight paths; hold a straight course; to teach the truth directly and correctly.*

We are to use the whole Word of Truth, discerning it properly to distinguish truth from error, so we can proceed on straight paths, teaching truth directly and correctly. Since the Word was designed for us as our sword in order that we might divide between truth and error, it should be evident that the words within it would harmonize rather than conflict and be pitted against one another in that process:

> [17] But he, knowing their thoughts, said unto them, **<u>Every king-dom divided against itself is brought to desolation</u>**; and <u>a house divided</u> against a house <u>falleth</u>. - Luke 11:17

There must be total Biblical harmony within the Kingdom of the singular Light of Life, or it will fall – even as the dual kingdom of the contra is the fallen realm. The Holy Spirit works in our hearts to harmonize the Word from cover to cover, and the contra spirit creates havoc through errant interpretations of the Word to steal away the harmony of the Word:

> [3] Endeavouring to keep **the unity of the Spirit** in the bond of peace.
>
> [4] There is **one** body, and **one** Spirit, even as ye are called in **one** hope of your calling;
>
> [5] **One** Lord, **one** faith, **one** baptism,
>
> [6] **One** God and Father of all, who is above all, and through all, and in you all. - Ephesians 4:3-6

As we see it, God's patterning is all about harmony, balance, and unity. This is Truth. Shema is about multiplicity within a unified singularity of essence. Our God is ONE, and so is the Word He provided for our use. This understanding encourages us to become holy as He is holy. As we walk in Tree of Life unity, we adhere to the guidance of the Spirit, while abiding in the Son, and obeying the Father. They are ONE.

Who Is Melchisedec?

The unity of Shema is further illustrated through the mysterious figure depicted as Melchisedec. There is very little mention of this figure in the Bible, and very little if anything is otherwise known about Melchisedec. However, as we work through this section, we will bring this figure into focus and begin to see how the singular unity of the Tree of Life message under girds the true Gospel of the Old and New Testaments. Although the spelling is slightly different, Melchizedek in the Old Testament is the same as Melchisedec in the New Testament.

We will begin with the first mention of Melchisedec in Genesis in the days of Abraham, while his name was yet Abram. (For ease of reading we will use the spellings of "Abraham" and "Melchisedec" throughout this section unless they are within Biblical quotations.)

Abraham was returning from a victory in war when he encountered Melchisedec at the Valley of Shaveh:

> [18] And **Melchizedek <u>king</u> of Salem** brought forth bread and wine: and he was **the <u>priest</u> of the most high God**.
>
> [19] And <u>he blessed</u> him, and said, Blessed be <u>Abram</u> of the most high God, possessor of heaven and earth:
>
> [20] And blessed be the most high God, which hath delivered thine enemies into thy hand. And <u>he gave him tithes</u> of all. - Genesis 14:18-20

Melchisedec was king of Salem. Salem means: *complete or <u>perfect peace</u>* which is symbolic of Heaven - God - the Tree of Life, from whence comes <u>peace that passes all understanding</u>:

> [7] And <u>the peace of God, which passeth all understanding</u>, shall keep your hearts and minds through Christ Jesus. - Philippians 4:7

Melchisedec brought forth bread and wine and blessed Abraham. It was a blessing by the priest of the Most High God, possessor of Heaven and earth; this was truly a blessing from the Spirit of the Tree of Life. Not only was Abraham blessed, but a form of communion (with the bread and wine) took place between Abraham and God. This was a precursor or a foreshadowing of the communion which Y'shua would one day offer mankind.

Melchisedec was a priest of the Most High God. What is meant here by "most high", and relative to what? Again, our focus is directed to the Heavenly – the Tree of Life. We believe this is a phrase which epitomizes the Spirit of the Tree of Life. The spiritual authority of the Melchisedecian priesthood is the same spiritual essence which emanates through the Father, the Son, and the Holy Spirit into the realm of man. Thus the Melchisedecian priesthood of the Most High God is the priesthood of the highest spiritual authority. Abraham realized that God had delivered his enemies into his hand. Not only did Melchisedec bless Abraham, but Abraham (in turn) paid homage to God through his offering of tithe to Melchisedec. By this action he was subscribing to this priesthood. This not only endorses the priesthood of Melchisedec, but it substantiates a spiritually rooted connection between God and man, to set the stage for God's covenant with Abraham in the following chapter. The interaction of Abraham with Melchisedec proclaims a linkage of the highest spiritual authority of the Heavenly realm to the earthly realm below. It can be seen as the Most High God spiritually sowing a seed of His Tree of Life into the realm of man.

The bread and wine being a type of communion underscores the interaction of the Heavenly with the earthly. It not only indicates the relevance of the priesthood of Melchisedec, but it establishes the significance of the Melchisedecian priesthood for our restoration to the Tree of Life. It implements the spiritual pathway for the return to God.

This restoration involves both the physical and spiritual aspects of man. Our spiritual advancement is initially dependent on physical alignment, but physical alignment is derived from a more spiritual source. The two are interwoven. The Levitical priesthood and its instructional base found in our Old Testament text would soon usher in the physical aspects of this spiritual authority.

As we proceed now to the New Testament, we will look at both priesthoods and come to realize how they interlock in the singular unity of the Tree of Life message.

Our New Testament text reminds us that Levi had not yet been born when Abraham met with Melchisedec. He was still in the seed of Abraham's loins. Levi would not be born for several generations in the future. Yet Abraham's payment of tithe to Melchisedec actually shows that the Levitical priesthood would be beneath that of the Melchisedecian. Though it would be steadfastly connected to the Melchisedecian priesthood through Abraham, it would be subordinate to it. We find this passage in the book of Hebrews to be instrumental in clarifying this relationship and the hierarchy of the two priesthoods:

> [4] <u>Now consider how great this man was, unto whom even the patriarch Abraham gave the tenth of the spoils</u>.

> [5] And verily they that are of the sons of Levi, who receive the office of the priesthood, have a commandment to take tithes of the people according to the law, that is, of their brethren, though they come out of the loins of Abraham:

> [6] But he whose descent is not counted from them received tithes of Abraham, and blessed him that had the promises.

> [7] And without all contradiction **the less is blessed of the better**.

> [8] And here men that die receive tithes; but there he receiveth them, of whom it is witnessed that he liveth.

> [9] And as I may so say, <u>Levi also</u>, who receiveth tithes, <u>payed tithes in Abraham</u>.

[10] For <u>he was yet in the loins of his father, when Melchisedec met him</u>. - Hebrews 7:4-10

In the Old Testament, Melchisedec represents the higher spiritual order of the Heavenly which is eternal in nature. In the New Testament, Hebrews chapter 7 also expounds on this eternal nature and attests to the succession of Y'shua into this priesthood:

[1] For this **Melchisedec, king of Salem, priest of the most high God**, who met Abraham returning from the slaughter of the kings, and blessed him;

[2] To whom also Abraham gave a tenth part of all; first being by interpretation **King of righteousness**, and after that also **King of Salem**, which is, **King of peace**;

[3] **Without father, without mother, without descent, having neither beginning of days, nor end of life**; but <u>made like</u> unto **the Son of God**; <u>abideth a priest continually</u>.

[15] And it is yet far more evident: for that after the similitude of Melchisedec there ariseth another priest,

[16] Who is made, not after the law of a carnal commandment, but after the power of an endless life.

[17] For he testifieth, **Thou art a priest for ever after the order of Melchisedec**. - Hebrews 7:1-3, 15-17

The reference to Melchisedec not descending from a father or a mother and having neither a beginning of days or end of life points to the eternal nature of the Heavenly order from which this priesthood is derived. So Melchisedec could not actually have been "made" in the technical sense as this would imply a beginning, but verse 3 says Melchisedec was "<u>made</u> like unto the Son of God". The words "made like" are a single Greek word, Strong's #G871 ("aphomoioō") - *to cause a model to pass off into an image or shape like it, to express itself in it, <u>to copy; to produce a facsimile</u>; to be made like, render similar; assimilate closely.* Thus we see that Melchisedec (being the priest of the Most High God) produced a spiritual Tree of Life copy or pattern for the priesthood of Y'shua, the actual Son of God, which is further illustrated in verses 15 and 16.

Our God is a God of pattern. This is evidenced in both the Temple and the priesthood of the Temple. Even as Moses was told to design the Tabernacle in the likeness of the Heavenly Temple, so too was the priesthood of Melchisedec patterned after the Heavenly:

> [5] Who serve unto the example and shadow of heavenly things,
> as Moses was admonished of God when he was about to make
> the tabernacle: for, See, saith he, that thou make all things accord-
> ing to the pattern shewed to thee in the mount. - Hebrews 8:5

The thread of spirituality that runs to earth from the Tree of Life is consistent and perpetual. This is illustrated through the eternal nature being shown by Melchisedec. The pattern of Y'shua's priesthood would naturally align with this eternal pattern of the Heavenly order. Hence "after the similitude of Melchisedec there ariseth another priest". The only begotten Son of God attained that which was patterned by the previous type and shadow of the Son of God as priest and king - Melchisedec of Abraham's day. For Y'shua however, the position of High Priest would be unending, even as the Heavenly priesthood itself is eternal:

> [17] For he testifieth, <u>Thou art a priest **for ever** after the order of</u>
> <u>Melchisedec</u>. - Hebrews 7:17

We would reference again the bread and wine presented by Melchisedec which represent the communion offered by Y'shua. This is further evidence of the type and shadow of the spiritual nature of this priesthood:

> [18] And **Melchizedek** king of Salem **brought forth bread and**
> **wine**: and he was the <u>priest</u> of the most high God. - Genesis 14:18

All references of Melchisedec after the Genesis narrative concerning Abraham show Y'shua being likened to Melchisedec. Indeed we see in Hebrews chapter 7 that Y'shua was <u>a high priest "after the order" of Melchisedec</u>:

> [21] (For those priests were made without an oath; <u>but this</u>
> <u>with an oath</u> by him that said unto him, **The Lord sware and**
> **will not repent, <u>Thou art a priest for ever after the order of</u>**
> **<u>Melchisedec</u>**:) - Hebrews 7:21

This phrase actually appears 7 times in the book of Hebrews. We even find it in the Psalms:

> [1] The LORD said unto my Lord, Sit thou at my right hand, until I
> make thine enemies thy footstool.
>
> [4] The LORD hath sworn, and will not repent, Thou art a priest for
> ever after the order of Melchizedek. - Psalms 110:1,4

<u>Sitting at the right hand</u> of Yahweh until He has made His <u>enemies His foot-</u>
<u>stool</u> is repeated again in the New Testament of Y'shua, so we know this

Psalm is a prophetic passage concerning Y'shua:

> [12] But this man, after he had offered one sacrifice for sins for ever, <u>sat down on the right hand of God</u>;
>
> [13] From henceforth expecting <u>till his enemies be made his footstool</u>.
>
> [14] For by one offering he hath perfected for ever them that are sanctified. - Hebrews 10:12-14

The wording of Psalms 110:4 is repeated virtually word for word in Hebrews 7:21:

> [4] **The LORD hath sworn, and will not repent, <u>Thou art a priest for ever after the order of Melchizedek</u>**. - Psalms 110:4
>
> [21] (For those priests were made without an oath; <u>but this with an oath</u> by him that said unto him, **The Lord sware and will not repent, <u>Thou art a priest for ever after the order of Melchisedec</u>**:) - Hebrews 7:21

As a side note, we find it awe-inspiring that our omniscient God knew Y'shua would attain to this priesthood even before His incarnation.

Let's take a closer look at exactly what "Thou art a <u>priest</u> for ever after the order of Melchisedec" means:

> [18] And **Melchizedek <u>king</u> of Salem** brought forth bread and wine: and he was **the <u>priest</u> of the most high God**. - Genesis 14:18

The word "priest" in Genesis 14:18 is Strong's #H3548 ("kohen") - *priest, principal officer or chief ruler, priest, principal officer or chief ruler, priest-king*. Then this combination of priest and king title is reiterated in the New Testament at the beginning of Hebrews 7:

> [1] For this **Melchisedec, king of Salem, priest of the most high God**, who met Abraham returning from the slaughter of the kings, and blessed him;
>
> [2] To whom also Abraham gave a tenth part of all; first being by interpretation **King of righteousness**, and after that also **King of Salem**, which is, **King of peace**; - Hebrews 7:1-2

Being of the Melchisedecian order, Y'shua will return to be king as well. This

Two Trees, Two Kingdoms, Two Kings

office and authority is over both the political and the religious order, as denoted by priest-king in the definition of "kohen" above. Indeed this is the same word used for "priest" in Psalms 110:4 above, which relates to Y'shua in our Hebrews text. The status of Melchisedec then is that of a ruler of the highest rank (chief ruler), both of a religious (priest) and governmental (king) nature.

The word "order" in the phrase "Thou art a priest for ever after the <u>order</u> of Melchisedec" is the same Greek word in each of the 7 references to this phrase. It is Strong's #G5010 ("taxis") - *an arranging, <u>arrangement</u>; <u>order</u>; <u>a fixed succession observing a fixed time</u>; due or right order, orderly <u>condition</u>; dignity; the post, <u>rank</u>; character, fashion, quality, style.*

The references repeatedly state that Y'shua is our High Priest "after the order" (in a fixed succession observing a fixed time, an arrangement or orderly condition of rank) which clearly denotes a specific cyclical patterning and timing of the Almighty. This will be further illustrated momentarily.

The name Melchisedec literally means: *king of righteousness* or *king of justice*. Both are significant to Y'shua. His Kingdom is one of righteousness:

> [8] But unto the Son he saith, Thy throne, O God, is for ever and ever: <u>a sceptre of righteousness is the sceptre of thy kingdom</u>. - Hebrews 1:8

On the other hand, Melchisedec's name denotes justification, and it is through faith in Y'shua that mankind is to be justified, rather than through the physical sacrificial system of the Levitical priesthood.

Thus we see how the phrase "Thou art a priest for ever after the <u>order</u> of Melchisedec" is meaningful to the fullness of the ministry of the Son of God. Melchisedec appeared first almost 2000 years before Y'shua in the days of Abraham, and prefigured the pattern for Y'shua. Then after Y'shua's resurrection we find that He was granted the stature of Melchisedec. Melchisedec's interaction with Abraham in Genesis initiated a spiraling cyclical advancement of the Tree of Life essence. It will culminate with Y'shua's return in this physical realm as priest and king of the highest spiritual authority.

We see in chapter 6 of Hebrews that Y'shua obtained the promise which became the anchor of the soul:

> [15] And so, <u>after he had patiently endured, **he obtained the promise**</u>.

[16] For men verily swear by the greater: and an oath for confirmation is to them an end of all strife.

[17] Wherein God, willing more abundantly to shew unto the <u>heirs of promise</u> the immutability of his counsel, **confirmed it by an oath**:

[18] That by two immutable things, in which it was impossible for God to lie, we might have a strong consolation, who have fled for refuge to lay hold upon the hope set before us:

[19] Which hope we have as <u>**an anchor of the soul**</u>, both sure and stedfast, and which **entereth into that within the veil**;

[20] Whither the **forerunner is for us entered**, even Jesus, <u>**made an high priest for ever after the order of Melchisedec**</u>. - Hebrews 6:15-20

Y'shua rent the veil that we could not rend, opening up the way for us to eventually go after Him. He entered that which was within the veil. What is it that is within the veil? This word "veil" is the Greek word Strong's #G2665 ("katapetasma") - *a veil spread out, a curtain; the name given to the two curtains in the temple at Jerusalem, one of them at the entrance to the temple separated the Holy Place from the outer court, the other veiled the Holy of Holies from the Holy Place*. It is the same word which is translated as "veil" in Hebrews 10, where we see it being related to the flesh:

[20] By **a new and living way**, which <u>he hath consecrated for us</u>, <u>**through the veil**</u>, **that is to say, his flesh**;

[21] And <u>having an high priest</u> <u>**over the house of God**</u>;

[22] Let us draw near **with a true heart in full assurance of faith**, having our hearts sprinkled from an evil conscience, and our bodies washed with pure water. - Hebrews 10:20-22

<u>The Complete Wordstudy Dictionary - New Testament</u> by Spiros Zodhiates offers more input regarding this word. It concurs that this veil was a typology expressed as flesh or body, but much more as well. He sees this veil as being a means of partitioning off the Heavenly realm from the earthly. Y'shua rent the veil of the flesh to receive a body that was not bound by the barriers of our 3-D world. At the same time, He burst through the veil that separated the earthly from the Heavenly and attained to the Heavenly realm with His new title – priest after the order of Melchisedec. The Tree of

Knowledge with its tainted version of good and evil was overcome, and the Tree of Life with its purity of the true Kingdom of Heaven came into view.

We must realize, however, that this change from the earthly to the Heavenly and crossing through the veil was contingent on fulfillment of the Levitical Law. With Y'shua's resurrection, He was able "by a new and living way" (Hebrews 10:20 above) to be made the priest of the Most High God "after the power of an endless life":

> [16] Who is made, not after the law of a carnal commandment, but **after the power of an endless life**. - Hebrews 7:16

This is the Tree of Life promise for Eternal Life! The commandments of the Levitical Law which relate to the carnality of the flesh had to be conquered before Eternal Life could be attained on the spiritual side of the veil. This transition was a victory of the highest order. Not only did He keep the Levitical Law, but He kept the full spiritual application of it which He projected in His earthly ministry. He was transitioned from His perfect compliance with the physical format of the Levitical priesthood to being the head of the spiritual format of the Melchisedecian priesthood. We see that the Tree of Life Levitical Law as introduced by Father is simply a physical application of a greatly advanced and superior spiritual version which pertains to the Melchisedecian priesthood. The Tree of Life physical Levitical Law under girds the Melchisedecian spiritual application of it. Both are associated with Y'shua's Melchisedecian priest-king position.

This is exemplified in our Hebrews 10:21 text which says "having an high priest over the house of God;":

> [21] And having an high priest **over the house of God**; -
> Hebrews 10:21

We believe this "house of God" and the Heavenly spiritual order of the Melchisedecian priesthood to be aspects of the Tree of Life itself. With Y'shua as our High Priest over the house of God, we now have the possibility and a promise for restoration into the Tree of Life ourselves through faith. Thus the crossing over of Y'shua opens the way to the Heavenly Kingdom for those who will follow Him. Until all that pertains to the fallen earthly realm is removed from us, we cannot cross over into the Heavenly Kingdom. Y'shua (in His perfection) was the only candidate who could cross this barrier. Now we can eventually cross into this Heavenly Kingdom as well "with a true heart in full assurance of faith" (Hebrews 10:22 above).

In summation, we would consider again the interaction between Melchisedec and Abraham as it is presented in the book of Hebrews:

> [1] For this **Melchisedec,** king of Salem, priest of the most high God, who **met Abraham** returning from the slaughter of the kings, and blessed him;
>
> [2] <u>To whom also Abraham gave a tenth part of all</u>; first being by interpretation King of righteousness, and after that also King of Salem, which is, King of peace;
>
> [3] Without father, without mother, without descent, having neither beginning of days, nor end of life; but <u>made like unto</u> the Son of God; abideth a priest continually.
>
> [4] Now consider how great this man was, <u>unto whom even the patriarch Abraham gave the tenth of the spoils</u>.
>
> [5] And verily they that are of <u>the sons of Levi, who receive the office of the priesthood</u>, have a commandment to take tithes of the people according to the law, that is, of their brethren, though they <u>come out of the loins of Abraham</u>:
>
> [6] <u>But he whose descent is not counted from them received tithes of Abraham</u>, and <u>blessed him that had the promises</u>.
>
> [7] And <u>without all contradiction the less is blessed of the better</u>. - Hebrews 7:1-7

The Levitical (physical) priesthood (which would collect tithe from the Hebrew people) would come from Abraham's loins (verse 5). Yet in this instance, Abraham paid tithe (one tenth of all) to the Melchisedecian (the spiritual) priesthood (verse 2). This passage points with a certainty to the greatness of the spiritual overshadowing the weaker physical (verse 7). The blessing of Abraham by Melchisedec (verse 1) is, however, evidence that the spiritual priesthood and Law under girded the physical. Likewise, the physical was based on the spiritual and then returns again to the spiritual through Y'shua - the cyclical patterning of God.

The ordination of the physical Law was derived from the spiritual Law of Heaven, and brought forth in Torah per our Old Testament text as our guidelines for physical obedience. Then (we shall see as the book proceeds) obedience to the physical aspects of the moral Law of Father is elemental and critical in the keeping of the more expansive spiritual Law. The spiritual (as revealed to us in our New Testament text) amplifies the physical so that we might more fully develop our spiritual relationship with Father.

The Tree of Life essence brought forth in the physical Law motivates man to conquer the carnality in the fleshly body he inhabits. Obedience to the physical moral guidelines of the Levitical Law, as it was intended by Father, is pivotal in the overcoming process spoken of in Revelation:

> [7] He that overcometh shall inherit all things; and I will be his God, and he shall be my son. - Revelation 21:7

> [14] Blessed are they that do his commandments, that they may have right to the Tree of Life, and may enter in through the gates into the city. - Revelation 22:14

This obedience to God's physical precepts is the first step in our progression to the weightier spiritual understanding which is built on it. It is an integral part of our walk of faith to prepare for crossing the veil. The spiritual elements of the Heavenly Law are broken down to their basal construct in the physical application of the Levitical Law. From there we can take the first steps of obedience, until we are equipped to elevate to the more complete spiritual understanding which Y'shua taught.

When mankind fell from grace and was ousted from the Heavenly realm to the earthly domain, he was no longer able to eat directly from the Tree of Life in the garden. As a result, his nutrition must be meted to him by God in minute morsels that are digestible to his fallen state. There was now a breach between the Tree of Life essence and the fallen state, and this breach must be resolved. The Levitical priesthood is instrumental in this process. Just as one cannot get a college degree without the elementary instruction which precedes his college courses, we must attain first to the Levitical to attain to the Melchisedecian.

We are destined to follow Y'shua through the veil and attain to the purity of the Melchisedecian state when we receive our new bodies. This necessitates that we first adhere to the Tree of Life's physical, Levitical instruction in order to properly advance to the desired spiritual state. Y'shua attained this spiritual advancement perfectly in order to repair the breach. This enables us to do what we could not do ourselves. Through His victory, we can attain to our intended Heavenly status once again. However, we are not to rest on His victory to the exclusion of our participation. We are obliged to emulate Him. He introduced the balance and harmony of the Heavenly realm into our 3-D world so we could begin to integrate the physical to the spiritual. This integration makes it possible to overcome and become one with Y'shua and the Father. He opened the door and provided the way for our path to restoration. We must now choose to enter that door and the path He provided for us.

The singularity of unity of the Tree of Life that runs through the Levitical and the Melchisedecian priesthoods has provided the following transitional steps: The spiritual authority of the Heavenly order embodied by Melchisedec in Abraham's day was the progenitor of a physical foundation. This foundation was the Levitical Law brought from Father to man through Moses. It was then amplified into a more spiritual construct by Y'shua in His teaching. Then the Holy Spirit was given in order to internalize this Heavenly spiritual Truth into the heart of man. Through this progression we are more equipped to comprehend the fuller implication of the Heavenly spiritual Tree of Life Law:

> [14] I press toward the mark for <u>the prize of the high calling</u> of God in Christ Jesus.
>
> [15] Let us therefore, as many as be perfect, <u>be thus minded</u>: and if in any thing ye be otherwise minded, God shall reveal even this unto you.
>
> [20] For our conversation is in heaven; from whence also <u>we look for the Saviour, the Lord Jesus Christ</u>:
>
> [21] <u>Who shall change our vile body, that it may be fashioned like unto his glorious body</u>, according to the working whereby he is able even to subdue all things unto himself. - Philippians 3:14-15, 20-21
>
> [11] But if the Spirit of him that raised up Jesus from the dead dwell in you, he that raised up Christ from the dead shall also <u>quicken your mortal bodies by his Spirit that dwelleth in you</u>. - Romans 8:11

All will be brought back full circle when we receive our new bodies. Corruption will no longer be possible, and we will be pure vessels before God under our High Priest after the order of Melchisedec.

It seems to be very evident when we consider the overall implications here, that the spiritual was the progenitor of the physical, which is (in turn) required for the spiritual. In other words, physical obedience is integral to spiritual advancement, and spiritual advancement promotes greater physical obedience. As long as we yet reside in these physical bodies, our attention to the requirements of the physical seem to be very critical to the process of overcoming.

Two Trees, Two Kingdoms, Two Kings

Only Y'shua overcame completely, and He understands our frailties. We now have an advocate in Him and can receive forgiveness through repentance to bridge the breach of our imperfections. Yet a measure of diligence (a verification of our repentant heart) is needed in our walk. Obedience to all of God's precepts (both physical and spiritual) is intrinsic to the process of man's Tree of Life restoration. Disregarding these precepts lends to divisiveness, a characteristic of the Tree of Knowledge of Good and Evil which embodies death. Attaining to these precepts leads to restoration and Life.

The personification of Melchisedec in our Bibles portrays a typology for the Spirit of the Tree of Life. This Spirit proceeds from the House of God through the Father and into the Son, then is provided by the Son from the Father to indwell man. This is Shema at work!

CHAPTER 4

APPLICATION

The more we worked with the Bible, the more readily we could see the danger of failing to maintain the singularity of the Tree of Life essence in our Biblical study. This failure would lead to a loss of intended Biblical harmony which would engender distortion in our thought process. In turn, our errant thoughts would generate false beliefs. These then would become entrenched and would lead to a hobbling spiritual walk. How would this walk emerge and what would it look like?

Symptoms of a Hobbling Walk

Obedience as it is commonly taught in today's church is centered around the Holy Spirit. We are told to follow the leading of the Spirit to secure our spiritual walk. In conjunction with this teaching, however, we are taught that God's Will is no longer relative to the Old Testament text. Because hearing from the Spirit is somewhat subjective, proper discernment of this guidance from the Spirit requires a filter of some nature. The expressly stated precepts of our Old Testament text are intended to provide just such a filter. Without understanding that the guidance of the Spirit is based on the expressly stated precepts of our Old Testament text, this subjectivity can set up for deception. The corrupting influence of the contra can then be easily confused with the leadership of the real, as the basis for discernment (Scriptural continuity) has been nullified. With the removal of these guidelines, the contra can then lead the unsuspecting Believer into errant thought and practice.

When our perception of God's Will comes to us from the true Spirit, the understanding that is infused by this Spirit will align with the precepts of His will that are expressed in Torah. If our perception of God's Will is being swayed by the contra spirit, it will often condone infractions of Father's expressly stated will. This perversion can then lead the Believer into a compromised walk by Father's standards.

As it relates to moral decisions, we don't need to look any further for God's Will than to the Word itself. Father has already given it to us and it is still valid. It is His will for us, yesterday, today, and always; and His Spirit will uphold it:

> [7] For there are three that bear record in heaven, the Father, the Word, and the Holy Ghost: and these three are one. - 1 John 5:7

> [8] Beware lest any man spoil you through philosophy and vain deceit, after the tradition of men, after the rudiments of the world, and not after Christ.

> [9] For in him dwelleth all the fulness of the Godhead bodily. - Colossians 2:8-9

> [8] Jesus Christ the same yesterday, and to day, and for ever. - Hebrews 13:8

Y'shua is one with the Father and the Holy Spirit, so this singularity of essence holds true throughout time. When we see a Believer walking in the ways of the world, chances are good that the contra gospel has been applied to his understanding. The "philosophy and vain deceit, after the traditions of men" and "rudiments of the world" have spoiled him.

Y'shua said to the Pharisees that they had left the commandments of God behind to follow their own traditions:

> [9] And he said unto them, Full well ye reject the commandment of God, that ye may keep your own tradition. - Mark 7:9

Unfortunately, we see that this could likewise be said today in regard to much of our religious system.

The contra belief system brings about a hobbling moral walk – one that aligns to the world rather than being set apart from it. The person who is led by this influence allows the flesh to depart from the constraints of God's instruction which was established for our benefit. It is often hard to distinguish this type of Believer from the average agnostic who has decent moral values, as the same spirit is in charge in both cases.

To hobble means: *to hamper, restrict or impede progress; to progress unevenly or with difficulty*. A hobbling walk can mean: *to walk lamely; to limp*. Our spiritual walk is certainly hobbled when our understanding is skewed by the pervasive contra messages of duality and division. On the other hand, our obedience to Father's instruction facilitates a graceful and adept walk:

[30] As for God, his **way** is perfect: **the word of the LORD is tried**: he is a buckler to all those that trust in him.

[31] For who is God save the LORD? or who is a rock save our God?

[32] It is God that girdeth me with strength, and **maketh my way perfect**.

[33] **He maketh my feet like hinds' feet, and setteth me upon my high places**. - Psalms 18:30-33

We have all experienced some degree of hobbling in our spiritual walk. It is not enough that we have to overcome our individual iniquities. In addition, we are subjected to spiritual guidance from a multiplicity of sources that are influenced and corrupted by the adversary. We have already established the existence of the contra gospel message, and now we want to take a closer look at how the hobbling walk is unwittingly being fostered in most churches today.

The contra gospel is formed around errant interpretation. Many theological constructs include both truth and error. While portions of the Biblical text may be interpreted properly, a skewed view of certain key portions of surrounding text can almost irreparably distort the resulting overall message. We should ask why there are so many denominations. If the Biblical text was interpreted properly by the clergy in every corner of the faith, there would be one church and only various geographical branches of this church rather than various denominational beliefs. Within Christendom today, each denomination believes their interpretation of key passages is the correct one. However, we see a common (almost universal) mistake regardless of the particular flavor of the theology. This mistake is the failure to pull forward the pure essence of the entire Biblical Scripture when forming any one particular strain of theology.

A study of Scripture which is fragmented or slanted to preconceived notions or biases will often result in incomplete truth or invalid conclusions. Our preconceptions are frequently based on teachings which we entertain, or (in the case of pastors) teachings which we must accept in order to be ordained by a particular denomination. Every televangelist, pastor and leader associated with a ministry endeavor will use Scripture in their teaching and ministry efforts. Unfortunately the messages built around these extracted Scriptural references are seldom formed around the context of the entirety of the Biblical text. When portions of Scripture are extracted in this manner without carrying forward the balance of Scriptural understanding, the extracted portion is usually misrepresented and the picture that is painted in the teaching is distorted. The use of the Biblical text (though misapplied) is what makes their teachings so plausible and actually increases the potential for danger. An unbalanced interpretation simply shreds the integrity of the congruency of the Biblical text by using only portions. This, in turn, leads to distortion of understanding. The obvious result is division in the body of Messiah by creating a multiplicity of denominational fronts.

Each denomination constructs a theological "box" of sorts around select portions of perceived "truth" while disregarding all portions of Biblical text which would contest their interpretations. All that falls outside of that box is viewed by that particular denomination as being errant – even heretical. These various denominational boxes overlap in agreement at times, but there are obvious areas of disagreement as well, where the boxes no longer overlap. A comparison of the various theological stances when moving from one denomination to another will prove this concept readily. How does such discrepancy occur? The only explanation is errant understanding relative to the Biblical text as a whole. Were it not for this, there would be total harmony in the body of faith today. Instead we have division. Such is the case when man fails to love God's Truth enough to put line on line and precept on precept to validate and integrate the entirety of God's Word properly:

> [9] <u>Whom shall he teach knowledge</u>? and <u>whom shall he make to understand doctrine</u>? them that are weaned from the milk, and drawn from the breasts.

> [10] For precept must be upon precept, precept upon precept; line upon line, line upon line; here a little, and there a little: - Isaiah 28:9-10

In 2 Thessalonians Paul warns about a lack of love for God's Truth. We find that the ramification of this lack of love is strong delusion:

> [10] And with all deceivableness of unrighteousness in them that perish; because **they received <u>not</u> the <u>love of the truth</u>**, that they might be saved.

> [11] And **for this cause <u>God shall send them strong delusion,</u> that they should believe a lie**:

> [12] That they all might be damned who believed not the truth, but had pleasure in unrighteousness. - 2 Thessalonians 2:10-12

Indeed the stronghold of the delusion fostered by the contra gospel is very difficult to break through. Paul emphasizes here the severity of such failure to realize and love Father's Truth. He indicates that it is such a grievance to God that God Himself will send this lie as a consequence. We sincerely believe that this truth which we are to love is the fullness of Torah Truth - presented in the written Torah (via Father), amplified by the living Torah (Y'shua), and directed by the indwelling Torah (the Holy Spirit). Anything that is extracted and segregated from that entirety is merely a partial truth and would not constitute love of His total Truth. Being Shema, God's Truth is singular in essence from the Old Testament to and through the New. <u>If we do not love this Truth as it is intended to be seen by the One who brought it into being, then (by default) we have subjected ourselves to His delusion.</u>

As difficult as it is to break through this stronghold, Father can break it. He knows the heart, and it is our belief that many who have been taught errant theology from the beginning of their faith, yet have a pure heart for God, will (by His mercy) be granted this breakthrough within His timing. We believe that they will find (through some source or other) His Truth.

In the meantime, if we have never understood and loved His Truth relative to the unity of the essence of the Godhead and the unity of the Word of God that presents it, we are extremely vulnerable to be fed and believe the lie that is commonly taught in Christendom. It is heart wrenching to realize that the same institution which can actually introduce one to the Savior of mankind is the institution that can potentially (and likely will) veer him off course after this introduction.

If we choose to reject the fullness of God's Truth, then we are seduced into belief of the lie (contra gospel). This then opens the door for us to walk in disobedience to Father's precepts because we no longer see the boundaries He established. If we do not desire God's total Truth at all cost, it will be very easy to eat of the wrong spiritual fruit and believe the lie (distortion of truth) that is being presented so often in our world today. God tries our hearts:

> [10] I the LORD search the heart, I try the reins, even to give every man according to his ways, and according to the fruit of his doings.
> - Jeremiah 17:10

How will our hearts measure up? Only those who fervently desire His Truth at all cost will find it:

> [8] For God is my record, how greatly I long after you all in the bowels of Jesus Christ.

[9] And this I pray, that your love may abound yet more and more in knowledge and in all judgment;

[10] That ye may approve things that are excellent; that ye may be sincere and without offense till the day of Christ;

[11] Being filled with the fruits of righteousness, which are by Jesus Christ, unto the glory and praise of God.

[27] … that ye stand fast in one spirit, with one mind striving together for the faith of the gospel; - Philippians 1:8-11, 27

To Slay or Not to Slay

Yahweh gave Saul (the king of the Hebrew people) a message:

[1] Samuel also said unto Saul, The LORD sent me to anoint thee to be king over his people, over Israel: now therefore hearken thou unto the voice of the words of the LORD.

[2] Thus saith the LORD of hosts, I remember that which Amalek did to Israel, how he laid wait for him in the way, when he came up from Egypt.

[3] Now go and smite Amalek, and utterly destroy all that they have, and spare them not; but slay both man and woman, infant and suckling, ox and sheep, camel and ass. - 1 Samuel 15:1-3

This is a type and shadow of what we are to do as Believers. The king is one who dictates. Within the Believer, the will of man dictates that which will be accomplished in our walk. The king (our will) is sent on a mission. Amalek is a name meaning: *valley dweller, one who licks*. It represents the contra. Being in the valley signifies being as low as one can get (similar to being on one's belly) and licking would be such as eating dust or licking the earth:

[14] And the LORD God said unto the serpent, Because thou hast done this, thou art cursed above all cattle, and above every beast of the field; upon thy belly shalt thou go, and dust shalt thou eat all the days of thy life: - Genesis 3:14

The spiritual message in this type and shadow is that the will of man must slay every aspect of our being that is controlled by or harbors the contra (no matter how innocent it may seem). We are to leave no shred of contra life remaining within our being. All aspects of the contra must be slain.

The ongoing struggle with Amalek (the contra) is typologically seen again in the book of Exodus, as well as the assured ultimate victory over him:

[14] And the LORD said unto Moses, Write this for a memorial in a book, and rehearse it in the ears of Joshua: for **I will utterly put out the remembrance of Amalek from under heaven**.

[15] And Moses built an altar, and called the name of it Jehovah-nissi:

[16] For he said, Because the LORD hath sworn that <u>the LORD will have war with Amalek from generation to generation</u>. - Exodus 17:14-16

Though Saul believed he was doing as God had said, he did not. The portion of the passage which relates Saul's failure to follow God's instructions is hard for us to read, but here it is:

[13] And Samuel came to Saul: and Saul said unto him, Blessed be thou of the LORD: **I have performed the commandment of the LORD**.

[14] And Samuel said, <u>What meaneth then this bleating of the sheep in mine ears</u>, and the lowing of the oxen which I hear?

[15] And Saul said, <u>They have brought them from the Amalekites: for the people spared the best of the sheep and of the oxen, to sacrifice unto the LORD thy God</u>; and the rest we have utterly destroyed.

[16] Then Samuel said unto Saul, Stay, and I will tell thee what the LORD hath said to me this night. And he said unto him, Say on.

[17] And Samuel said, When thou wast little in thine own sight, wast thou not made the head of the tribes of Israel, and the LORD anointed thee king over Israel?

[18] And **the LORD sent thee** <u>on a journey, and said,</u> **Go and utterly destroy the sinners the Amalekites**<u>, and fight against them</u> **until they be consumed**.

[19] <u>Wherefore then didst thou</u> **not obey** <u>the voice of the LORD,</u> but didst fly upon the spoil, and **didst evil in the sight of the LORD**?

[20] And Saul said unto Samuel, Yea, **I have obeyed the voice of the LORD,** and have gone the way which the LORD sent me,

> and **have brought Agag the king of Amalek**, and have utterly destroyed the Amalekites.
>
> [21] But the people **took of the spoil, sheep and oxen**, the chief of the things which should have been utterly destroyed, to sacrifice unto the LORD thy God in Gilgal.
>
> [22] And Samuel said, **Hath the LORD as great delight in burnt offerings and sacrifices, as in obeying the voice of the LORD**? Behold, **<u>to obey is better than sacrifice</u>**, and to hearken than the fat of rams.
>
> [23] <u>For rebellion is as the sin of witchcraft, and stubbornness is as iniquity and idolatry</u>. **Because thou hast rejected the word of the LORD, he hath also rejected thee from being king**. - 1 Samuel 15:13-23

<u>King Saul thought he had obeyed God, but by altering God's intent, he was mixing the ways of man with God's instructions which caused him to fall far short of faithfully completing the mission God had given him</u>.

Isn't that what is happening often today? We are taught that to walk in the Spirit is the perfect sacrifice, and that to do so correctly we must leave the Law behind. When we fall prey to this understanding <u>we think we are obeying God</u>. <u>However, by altering God's intent we are mixing the ways of man with God's instructions</u>. <u>This causes us to fall short of faithfully completing the mission God has given us</u> – the mission to become holy and set apart for God's purposes. We fail to properly destroy the enemy within. Heeding the guidance we perceive through the Spirit is commonly viewed by Christendom as sacrifice. This passage helps us see that any such sacrificial activity is to be centered around obedience:

> [22] And Samuel said, **Hath the LORD as great delight in burnt offerings and sacrifices, as in obeying the voice of the LORD**? Behold, **<u>to obey is better than sacrifice</u>**, and to hearken than the fat of rams. - 1 Samuel 15:22

If our sacrificial acts are not framed by obedience to God's total Truth, then they are inadequate sacrificial acts. The "voice of the Lord (Yahweh, in the Hebrew)" as found in this verse is that which is projected by the Spirit. In our current life typology, however, the voice of the Spirit must enumerate and confirm the voice of Yahweh which was revealed to us in Torah. It is all one voice: the voice of the Spirit will not be in conflict with that of Torah. By ignoring Father's precepts in order to attain a more perfect "walk in the

Spirit", we are listening to the contra voice rather than slaying it within us. This then is "evil" in Yahweh's sight per verse 19 of this passage. Our sacrifice of "walking in the Spirit" is not adequate BECAUSE it is not coupled with obedience to the precepts of the Father. When the mind begins to embrace the contra gospel it brings diversion from Father's instructions and iniquity follows. This is as <u>wickedness</u> in Father's eyes:

> [5] <u>We have sinned, and have committed iniquity, and have done wickedly, and have rebelled</u>, even **by departing from thy precepts and from thy judgments**: - Daniel 9:5

The departure from God's precepts in this verse, and the iniquity and rebellion aspect which God sees as the result, correlates well with verse 23 of our 1 Samuel passage:

> [23] <u>For rebellion is as the sin of witchcraft, and stubbornness is as iniquity and idolatry</u>. **Because thou hast rejected the word of the LORD**, he hath also rejected thee from being king. - **1 Samuel 15:23**

Other significant references in Jeremiah and Proverbs might apply as well:

> [14] O Jerusalem, wash thine heart from <u>wickedness</u>, that thou mayest be saved. <u>How long shall thy vain thoughts lodge within thee</u>? - Jeremiah 4:14

> [18] Thy way and thy doings have procured these things unto thee; <u>this is thy wickedness</u>, because it is bitter, because <u>it reacheth unto thine heart</u>. - Jeremiah 4:18

> [6] Righteousness keepeth him that is upright in the way: but <u>wickedness overthroweth the sinner</u>. - Proverbs 13:6

> [27] **<u>The sacrifice of the wicked is abomination</u>**: how <u>much more, when he bringeth it with a wicked mind</u>? - Proverbs 21:27

Here we see that if one is in wickedness (outside the Father's precepts), the sacrifice he offers is not acceptable. Thus the sacrifice of "walking in the Spirit" is inappropriate if this walk is outside of the parameters of the Father's instruction. Not only is this sacrifice not acceptable, we cringe when we read that it is viewed by Father as abomination per this last verse above. Such disobedience was so grievous to Yahweh that Saul was rejected from continuing as king. He lost his right to reign. We are supposed to reign and rule with Y'shua during His Millennial reign:

> [4] And I saw thrones, and they sat upon them, and judgment was given unto them: and I saw the souls of them that were beheaded for the witness of Jesus, and for the word of God, and which had not worshipped the beast, neither his image, neither had received his mark upon their foreheads, or in their hands; <u>and they lived and reigned with Christ a thousand years</u>. - Revelation 20:4

Note that it is those who overcome who are allowed to do so:

> [26] And <u>he that overcometh</u>, and keepeth my works unto the end, to him will I give power over the nations:
>
> [27] And <u>he shall rule</u> them with a rod of iron; as the vessels of a potter shall they be broken to shivers: even as I received of my Father. - Revelation 2:26-27

If we do not have the longing and determination to rule over our own fleshly desires, then we are not fit material to rule with Y'shua in the hereafter:

> [12] Therefore, brethren, we are debtors, not to the flesh, to live after the flesh.
>
> [13] For if ye live after the flesh, ye shall die: but if ye through the Spirit do mortify the deeds of the body, ye shall live. - Romans 8:12-13

We overcome when we are diligent in our endeavor to slay every aspect of that which would exalt itself above the righteous character of Father:

> [24] And <u>they that are Christ's</u> **have crucified the flesh with the affections and lusts**. - Galatians 5:24

That is His mission for all Believers. That does not mean we will be perfect at keeping all of the jots and tittles of the Law, but it does mean that we will be conscientious to slay all that rebels against God's holiness in our character and ways – all that rebels against the instructions in our Bibles and the guidance of the Holy Spirit within. Only as we are about this process will we be able to love God's Truth fully, which includes all of His precepts.

We are to grant Father our obedience, and determine to keep all of the precepts which comprise His moral character, not viewing any such precepts as a hindrance to our sacrificial walk in the Spirit, but rather as superimposed parameters FOR that walk. We are to understand that walking in the Spirit must not be separate from the precepts of Father, but that a true walk is in conjunction with them. We are to apprehend the concept that obedience is the foundation to our relationship with Father and the first step to a fruitful walk in the His Spirit.

Jeremiah shows us that we are to learn from the wickedness of our contra mindset and the sinful state which it engenders. We are to learn that we have forsaken Yahweh and that His fear is no longer in us:

> [19] <u>Thine own wickedness shall correct thee, and thy backslidings shall reprove thee</u>: <u>know therefore and see that it is an evil thing and bitter, that thou hast forsaken the LORD thy God, and that my fear is not in thee, saith the Lord GOD of hosts</u>. - Jeremiah 2:19

Then we are to correct the problem by coming back to the precepts of Father and abiding within them WHILE walking in the Spirit. To slay the contra is to slay the flesh which rebels against the structured authority Father put into place - to embrace Father's ways as the initial stage of a true walk in the Spirit:

> [4] <u>That the righteousness of the law might be fulfilled in us, **who walk not after the flesh**, but after the Spirit</u>. - Romans 8:4

The Believer's Accountability

We see a tremendous falsehood and danger is being told that EVERYTHING was accomplished at the cross – that we have no need to be accountable after receiving our atonement. If this were true, why would Peter warn us to "be diligent" that we may be found "blameless"?:

> [14] Wherefore, beloved, seeing that ye look for such things, **be diligent that ye may be found of him in peace, without spot, and blameless**. - 2 Peter 3:14

If the totality of our sanctification was accomplished on our initial belief, then why would we have to be diligent in our walk at all? Why would we have need for the refiner's fire?:

> [2] But who may abide the day of his coming? and who shall stand when he appeareth? for he is like **a refiner's fire**, and like fullers' soap: - Malachi 3:2

Why would we need to be a living sacrifice to God?:

> [1] I beseech you therefore, brethren, by the mercies of God, that ye **present your bodies a living sacrifice**, holy, acceptable unto God, which is <u>your reasonable service</u>. - Romans 12:1

Two Trees, Two Kingdoms, Two Kings

Why would we be told to deny ourselves and take up our cross to follow Y'shua?:

> [24] Then said Jesus unto his disciples, If any man will come after me, **let him deny himself, and take up his cross, and follow me**. - Matthew 16:24

Why would we be shown to work out our salvation AFTER belief on Y'shua with fear and trembling?:

> [12] Wherefore, my beloved, **as ye have** always **obeyed**, not as in my presence only, but now much more in my absence, **work out your own salvation with fear and trembling**. - Philippians 2:12

Notice in this verse that the working out of our salvation is linked to obedience. In his letter to the Philippians, Paul is verifying the importance of continued obedience to Scriptural principles of the day which were assuredly Torah based. He seems to be stressing here that Torah instruction is elemental to our salvation process.

Paul understood. It is just man's interpretation of Paul's writings that twists his intent.

Paul is praising the Philippians for their obedience, and even as they have to the present time been obedient, he is admonishing them not to turn from this obedience, in order that their salvation would be worked out. This working-out process is our sanctification. It is begun at the time of belief and accomplished THROUGHOUT our walk of faith. It then culminates in our salvation at the end of this walk of faith.

We will discuss the fullness of the term "faith" further into the book, but in the meantime let us address three other terms used here as they relate to Paul's writings in our New Testament text. They are justification, sanctification, and salvation, including various forms of these words. We will cover the Greek word and definition for each. Then we will relate each to the process we see in Paul's writings that enables our change from corruptible to incorruptible (1 Corinthians 15:50-55).

The first of these three terms is "justification". The word "justified" is Strong's #G1344 ("dikaioō") - *to render righteous or such he ought to be; to show, exhibit, evince, one to be righteous, such as he is and wishes himself to be considered; to declare, pronounce, one to be just, righteous, or* **such as he ought to be**.

This seems to show justification as being a <u>positional</u> rendering, rather than a pronouncement of something attained on a personal level. It is a declaration of sorts which deems one to be seen as just or righteous. Within the definition we see this person being declared righteous <u>as he OUGHT TO BE</u>. It is the <u>absolution of the sins of our past</u> to a purified state so that we may enter into relationship with the Lord:

> [25] Whom God hath set forth to be a propitiation through faith in his blood, to declare his righteousness for the <u>remission of sins that are past</u>, through the forbearance of God; - Romans 3:25

> [30] Moreover whom he did predestinate, them he also called: and whom he called, them he also justified: and whom he justified, them he also glorified. - Romans 8:30

We see justification as being the initial step of the "sanctification" process which leads to this glorification. We are declared to be righteous (as we ought to be), and it is our new obligation to leave behind the sins of our past and follow through to remain blameless in our walk as a Believer. This walk then becomes the process of sanctification. The word "sanctification" is Strong's #G37 ("hagiazō") - *to render or acknowledge, or <u>to be venerable or hallow;</u> <u>to separate from profane things and dedicate to God; consecrate things to God;</u> dedicate people to God; to purify; <u>to cleanse externally;</u> to purify by expiation: free from the guilt of sin; <u>to purify internally by renewing of the soul</u>.*

Justification initiates the sanctification process with our initial purification through expiation (atonement). This is the first great accomplishment of Y'shua at the cross. It is followed closely with forgiveness through repentance when we fall short of God's ways. Obedience to His ways is front and center to our walk of sanctification. Y'shua (through the Father) provided us with the Holy Spirit to draw us to and guide us through our spiritual growth in a walk of faith. Speaking of the Holy Spirit, Y'shua says:

> [8] And when he is come, <u>he will reprove the world of sin, and of righteousness, and of judgment</u>: - John 16:8

Sanctification is to engage in this walk, and (as we will cover a bit later) it is actually proof of our very engagement (betrothal) to our Bridegroom. This walk is God's design for Believers – effecting the sanctification process through consecration to God (being set apart from the world to God and His ways). As we have seen already, it is our reasonable service to become the living sacrifice of Romans 12:1. It is a means to honor Y'shua with gratitude and dedication for the gift He wrought for us.

Two Trees, Two Kingdoms, Two Kings

Implied in this process is separation from profane things and a turn to the ways of God – the pathway which leads to ultimately being acknowledged as venerable or hallowed. The route to full sanctification then involves the separation from the profane in every aspect of our being, spiritual (soul and spirit) as well as physical (body). In this manner we are totally blameless before God:

> [23] And the very God of peace sanctify you wholly; and I pray God your whole spirit and soul and body be preserved blameless unto the coming of our Lord Jesus Christ. - 1 Thessalonians 5:23

This sanctification process then would be the progression from justification at our initial belief (when our sins of the past are purged) to our glorification (when the corruptible is made incorruptible and we receive our incorruptible immortal bodies). The whole process (sanctification) then is the working out of our salvation per Philippians 2:12 above. This walk of sanctification to holiness is contingent on obedience to the ways of God as shown first in Torah:

> [7] Sanctify yourselves therefore, and be ye holy: for I am the LORD your God.
>
> [8] And ye shall keep my statutes, and do them: I am the LORD which sanctify you. - Leviticus 20:7-8

As we keep His precepts, we abstain from the things He sees as profane, and our journey to holiness proceeds. This is the overcoming process of Revelation which allows us to eat of the Tree of Life once again:

> [7] He that hath an ear, let him hear what the Spirit saith unto the churches; To him that overcometh will I give to eat of the tree of life, which is in the midst of the paradise of God. - Revelation 2:7

"Salvation" would then be the end result of this process, the deliverance from the mortal body and inheritance of the glorified state of incorruptibility - restoration to God and His Kingdom - a reward from God for adhering to the sanctification process throughout the walk of faith to its successful conclusion:

> [5] Who are kept by the power of God **through faith** unto salvation ready to be revealed **in the last time**.
>
> [7] That the **trial of your faith**, being much more precious than of gold that perisheth, though it be tried with fire, might be found unto praise and honour and glory at the appearing of Jesus Christ:

> [9] Receiving <u>the **end** of your faith</u>, even the **salvation** of your <u>souls</u>. - 1 Peter 1:5, 7 and 9

The term "salvation" means virtually the same thing when traversing from the Old Testament to the New. In the Old Testament it is primarily Strong's #H3467 - ("yasha'") - *to save, be saved, be delivered; to be liberated, be saved; be victorious.* There are two other Hebrew words that stem from this root which are sometimes used. The first is Strong's #H3444 ("yĕshuw'ah") - *salvation, deliverance; welfare, prosperity; salvation (by God); victory.* The second is Strong's #H3468 ("yesha'") - *deliverance, salvation, rescue, safety, welfare; prosperity; victory.* In the Greek, it is usually Strong's #G4991 ("sōtēria") - *deliverance, preservation, safety, the soul's salvation, future salvation, the sum of benefits and blessings which the Christians, redeemed from all earthly ills, will enjoy after the visible return of Christ from Heaven in the consummated and eternal Kingdom of God.* On occasion it is the related form of this Greek word, Strong's #G4992 ("sōtērios") which means: *the one who brings "soteria".* It is obvious that all of the meanings for the relative terms are very much related and mean the same basic thing: *rescue, deliverance, and victory - and that this is accomplished by God.*

We see how Paul's words work with Peter's to express this reality:

> [8] For **by grace are ye saved <u>through faith</u>**; and that not of yourselves: it is the gift of God: - Ephesians 2:8

Indeed we cannot provide for our own salvation. <u>God provides the initial justification</u> on our belief <u>and gives us the indwelling Holy Spirit to guide us through our walk of faith</u>. At the conclusion of the sanctification process, the Glory of salvation is manifested. Thus our salvation is in God's hands from start to finish:

> [9] Receiving the <u>**end** of your faith</u>, even the **salvation of your souls**. - 1 Peter 1:9

We are to take this salvation process seriously and walk in those things which have been shown "from the first" by Father, heeding them earnestly in our walk. We are cautioned of this in Hebrews:

> [1] Therefore we ought to <u>give the more earnest heed to the things which we have heard</u>, lest at any time we should let them slip.
>
> [2] For if the word spoken by angels was stedfast, and every transgression and <u>disobedience received a just recompence of reward</u>;

> [3] <u>How shall we escape, if we neglect so great salvation</u>; <u>which at</u>
> <u>the first began to be spoken by the Lord</u>, and was confirmed unto
> us by them that heard him; - Hebrews 2:1-3

The "recompense of reward" in verse 2 lies ahead if we fail to do so. It would be a negative "reward" for disobedience. Obviously the term "rewards" in the Biblical sense can be associated with either pleasant OR unpleasant consequences which result from our actions.

The walk of faith brings forth the sanctification process which culminates in salvation. **This walk of faith too is a gift of God – not of ourselves.** We are given power to become sons of God, but that power is a GIFT to us, not a mantle FORCED ON us. It is given through the Holy Spirit, and we must choose not to quench the power the Spirit provides to us:

> [19] Quench not the Spirit. - 1 Thessalonians 5:19

This instruction would not have been necessary if quenching the Spirit was impossible. We have a choice in the matter. We have to surrender to the Spirit's influence and allow the Holy Spirit (the true essence of the Tree of Life) to lead us through it. Any works we try to do on our own will not stand before the Throne, as they may well be influenced by the inclination of our own mind and the subtle directives of the contra spirit – man's version of good. We must be led by the Holy Spirit, and the Spirit will lead us with God's good, which will align with the parameters of the Father's precepts. These works WILL stand before the Throne.

The following four verses then point to the Holy Spirit's leading us through this sanctification process as the means to becoming blameless:

> [12] Wherefore, my beloved, as ye have always **obey**ed, not as in
> my presence only, but now much more in my absence, work out
> your own salvation with fear and trembling.

> [13] For it is **God** which <u>worketh in you</u> both **to will and to do of**
> **his good pleasure**.

> [14] Do all things without murmurings and disputings:

> [15] **That ye may be blameless and harmless**, the <u>sons of God,</u>
> <u>without rebuke</u>, <u>in the midst of a crooked and perverse nation,</u>
> among whom ye shine <u>as lights in the world</u>; - Philippians 2:12-15

The instruction in verse 14 to "do" implies that we <u>can</u> choose not to "do". Even though God's Spirit is working within us to do Father's will, we can choose to quench this guiding power. We see here the need to combine obedience to Father's precepts (as revealed in the Holy Word) with a yielding to the Father's personal will for each of us (as revealed by the Holy Spirit). It is in this manner that we are seen as blameless - His "sons", with no rebuke being needed. This power provided by the Spirit to attain the title of His "sons" was referenced as well in John:

> [12] But as many as received him, to them <u>gave he power to become</u> the sons of God, even to them that believe on his name: - John 1:12

It is not an automatic process, but one by which we are empowered to "become" His "sons" through our walk of sanctification. This is accomplished as we choose to yield to (rather than to quench) the Spirit within us.

During this process we are to yield to the power of the Spirit to cleanse both the physical and spiritual portions of our being in the fear of God:

> [1] Having therefore these promises, dearly beloved, let us cleanse ourselves from all filthiness of the **flesh and spirit, perfecting holiness in the fear of God**. - 2 Corinthians 7:1

We can THEN be the proper example to this crooked and perverse nation, shining as lights in the world around us. Verse 13 of the above Philippians text says the Father works in us to WILL (relating to the spiritual) and to DO (relating to the physical) OF HIS GOOD PLEASURE. How could our determination in our will or our performance by our body of anything which violates His precepts ever be seen as being OF HIS GOOD PLEASURE? It is only when we "WILL AND DO OF HIS GOOD PLEASURE" that we may be seen as blameless and harmless in the fullness of our beings. This good pleasure is to be done while we are yet in the midst of a crooked and perverse nation. Indeed we are there!

Belief on the blood of Y'shua provides our initial justification, reopening the path to Father, and making us acceptable in His sight through His beloved Son. Then we begin to tend to our sanctification, the process by which we REMAIN acceptable (blameless). This is why Paul prayed for the Brethren that they might be found blameless at the return of Y'shua. They were already justified, but their continued state of blamelessness was not assured at their conversion:

> [23] And the very God of peace sanctify you wholly; and **I pray** God your whole spirit and soul and body be preserved blameless unto the coming of our Lord Jesus Christ. - 1 Thessalonians 5:23

Two Trees, Two Kingdoms, Two Kings

Speaking to the Brethren, John says we all still sin:

> [8] If we say that we have no sin, we deceive ourselves, and the truth is not in us. - 1 John 1:8

As Believers we strive to overcome sin, but nobody is going to keep the Law perfectly, and when we fail we can turn to Y'shua:

> [1] My little children, these things write I unto you, that ye <u>sin not</u>. And <u>if any man sin, we have an advocate with the Father, Jesus Christ the righteous</u>: - 1 John 2:1

Father recognizes that even after our belief we are still human ("as dust") and has therefore provided an advocate via Y'shua for the removal of sin for those who "fear" Him (strive to draw nigh to His ways):

> [12] <u>As far as the east is from the west, so far hath he removed our transgressions from us</u>.

> [13] Like as a father pitieth his children, so <u>the LORD pitieth **them that fear him**</u>.

> [14] For he knoweth our frame; <u>he remembereth that we are dust</u>. - Psalms 103:12-14

In fact "fear" of the Lord is nearly always linked with keeping His commandments:

> [1] Praise ye the LORD. Blessed is the man that **feareth the LORD**, that <u>delighteth greatly in his commandments</u>. - Psalms 112:1

> [10] The **fear of the LORD** is the beginning of wisdom: a good understanding have all they that <u>do his commandments</u>: his praise endureth for ever. - Psalms 111:10

In this last verse we see that it is also the beginning of wisdom. When we fear God properly we will be striving to keep His commandments, and will know by our awareness of these precepts when we have transgressed. We will then confess our failures and our advocate Y'shua will provide for our cleansing:

> [9] <u>**If we confess our sins,** he is faithful and just to forgive us our sins, and to cleanse us from all unrighteousness</u>. - 1 John 1:9

The word "IF" in 1 John 1:9 above makes this a conditional promise. It is therefore very important that we recognize and confess our sins after belief.

We must be able to recognize our failures in order to confess them, which is a necessity in the redemptive plan of God. By being cleansed and forgiven we remain in a blameless state.

New Testament Scripture very clearly reveals to us how to recognize sin for what it is. John tells us that sin is transgression of the Law, and Paul tells us that it is by the Law that we understand what sin is:

> [4] Whosoever committeth sin transgresseth also the law: for **sin is the transgression of the law**. - 1 John 3:4

> [20] Therefore by the deeds of the law there shall no flesh be justified in his sight: for **by the law is the knowledge of sin**. - Romans 3:20

Therefore <u>it is imperative to understand and acknowledge Father's moral precepts of the Law so we will know when we have broken it</u>. Only then will we know to confess our shortcomings and be cleansed again to blamelessness.

This is the way one remains in good standing, but many will not be found in blamelessness when it is time to give account. For instance, one who has turned from the holy commandment is as a dog who returns to his vomit:

> [21] For it had been better for them not to have known the way of righteousness, than, after they have known it, <u>to turn from the holy commandment delivered unto them</u>.

> [22] But it is happened unto them according to the true proverb, <u>The dog is turned to his own vomit again</u>; and the sow that was washed to her wallowing in the mire. - 2 Peter 2:21-22

Abiding within the WILL of God produces fruit which proves that the sanctification process is on track within the spiritual man:

> [9] (For the fruit of the Spirit is in all goodness and righteousness and truth;)

> [10] Proving what is acceptable unto the Lord. - Ephesians 5:9-10

> [22] But the fruit of the Spirit is love, joy, peace, longsuffering, gentleness, goodness, faith,

> [23] Meekness, temperance: against such there is no law.

> [24] And they that are Christ's have crucified the flesh with the affections and lusts.

> [25] If we live in the Spirit, let us also walk in the Spirit. -
> Galatians 5:22-25

As we have indicated, the walk in the Spirit is the walk of faith which carries us through the sanctification process. This walk produces spiritual fruit which is pleasing to God. Within this walk we are to be circumspect and focused on the will of God:

> [15] See then that ye <u>walk circumspectly</u>, not as fools, but as wise,
>
> [16] Redeeming the time, because the days are evil.
>
> [17] Wherefore be ye not unwise, but <u>understanding what the will of the Lord is</u>. - Ephesians 5:15-17

How can we understand what God's will is when we reject His heart (Torah)? His will is expressly stated in the principles of Torah so that we can draw near to His heart and honor Him properly. The will of God begins with the physical aspect which is found in our Old Testament text, and builds on that foundation with the spiritual aspect as it is revealed in our New Testament text.

The New Testament is in the Old concealed, and the Old Testament is in the New revealed. The New does not REPLACE the Old, it serves to amplify and shed light on the Old so we will understand more fully the heart of the Father.

The laws of Torah in our Old Testament text provide the parameters for our walk of faith AND provide the structure over which the spiritual Law of the New Testament lies. By combining the Word of God (Old Testament and New) with the impartation of the indwelling Spirit of God, we come to realize the fullness of faith we were intended to find.

The walk of faith is the means by which Father's will is manifested through our lives to glorify Father and benefit our fellow man. This walk of faith is intended to be within the parameters of Father's precepts as given to us in our Old Testament text. Obedience to DO the physical Law brings the physical body into blamelessness. Returning to our 1 Thessalonians text, Paul points to the necessity of the combination of spiritual and physical alignment (spirit, soul, and body) in order to be wholly sanctified:

> [23] And the very God of peace **sanctify you wholly**; and I pray
> God your whole <u>spirit and soul and body</u> be preserved blameless
> unto the coming of our Lord Jesus Christ. - 1 Thessalonians 5:23

This then is the voice of the true Spirit of God – the instruction to observe the will of God by being diligent in our obedience to both the physical and spiritual aspects of the Law, Old Testament and New. Abiding within the will of the Father is an integral aspect of our worthiness to enter into Heaven:

> [21] <u>Not every one that saith unto me, Lord, Lord, shall enter into the kingdom of heaven</u>; **but <u>he that doeth the will of my Father which is in heaven</u>**. - Matthew 7:21

Father's commandments are an intrinsic part of His Will, and they are carried forth by Y'shua, even as they were first given in written Torah from the beginning. He walked in them to be our blemish-free sacrifice. John's words are pivotal:

> [3] And hereby we do know that we know him, if we keep his commandments.

> [4] <u>He that saith, I know him, and keepeth not his commandments, is a liar, and **the truth** is not in him</u>.

> [5] But <u>whoso keepeth his word, in him verily is the love of God perfected</u>: hereby know we that we are in him.

> [6] <u>He that saith he abideth in him ought himself also so to walk, even as he walked</u>.

> [7] Brethren, I write <u>no new commandment</u> unto you, <u>but an old commandment which ye had from the beginning</u>. **The old commandment is the word which ye have heard from the beginning**. - 1 John 2:3-7

Here it is, if we have "eyes to see". THE TRUTH is in the one who keeps Father's commandments, as they are that which we have heard from the beginning – the Old Testament Torah. There is no new command, but only that which was from the beginning. Conversely, the one who departs from Father's commandments has not the truth. Do we love His TRUTH? How can we say we do if we are not keeping His commandments which are from the beginning?

The Holy Spirit is dispatched to see us through our walk of sanctification. This Spirit will not then divert us from that very thing that is to bring us into blamelessness. This Spirit will not deter us from the moral precepts of Torah which would jeopardize our standing before God.

Conversely, the contra voice will come through with great authority once the contra gospel message is embraced by the mind. This voice will assure us that

Two Trees, Two Kingdoms, Two Kings

Torah Law no longer has a place in our lives today – that Calvary changed all of that. It is amazing how many Scriptural passages must be ignored in order to come to that conclusion.

The acceptance of the contra message grants authority to this voice. To accept these teachings of man is to try to shortcut the system ordained by God:

> [6] He answered and said unto them, Well hath Esaias prophesied of you hypocrites, as it is written, <u>This people honoureth me with their lips, but their heart is far from me</u>.
>
> [7] Howbeit in vain do they worship me, <u>teaching for doctrines the commandments of men</u>.
>
> [8] For **laying aside the commandment of God**, **ye hold the tradition of men**, as the washing of pots and cups: and many other such like things ye do.
>
> [9] And he said unto them, Full well <u>ye reject the commandment of God</u>, <u>that ye may keep your own tradition</u>. - Mark 7:6-9

The contra teaching insists that any focus on Torah Law impedes our walk in the Spirit. We would say that the only walk that is impeded by focus on Torah Law is the walk in the contra spirit. Contra teaching (through lack of focus on Torah Law) effects a hobbling walk, truly an impediment to a blameless walk in the true Spirit. The contra message is designed to put the contra spirit in place of God's true Spirit, so the departure from the Law is a good place to start. To be taught to just walk in the Spirit when the boundaries established by God's Torah are removed makes it far too easy for the wrong spirit to take charge and direct our walk.

Both spirits have voices which are usually internal and inaudible, but rather a perception within the mind. Therefore, the hearing of them is a somewhat subjective matter. Once the understanding of the singularity of Shema Truth is removed, there are no longer any guidelines to validate that it is the correct Spirit which is doing the guiding. When the wrong one gains control and justifies walking in violation to the Father's precepts, the Believer invariably falls into iniquity and causes the physical body to fall short of blamelessness. The spiritual aspects of man will also fall short of blamelessness when the contra spirit guides the walk, because the Father's will for such a one can never be fully worked out in that lifestyle.

The contra gospel simply obliterates the cohesive system Father designed for total sanctification. Please understand that the contra spirit will not drag one into egregious sin right away. That would be too obvious, and the enemy is much too smart for that. It is a very gradual process, but unless something deters this influence, it can lead to profound departure from God's Way. Even a seemingly harmless minor departure is still a departure, and the adversary is extremely cunning and subtle to prompt these departures by counterfeiting God's good. Unless something happens to awaken the one who has embraced the contra gospel, the contra spirit will almost invariably succeed in undermining the true intent of God in the Believer's life, If not curtailed, it will stifle and possibly totally derail the sanctification process.

The question now becomes one of how God's expectation meets with man's perception of it. Where does the "Law" fit into the walk of the Believer today? When we read Paul's writings, are we getting the proper picture of what he even means by this term "law", and is it always used in the same manner?

Keys to Discernment

Part of the confusion when interpreting New Testament text is failure to understand the Hebrew linguistic style used by both Y'shua and Paul. This style often creates paradoxical examples to drive home a point. Unless one understands this linguistic style, a literal rendering can cause errant understanding. For instance Y'shua said in one passage to honor one's father and mother:

> [19] Honour thy father and thy mother: and, Thou shalt love thy neighbour as thyself. - Matthew 19:19

Then He says we must hate them in order to be His disciple:

> [26] If any man come to me, and hate not his father, and mother, and wife, and children, and brethren, and sisters, yea, and his own life also, he cannot be my disciple – Luke 14:26

In order to properly honor one's father and mother, one must put aside any ill feelings and show them love. So which of Y'shua's sayings is right? Well, when we view it through paradoxical relativity glasses, both are right. He was not really saying we must hate them. To do so would not honor them. He was overstating the obvious in order to make a point. His point was that we should have so much more love for Him that even the love we feel for our own parents would be (relatively) as "hate". We find the clarity of the relativity in another verse of Matthew where Y'shua says:

> [37] He that loveth father or mother more than me is not worthy of

> me: and he that loveth son or daughter more than me is not worthy
> of me. - Matthew 10:37

Another example might be Paul's words regarding circumcision:

> [2] Behold, I Paul say unto you, that <u>if ye be circumcised</u>, **Christ
> shall profit you nothing**.

> [3] For I testify again to every man that is circumcised, that <u>he is a
> debtor to do the whole law</u>. - Galatians 5:2-3

Here it sounds like Paul refutes the practice of circumcision for the Believer, implying that the Believer who is circumcised invalidates his salvation through Y'shua. Yet a few verses later Paul indicates that he preaches circumcision (Galatians 5:11):

> [11] And I, brethren, if **I yet preach circumcision**, why do I yet
> suffer persecution? then is the offense of the cross ceased. -
> Galatians 5:11

In fact, he has Timothy circumcised:

> [1] Then came he to Derbe and Lystra: and, behold, a certain
> disciple was there, named <u>Timotheus</u>, the son of a certain woman,
> which was a Jewess, and believed; but his father was a Greek:

> [2] Which was well reported of by the brethren that were at Lystra
> and Iconium.

> [3] Him would **Paul** <u>have to go forth with him; and</u> **took and cir-
> cumcised him** because of the Jews which were in those quarters:
> for they knew all that his father was a Greek. - Acts 16:1-3

Why would Paul teach circumcision and have Timothy circumcised (after believing) if it would make Timothy a debtor to the whole Law and make Y'shua of no effect to him? If Paul's words of Galatians above were to be taken literally, Paul would have been damning Timothy by having him circumcised. Obviously this is not the case. The answer is paradoxical relativity reasoning.

Paul was making a point regarding the Believer's justification by using the example of circumcision, a part of the Law of Torah – a key sign of the Torah observant male. Paul acknowledges the link of circumcision to the Law when he says that it would make one a debtor to the whole Law in Galatians 5:3 above.

The Law in and of itself is holy, just, and good:

> [12] Wherefore the law is holy, and the commandment holy, and just, and good. - Romans 7:12

Thus circumcision (being a part of the Law) is likewise holy, just and good. However, when putting on the paradoxical relativity eyeglasses, we see that if the male Believer enters into circumcision <u>in an effort to be justified</u>, he effectively annuls the profitability of the cross, as only Y'shua can provide our justification:

> [4] Christ is become of no effect unto you, whosoever of you are **justified by the law**; ye are **fallen from grace**. - Galatians 5:4

The point he is making about justification by going to this extreme can be easily misinterpreted if the fullness of Biblical context and the understanding of linguistic style is not considered. Paul is not encouraging people to abstain from circumcision, but to enter into it with the right perspective. While it is one of the commandments of God, it is only a small part of "keeping the commandments of God", and not to be construed as a means to justify man to God:

> [19] Circumcision is nothing, and uncircumcision is nothing, <u>but the keeping of the commandments of God</u>. - 1 Corinthians 7:19

He knows that God intends for His male children to be circumcised in the flesh, an outward sign of crucifying the flesh and being in covenant with Him, so he still taught it. In fact, we who are grafted into Israel by belief (strangers among the children of Israel) are not to be allowed into the Millennial Temple without it:

> [9] Thus saith the Lord GOD; No stranger, <u>uncircumcised in heart, nor</u> **uncircumcised in flesh**, shall enter into my sanctuary, of any <u>stranger that is among the children of Israel</u>. - Ezekiel 44:9

Those who try to build a doctrine around Paul's words of Galatians 5:2-3 without bringing the entirety of the Word into perspective may actually be shutting themselves out of the Temple during the Millennial reign. This is why it so important for us to have our foundation well grounded in Torah when reading New Testament Scripture.

Paul was raised with an understanding of Torah, being a Jew who was tutored by Gamaliel, commonly known as THE premier teacher of the Law in the first century AD:

> [3] I am verily a man which am <u>a Jew</u>, born in Tarsus, a city in Cilicia, yet <u>brought up</u> in this city <u>at the feet of Gamaliel</u>, and <u>taught according to the **perfect manner of the law** of the fathers</u>, and was zealous toward God, as ye all are this day. - Acts 22:3

It seems obvious to us that God selected a man of Paul's background (who had a thorough understanding of the PERFECT manner of the Law) to write much of our New Testament text for a specific reason. He knew that Paul would be able to see the link between the perfect manner of the Law (Truth) he had been taught and the spiritual application (amplified Truth) that would be revealed to him by the Holy Spirit.

Paradoxical relativity reasoning prevails throughout Paul's writings and if we do not understand that, then a lot of what Paul says can be extracted from its context and very easily misinterpreted.

To further complicate man's understanding of Pauline epistles, today's institutional theology almost always construes the word "law" (as used in Paul's writings) to mean: *Old Testament Torah*. The word "Torah" actually means: *teaching or instruction*. It is the expression of the heart of God in written form. While it contains the basic foundational structure of "law" in written form, it is much broader than a list of dos and don'ts. It is the application of Father's heart in our physical realm. <u>Actually Paul's use of the word "law" seldom means: *Torah Law* in its pure form</u>. Paul uses the term "law" in a variety of applications, and sometimes it will appear that he is against the "law" while other times he will seem to be for it. Often when Paul refers to the "law" he is not even indicating the Law of Torah at all. Yet other times when he does mean: *Torah Law*, he is actually referring disdainfully to the Pharisaical perversion of Father's pure Torah rather than the undefiled version of it. The Pharisees had added to the Law until it had become traditions of men rather than God's holy intent:

> [1] Then came to Jesus scribes and **Pharisees**, which were of Jerusalem, saying,
>
> [2] Why do thy disciples transgress the tradition of the elders? for they wash not their hands when they eat bread.
>
> [3] But he answered and said unto them, <u>Why do ye also transgress the commandment of God by your tradition?</u>
>
> [4] For God commanded, saying, Honour thy father and mother: and, He that curseth father or mother, let him die the death.

[5] But ye say, Whosoever shall say to his father or his mother, It is a gift, by whatsoever thou mightest be profited by me;

[6] And honour not his father or his mother, he shall be free. Thus have <u>ye made the commandment of God of none effect by your tradition</u>. - Matthew 15:1-6

At other times when Paul uses the term "law", he is actually referring to the penalty that is coupled to God's Law rather than referring to the Law itself. He also understands that there are both physical and spiritual applications of God's Law, and it is easy to misunderstand which one he is referencing without a discerning eye. He often refers to the "law" of sin and death and the bondage associated with it as well. His words in any particular portion of text must be carefully studied in order to properly understand the flow of thought he is conveying, which type of "law" he is referencing, and what aspect of that "law" is pertinent.

The contra gospel is dependent on the deviation which occurs from inordinately construing almost every mention of the word "law" in Pauline epistles to mean: *Old Testament Torah Law*. Due to the specific wording in Paul's writings, it is easy to jump to conclusions that support the contra gospel message instead of digging out the true intent of Paul's words which support the true Gospel message. Seeing Paul's words in their proper context is amazingly straightforward and transparent, once we come to understand that his intended message is always in alignment with Torah. Paul understood the singularity of the Tree of Life essence and had a fully grounded spiritual understanding through the Holy Spirit. When properly discerned, his inspired understanding (and therefore his writing) maintains total integrity with the Old Testament Torah principles.

Again, the context one needs to use in order to properly interpret Paul's writings is not just a few words around a referenced verse, but rather the entire Biblical text, including the Old Testament text which he knew inside and out – the same text which Paul knew his first century audience likewise understood. Paul expects the reader or hearer to put his words WITHIN the parameters of Father's Torah. This would be the Hebraic style of cyclical instruction which Paul understood and used. Any implication drawn from his words should be viewed with this understanding rather than being isolated from Torah in the linear instructional fashion often used in today's pulpits of western thought.

In his writing Paul presumed that his audience was totally familiar with the Scriptures, which (at the time of his writing) only consisted of the Torah, the prophets, Psalms and the various other writings from our Old Testament. He knew that they would never interpret his words as being in conflict with the instructions of the Father, as recorded in our Old Testament text. He intended his words to uphold the principles found within these Old Testament Scriptures. We will see multitudes of evidence to validate this claim as the book proceeds. We will look at the words of Paul which are often misinterpreted, and will put them into the context of the entirety of God's Word. The picture that emerges is quite estranged from the gospel message we often hear today.

CHAPTER 5

RELATIVITY OF LAW

Possibly the hardest hurdle in our new understanding was how the concept of "law" in Paul's epistles integrated with this emerging picture. How did it fit with the singularity pattern? If we were committed to viewing the harmony of the entire Biblical text as a congruent whole, what part did the Law play in this perspective?

Law – Is it Obsolete?

There is much contention within the body of Messiah today regarding whether or not the Law should be observed. It seems that whether or not we choose to observe Father's Law might result in the honoring or dishonoring of the One who gave it to us. Paul has this to say in Romans:

> [23] Thou that makest thy boast of the law, through <u>breaking the law dishonourest thou God</u>? - Romans 2:23

Though this verse is coming from the back side to prove a point, it is clear that Paul understands that the breaking of the Law dishonors God. Would he then teach man that there is no harm in doing so? Often quotes from Paul's epistles are used to justify the rejection of Law for today, but if we are unbiased and diligent to seek his true intent, we can see otherwise. In future chapters, we will cite many of Paul's references that are misinterpreted today and will work through them to see what they really do and don't say. There are other New Testament passages to be addressed in this respect as well. There are actually many portions of text that undeniably uphold the Law and even verify the importance of it in our lives today.

Much of the Scripture that is used to paint the distorted contra picture is centered around the new priesthood and covenant of Hebrews 7 and 8, which we will dissect shortly as well. Yes, there is a new priesthood coming, but

Two Trees, Two Kingdoms, Two Kings

any teaching that uses this new priesthood to promote the idea that Father's precepts are no longer a consideration is a thorny fruit, and any voice that concurs with this teaching is not the right voice. That picture simply shreds the integrity of the singularity of the Father's Word that we know as our Bible. Such division is destructive beyond measure.

Before we work with Paul further, we would acknowledge that he was not the only source for things that could be wrongfully interpreted to support the abolition of Law today. Another such verse is found in John:

> [17] For the law was given by Moses, *but* grace and truth came by Jesus Christ. - John 1:17

Some might use this verse out of context to contrast the inferiority of Moses to Y'shua, and therefore diminish the status of the Law brought by Moses. We must remember though, that it was the Father who actually provided the Law which Moses simply brought forward. Likewise, some see this verse as implying that the Law was inferior to grace and Truth. This is due to what appears (in our translated text) to imply a contrast between the first part of the sentence and the last. The implication that the Law (a direct extraction from the Word of Father) was meaningless compared to the Truth which Y'shua brought forth, would have to come at the expense of numerous other portions of Scripture.

In Y'shua's prayer to the Father in John, He says:

> [17] Sanctify them through thy truth: <u>thy word is truth</u>. - John 17:17

If the Word (which contains the Law) is not Truth, then why would Y'shua speak what He did to Father in prayer in this verse? Even the book of Psalms confirms that the Law is Truth:

> [142] Thy righteousness is an everlasting righteousness, and **thy law is the truth**. - Psalms 119:142

When we harmonize Scripture we see that the Law too is Truth. Both the Law and Y'shua are Truth because they are of one and the same essence. Y'shua is the Torah come to life, bringing WITH Him grace. The word "but" in John 1:17 was added to the Biblical text when it was translated, as noted by its italicized font. Without it we get a different view. If we remove it to see what was originally said, this verse is actually showing this progression – not pitting one part of the sentence against the other. For the <u>Law (Truth)</u> was given by Moses, <u>grace **AND** Truth</u> came by Jesus Christ.

It is showing that Y'shua was not only the Truth of the Law brought forward, but as He brought it forward He did so this time in grace, providing redemption for our inability to keep that Law. The word "and" can actually imply that the Torah Law itself was Truth without this measure of grace, but Y'shua brought both the Truth of Torah AND the manifestation of the grace. It would be by this grace that man could be saved from the penalty imposed by the failure to keep the Law. Paul references this penalty as the curse associated with the Law. Y'shua took our penalty on Himself:

> [13] <u>Christ hath redeemed us from **the curse of the law**</u>, being made a curse for us: for it is written, Cursed is every one that hangeth on a tree: - Galatians 3:13

Further, Y'shua expanded on the Truth of the written Torah to provide us spiritual insight regarding the Father's precepts, bringing the Law to life in a more meaningful manner. The Father brought man the written Torah through Moses, then sent Y'shua to us as the living Torah, full of BOTH grace AND Truth:

> [14] And **the Word was made flesh**, and dwelt among us, (and we beheld his glory, the glory as of the only begotten of the Father,) <u>full of grace and truth</u>. - John 1:14

To see John 1:17 as pitting the Law against grace would be a prime example of what happens when deception sets in. By ignoring the entirety of the Word we can easily misapply certain portions of the Word and adjust them to align with our belief. This is a snare of major magnitude.

What Did Y'shua Relate About the Law?

There are two spiritual commandments given by Y'shua on which all others that stem from Old Testament Torah hang. These two major commandments don't negate any of the previous commandments, but merely summarize them under their broader spiritual application. If these two summary commandments negated the other portions of the Law then there would be nothing left to hang or be suspended on them. The physical laws <u>hang on</u> these two New Testament commandments:

> [37] Jesus said unto him, Thou shalt **love the Lord thy God** with all thy heart, and with all thy soul, and with all thy mind.

> [38] This is the <u>first and great commandment</u>.

> [39] And the second is like unto it, Thou shalt **love thy neighbour** as thyself.
>
> [40] **On these two commandments hang all the law and the prophets**. - Matthew 22:37-40

Actually, these two commands were first mentioned in Old Testament Torah instruction:

> [5] And thou shalt **love the LORD thy God** with all thine heart, and with all thy soul, and with all thy might. - Deuteronomy 6:5
>
> [18] Thou shalt not avenge, nor bear any grudge against the children of thy people, but thou shalt **love thy neighbour as thyself**: I am the LORD. - Leviticus 19:18

Accordingly, these two commandments spoken by Y'shua were not new commandments as is typically taught today. Y'shua was just repeating to us what Torah had already commanded. Our Matthew reference tells us that the first one was the more important of the two. If loving the Lord our God is the greatest commandment which Y'shua carried forth, then we should be told somewhere how to do it. We find our answer by looking to 1 John:

> [3] For **this is the love of God, that we keep his commandments**: and his commandments are not grievous. - 1 John 5:3

This is a bookmark text. It feeds us a truth that we must realize in order to love God properly, the greatest commandment of all. We cannot love Father fully in order to obey the first of the spiritual commandments Y'shua gave us, without first keeping the basic commandments Father gave us in Torah. First comes the physical (or natural), then the spiritual. It is a pattern of God:

> [46] Howbeit that was not first which is spiritual, but that which is natural; and afterward that which is spiritual. - 1 Corinthians 15:46

It is by adhering to the Torah precepts of Father that we show Him we love Him properly. The two go hand in hand. The church often teaches us to love the Son, but seldom brings the Father into the picture at all. Y'shua did not just come merely to provide atonement for our sins. The atonement He accomplished was to implement a much greater objective - to reunite us with the Father:

> [6] Jesus saith unto him, I am the way, the truth, and the life: **NO MAN COMETH UNTO THE FATHER, BUT BY ME**. - John 14:6

That is perhaps the most profound principle of the faith, and very few see it. The Son was sent in order to restore the Way back to the Father. It is critical that we realize this. The forgiveness of sins is often taught as the <u>purpose</u> for which the Son came. That is only a part of the picture. In the broader sense it was <u>simply the means</u> by which He would restore us to Father, repairing the breach which our ancestors Adam and Eve wrought between Father and mankind in Eden.

Prophesying of Y'shua's arrival in the future, Isaiah's words are very significant:

> [12] And they that shall be of thee shall build the old waste places: thou shalt raise up the foundations of many generations; and thou shalt be called, **The repairer of the breach**, **The restorer of paths to dwell in**. - Isaiah 58:12

We are to love and honor the Father, just as we do the Son. We are certainly not shown anywhere to ignore the Father, and both are to reside with us:

> [23] Jesus answered and said unto him, <u>If a man love me, he will keep my words</u>: and <u>**my Father**</u> **will love him, and** <u>**we**</u> **will come unto him, and make our abode with him**. - John 14:23

If the Father is also to abide with us, why would we want to grieve Him by turning our back on His precepts? Actually this verse seems to imply that the Father's abiding with us is <u>hinged on</u> our keeping Y'shua's words, and His words indicate that we should honor the Father's Law:

> [17] Think not that I am come to destroy the law, or the prophets: I am not come to destroy, but to fulfil.

> [18] For verily I say unto you, Till heaven and earth pass, one jot or one tittle shall in no wise pass from the law, <u>till all be fulfilled</u>.

> [19] <u>Whosoever therefore shall break one of these least com-mandments, and shall teach men so, he shall be called the least in the kingdom of heaven: but whosoever shall do and teach them, the same shall be called great in the kingdom of heaven</u>. - Matthew 5:17-19

Y'shua informs us quite clearly that the Father's Law will be in effect until ALL is fulfilled. This fulfillment of all things will be evidenced by the passing away of Heaven and earth, which has not yet occurred. In the meantime, we are not to break even the least of these laws or teach others that it is accept-able to do so.

Two Trees, Two Kingdoms, Two Kings

In John's epistles we are shown that in order for us to continue in BOTH the Son AND the Father we must retain within us that which we heard from the beginning:

> [24] <u>Let that therefore abide in you, **which ye have heard from the beginning**. If that which ye have heard from the beginning shall remain in you, ye also shall continue **in the Son, and in the Father.**</u> - 1 John 2:24

Even if we come to Messiah through the New Testament in our corporate church system, words such as these in John's epistles should direct us back to the Old Testament to discover the foundation for our faith. It was Torah which was taught to God's children "from the beginning". The commandments of Torah are then reinforced throughout the balance of the Biblical text, if one hears it with ears to hear, and reads it with eyes to see:

> [7] The works of his hands are verity and judgment; **all his commandments are sure**.
>
> [8] **They stand fast for ever and ever**, and are done in truth and uprightness.
>
> [9] <u>He sent redemption unto his people</u>: **he hath commanded his covenant for ever**: holy and <u>reverend is his name</u>.
>
> [10] The fear of the LORD is the beginning of wisdom: **a good understanding have all they that do his commandments**: his praise endureth for ever. - Psalms 111:7-10

We will show a bit later how the new covenant found in the book of Hebrews is not (as it is commonly taught) a <u>replacement of</u> the old, as this would negate the words of verse 9 here that "he hath commanded his covenant for ever". We know that the redemption Father sent His people was Y'shua. Even after the reference to this redemption in verse 9, we see Father's insistence of keeping His commandments, and it is sealed with His reverend name. It is important to note in Hosea, however, that in spite of His redemptive measures His ways are not followed:

> [13] Woe unto them! for <u>they have fled from me</u>: destruction unto them! because <u>they have transgressed against me</u>: **though I have redeemed them**, yet <u>they have spoken lies against me</u>.
>
> [16] **They return, but not to the most High:** <u>they are like a deceitful bow</u>: ... - Hosea 7:13, 16

It was never God's intent to receive and walk in Y'shua to the exclusion of the Father, but (as Y'shua indicates in the Gospel of John) we are to be one IN them even as they are one with each other:

> [21] That they all may be one; **as thou, Father, art in me, and I in thee, <u>that they also may be one IN us</u>**: that the world may believe that thou hast sent me. - John 17:21

This was to be accomplished **through the Father's name and the Truth of His Word**:

> [11] And now I am no more in the world, but these are in the world, and I come to thee. Holy Father, <u>keep **through thine own name those whom thou hast given me**</u>, **that they may be one, as we are**.

> [17] <u>Sanctify</u> them **through thy truth**: thy **word** is truth. - John 17:11 & 17

Thus it is Father's Word (which is primarily Old Testament Torah) that is to sanctify us, and His Word (Torah) is Truth. The Truth of the physical aspects of Torah was the foundation for the amplified spiritual Truth which followed. When this sanctification is completed, we will be as one with the Father and the Son, per Y'shua's prayer in John 17:21 above. It is voiced again in Hebrews:

> [11] **For both he that sanctifieth and they who are sanctified are all of one**: for which cause he is not ashamed to call them brethren, - Hebrews 2:11

Thus we see that our walk of sanctification is to involve both the Father and the Son, and is intricately bound to Torah Truth and Law:

> [17] And he said unto him, Why callest thou me good? there is none good but one, that is, God: but **if thou wilt enter into life, keep the commandments**. - Matthew 19:17

> [14] **Blessed are they that do his commandments, that they may have right to the Tree of Life**, and may enter in through the gates into the city. - Revelation 22:14

The emphasis must be to keep the physical <u>as the beginning</u> of keeping the spiritual. It is through <u>keeping the physical Law</u> that we show our love to Father. While the physical Law is more concrete, the spiritual Law is discerned as the Holy Spirit shows us how it correlates to the physical. Because it overlies the physical, it would be incomplete without the structural foundation of the physical beneath it.

An example of this would be the words of Y'shua:

> [27] Ye have heard that it was said by them of old time, Thou shalt not commit adultery:

> [28] But I say unto you, That whosoever looketh on a woman to lust after her hath committed adultery with her already in his heart. - Matthew 5:27-28

Not lusting after a woman in the heart is the spiritual aspect of the Law which applies to the heart and mind. It amplifies the physical Law which is the seventh of the ten basic Torah commandments – the prohibition of physical intimate relations outside of marriage. The spiritual concept of lusting after a woman does not replace the Law relative to physical adultery, it accentuates it and allows us to see the more expansive spiritual application of it. The spiritual intent in Heaven gave birth to the physical precept on earth through Torah instruction. Later after Y'shua came, the physical was amplified by the spiritual to give us insight to the broader Heavenly purpose of God's original intent. That which was given to us first was the natural or earthly physical version, which was followed by the Heavenly spiritual version:

> [45] And so it is written, The first man Adam was made a living soul; the last Adam was made a quickening spirit.

> [46] Howbeit that was not <u>first</u> which is spiritual, but <u>that which is natural</u>; and <u>afterward that which is spiritual</u>.

> [47] The <u>first</u> man is of the earth, <u>earthy</u>: the <u>second</u> man is the Lord <u>from heaven</u>. - 1 Corinthians 15:45-47

The structure of the physical provided the basis for our understanding of the spiritual. Overlying the physical with the spiritual helps us to bring the thoughts of the mind and heart (the inner man) under obedience, so the body (the outer man) does not sin in the physical state:

> [5] Casting down imaginations, and every high thing that exalteth itself against the knowledge of God, and bringing into captivity every thought to the obedience of Christ; - 2 Corinthians 10:5

The act of adultery is the physical application, but if we abstain from even the indulgence of such thoughts (the spiritual application), then the physical will not become an issue. Physical iniquity follows spiritual transgression.

As we keep Father's physical commandments, we are shown how to love Him even more fully by adhering to the spiritual application as well. As we keep the spiritual in accordance with the Spirit of God, the physical will more easily fall into place. As we keep His commandments that relate to our fellow man we learn how to apply the spiritual Law toward them as well, loving them even more fully than we otherwise would. In this way are the two commandments given to us by Y'shua honored.

The natural man (one who has not yet found Y'shua and therefore has not received the indwelling of the Holy Spirit) can actually walk in the physical commandments to some degree of success. However, keeping the physical Law will not provide for his justification:

> [16] ... for by the works of the law shall no flesh be justified. - Galatians 2:16

He will likewise stumble over the spiritual aspects of the Law which are conveyed by the Holy Spirit, because they are spiritually discerned:

> [14] But <u>the natural man receiveth not the things of the Spirit of God</u>: for they are foolishness unto him: neither can he know them, because they are <u>spiritually discerned</u>. - 1 Corinthians 2:14

Going back to the beginning, we were given strict orders NOT to add to or detract from the written commandments as they were first given:

> [2] <u>Ye shall not add unto the word which I command you</u>, <u>neither shall ye diminish ought from it</u>, that ye may <u>keep the commandments of the LORD your God</u> which I command you. - Deuteronomy 4:2

It seems Father knew this would happen in the end days. Isn't that exactly what the increasingly popular interpretation of Paul's teachings accomplishes – removing the Law which Father AND Y'shua said (in Matthew 5:18 above) was never to be removed? On the other hand, the Pharisees had added so many extra measures to Torah precepts that they had totally obscured the original intent. We take issue with both manners of infraction of this Deuteronomy 4:2 text.

Further validation that the Law is still to be acknowledged today is found in 1 John when he says:

> [7] Brethren, I write no new commandment unto you, but an
> old commandment which ye had from the beginning. The old

> commandment is the word which ye have heard from the beginning. - 1 John 2:7
>
> [5] And now I beseech thee, lady, not as though I wrote a new commandment unto thee, but that which we had from the beginning, that we love one another.
>
> [6] And <u>this is love, that we walk after his commandments. This is the commandment, That, as ye have heard from the beginning, ye should walk in it</u>. - 2 John 1:5-6

As we will further explain a bit later, the reference to Ephraim can be a metaphor for (or a deeper prophetic implication of) the spiritual house we call Christianity. Israel can be understood as the broader description of this house – emphasizing the people within it. Accordingly, some wording in Hosea disturbs us greatly:

> [3] I know Ephraim, and Israel is not hid from me: for now, O Ephraim, thou committest whoredom, and <u>Israel is defiled</u>.
>
> [4] <u>They will not frame their doings to turn unto their God</u>: for the spirit of whoredoms is in the midst of them, and they have not known the LORD. - Hosea 5:3-4
>
> [12] <u>I have written to him the great things of my **law**, but they were counted as **a strange thing**</u>. - Hosea 8:12

What God sees as being great, the church sees as being a strange thing. The words "strange thing" are a single Hebrew word, Strong's #H2114 ("zuwr") - *the basic meaning of this word is to turn aside; to be a stranger, a person outside the family, the adulterous woman, to go astray, to be wayward.* The church's disregard for Torah observance today grieves us because we can see the indignant displeasure indicated by God's words here - how treating His great Law as being strange or foreign is so troubling to Him. "They have not <u>known</u>" Him (verse 4 above).

It is critical to our walk of faith to be true to Father's precepts. If the Word is our filter, then we can not throw major chunks of it away and filter through only those parts that remain to our liking. Any doctrinal stance we embrace must filter through the entirety of the Biblical text. To fail to do so is to fail to be Berean. The theology of our end days is ladened with land mines, and if we fail to be Bereans in this day of rampant deception, we are destined to fall prey to that deception. While Paul's words convey truth, the interpretations of them that are common today are filled with falsehood that will lead to the broad path, and we MUST be Bereans to see it. Recall that Paul praised the Bereans for searching out his own teachings in the Scriptures (the Old Testament [Torah] in his day) to understand his message. He would expect us to do likewise. Only by doing so can we see what our New Testament text is really saying.

Bitter Waters

> [23] And when they came to Marah, <u>they could not drink of the</u> <u>**waters** of Marah, for they **were bitter**</u>: therefore the name of it was called Marah.
>
> [24] And the people murmured against Moses, saying, What shall we drink?
>
> [25] And he cried unto the LORD; and <u>the LORD shewed him **a**</u> <u>**tree**, which when he had cast into the waters, the **waters** were</u> <u>**made sweet**: there he made for them a statute and an ordinance,</u> <u>and there **he proved them**</u>,
>
> [26] And said, <u>If thou wilt diligently hearken to the voice of the</u> <u>LORD thy God, and wilt do that which is right in his sight, and wilt</u> <u>give ear to his commandments, and keep all his statutes, I will put</u> <u>none of these diseases upon thee, which I have brought upon the</u> <u>Egyptians: for I am the LORD that healeth thee</u>. - Exodus 15:23-26

The proper name Marah is Strong's #H4785 ("Marah") - *bitter*. Mary (the mother of Y'shua) is Strong's #G3137 ("Maria"). Its roots go back to the Hebrew word, Strong's #H4784 ("marah") - *bitter, to be contentious, be rebellious, be refractory, be disobedient towards, be rebellious against God*. It appears that #H4785 is the Hebraic name derived from the meaning of its roots in #H4784. Therefore, the names Marah and Mary the mother of Y'shua are linked.

The word "waters" of verse 23 is Strong's #H4325 ("mayim"). The lexicon notes indicate that this word can allude to waters in a reproductive sense. This may be an intentional double meaning embodied in the language by the Creator. His masterful linguistic design may be pointing us to a relevant parallel passage of significance:

> [18] Now the birth of Jesus Christ was on this wise: <u>When as his</u> <u>mother Mary was espoused to Joseph, before they came together,</u> <u>she was found with child of the Holy Ghost</u>.
>
> [19] Then Joseph her husband, being a just man, and not willing to make her a publick example, was minded to put her away privily.

> [20] But while he thought on these things, behold, the angel of the Lord appeared unto him in a dream, saying, Joseph, thou son of David, <u>fear not to take unto thee Mary thy wife: for that which is conceived in her is of the Holy Ghost</u>.
>
> [21] And <u>she shall bring forth a son</u>, and thou shalt call his name JESUS: for <u>he shall save his people from their sins</u>. - Matthew 1:18-21

The waters within Mary can be considered as bitter and rebellious. This is not in any way implying that Mary was personally anything less than chaste, honorable and upstanding. It is simply a fact relative to the human state that our bodies and reproductive capacities are contaminated with the sin nature after the fall. It is simply the flaw of humankind in the post-fall condition, and Father was about to turn this around.

Just as we found in the Old Testament text relative to Marah, God is now turning bitter to sweet in the New Testament era. Into Mary's waters was put a tree, and the waters were made sweet. This tree was not of Joseph, nor was it of human origin. This tree was the Tree of Life being brought forth as Y'shua into and through Mary by the Holy Ghost. This tree was a pure source which would sweeten the water from which mankind would be able to drink to bring them to salvation. It would ultimately turn them from bitter (corrupted) to sweet (incorruptible). To continue the thought process of our Exodus passage where the water was made sweet, verses 25-26 say that this was <u>to prove man</u> – to see if man would then choose to walk in His ways so he could be healed.

Are we beginning to see that the role of Y'shua was to restore the breach, giving us all that we need (the Way, the Truth, and the Life) in order to prove us before the Father? He would provide the Way (the narrow way) back to Father. He would impart the Truth we need to understand how to walk in the Way. Then He would grant us access to the resurrected Life so we might be able to remain in the Way. All of Y'shua's provision was put into our hands along with the freedom to choose – to choose whether or not to enter and then stay on the narrow way He opened up to us. Thus could we be proven before Father – proven as being those who love Him and His Law. Will we be proven to honor His Way and walk with Him in obedience? Will we be proven to decline to obey, choosing instead the way of the world and the traditions of men? Which course will we individually choose?:

> [25] And he cried unto the LORD; and the LORD shewed him a tree, which when he had cast into the waters, the waters were

made sweet: there he made for them a statute and an ordinance, and there he **proved** them,

[26] And said, <u>If thou wilt diligently hearken to the voice of the LORD thy God, and wilt do that which is right in his sight, and wilt give ear to his commandments, and keep all his statutes</u>, I will put none of these diseases upon thee, which I have brought upon the Egyptians: for <u>I am the LORD that healeth thee</u>. - Exodus 15:25-26

The word "proved" in verse 25 is Strong's #H5254 ("nacah") - *to test, try, prove, tempt, assay, put to the proof or test*. That is exactly what Y'shua did. He came to proclaim that which He heard from the Father, and to encourage those who professed His name to follow the ways of the Father:

[50] And I know that his commandment is life everlasting: whatsoever I speak therefore, even as the Father said unto me, so I speak. - John 12:50

[17] And he said unto him, Why callest thou me good? there is none good but one, that is, God: but if thou wilt enter into life, keep the commandments. - Matthew 19:17

The above Exodus text concerning the water of Marah indicates in verse 26 that Father is the healer of mankind. Accordingly, good health in the earthly realm can be a reward of obedience to Father's commandments, and the avoidance of disease may be conditional to keeping the commandments. Though we know that failure to keep the commandments is not the sole reason for disease in our day, might it have bearing in a large number of cases? In reality (especially in today's modern lifestyles) there are many who are not keeping some of God's ways, failing to understand that it is a problem in His eyes.

If we look even one step further to our predominant spiritual disease of sin, lack of obedience may be a barrier to the healing that makes us WHOLE at the conclusion of our earthly sojourn when our corruptible state is to be transitioned into the incorruptible state. That too may be heavily linked to the commitment to abide within the Father's statutes after the bitter is made sweet. He <u>proves</u> us after our belief in Y'shua turns our bitter to sweet. If we profess the name of Y'shua and yet turn from the "Way" which He tells us to walk (rebelling against His commandments and statutes), then we profess with our mouths the Tree of Life which Y'shua provides, but reject it by the way we live our lives. In essence we then return spiritually (at least to some degree) to the bitter waters:

[8] This people draweth nigh unto me with their mouth, and

> honoureth me with their lips; but their heart is far from me. -
> Matthew 15:8

We bring hypocrisy into our walk when we speak a profession of Y'shua, then walk in denial of the path He entreated us to follow. This spites the Spirit of Grace by which we were saved, bringing into jeopardy the spiritual healing which is to follow for those who adhere to the ways of the Father:

> [17] And he said unto him, Why callest thou me good? there is none good but one, that is, God: but <u>if thou wilt enter into life, keep the commandments</u>. - Matthew 19:17

We are free to push aside the moral precepts presented by Father, even after our Belief on Y'shua, but doing so may be at a great cost.

Moral and Ceremonial Laws

Christendom commonly categorizes the various aspects of the Law under either moral or ceremonial headings. We essentially agree with these general headings. However, while Christendom typically relegates both categories to the sidelines of the faith, we do not. We distinguish between these headings relative to the way the Laws beneath them are to be treated. The ceremonial portion includes such aspects as rituals, observances, and corrective measures. The moral segment expresses the expectations of our God relative to the conduct of His children. Since we will discuss the individual aspects of the Law as we proceed, we will not cover them now.

There are multiple Hebrew words that we associate with the term "law" in our English language. Some of these are ordinances, statutes, commandments, and precepts. There is considerable overlapping with the words ordinances, statutes, and commandments, and many of the Hebrew words that are so translated fluctuate from one to the other throughout the text. This would imply a great deal of similarity in their meaning. The one that stands out from the rest seems to be the Hebrew word which is usually translated as "**precepts**". This word is Strong's #H6490 ("piqquwd") - *precept, statute*. It is translated "precept(s)" 21 times, "commandment(s)" two times, and "statute(s)" one time. Therefore, it is predominantly presented as being a "precept" in contrast to an ordinance, statute, or commandment. The term precept carries a slightly different connotation than the other three words. It indicates <u>a rule or **principle** prescribing a particular course of action or conduct</u>. It is more of a moral code. It is primarily this context of "precepts" of the Law (the moral principles) which we will address throughout the book.

The moral codes were imposed to point us to Father's more spiritual design for our lives. They are Father's heart, and we are not to trample His heart under our feet. We believe they are to be observed continually, as long as we have life and breath.

The important concept being presented at this point is the difference in the relativity of the various aspects of God's Law in our lives today. As we have come to understand God's imprint on our hearts, the ceremonial aspects of the Law were given to the people for a time. They pointed to various segments of God's plan for mankind which must be fulfilled by Y'shua. Each aspect of these Laws was to be observed until its complete fulfillment:

> [17] Think not that I am come to destroy the law, or the prophets: **I am not come to destroy, but to fulfil**. - Matthew 5:17

Again, the word "fulfil" here is Strong's #G4137 ("plēroō") - *to make full, to fill to the full; to cause to abound, to furnish or supply liberally; to fill to the top: so that nothing shall be wanting to full measure; to make complete in every particular, to render perfect; to carry through to the end, to accomplish, carry out, (some undertaking); in matters of duty: to perform, execute of sayings, promises, prophecies, to bring to pass, ratify, accomplish; to cause God's will (as made known in the law) to be obeyed as it should be, and God's promises (given through the prophets) to receive fulfillment.*

We mentioned earlier that Y'shua came to bring us fuller understanding in His teachings, but He also came that He might bring completion to all that they represent. The former has been accomplished already, but the latter is still unfolding.

Corrective Measures

As the Law relates to man's relationship to other men, the Law allows for corrective measures to deter improper behavior. At times there is need for the legal system to provide restitution for wrongs, or to secure a dangerous offender. However, in this era of grace after Y'shua, the need for severe consequence has been tempered. There is little demand for such extreme corrective measures as stoning an offender. The arrival of Y'shua brought forgiveness to the forefront, and through this forgiveness, the offender may be granted at least a degree of reprieve:

> [38] Ye have heard that it hath been said, An eye for an eye, and a tooth for a tooth:

> [39] But I say unto you, That ye resist not evil: but whosoever shall smite thee on thy right cheek, turn to him the other also.
>
> [40] And if any man will sue thee at the law, and take away thy coat, let him have thy cloke also.
>
> [41] And whosoever shall compel thee to go a mile, go with him twain. - Matthew 5:38-41

While judgment is at times still needed, it is now to be tempered with mercy:

> [13] For he shall have judgment without mercy, that hath shewed no mercy; and mercy rejoiceth against judgment. - James 2:13

A secondary aspect of corrective measures was to separate the unclean person from the clean so there would be no cross-contamination. It was usually due to contagious disease, menstruation, or some other unclean condition. Quarantining was the typical procedure to deal with this problem. Our hygienic capabilities are considerably different today, largely enabling modern society to bypass such measures as menstruation quarantine, etc. God is all about dividing the holy from the unholy and the clean from the unclean, so if we aspire to be pleasing to Him we should view this seriously:

> [10] And that ye may put difference between holy and unholy, and between unclean and clean; - Leviticus 10:10

When it comes to the dietary restrictions of the Law, we will discuss briefly now the eating of things which God says are unclean. Since eating these things involves internalizing and taking into the digestive tract the unclean thing (which we are admonished in great detail not to do), we believe it actually encroaches on the category of moral principles.

Paul even reiterates this separation of clean from unclean when he warns us not to <u>touch</u> the unclean thing in order that God will receive us:

> [17] Wherefore come out from among them, and be ye separate, saith the Lord, and **touch not the unclean thing**; and I will receive you, - 2 Corinthians 6:17

While this particular reference is relative to the infidel, God's standards of clean and unclean extend much further, and the principle is still active. To eat unclean meat is to not only touch it but to actually internalize it!

The punitive aspects of the Law have become somewhat conditional. However, the underlying desires of Father should still be honored at all times. The moral precepts are the very heart of the Father Himself, and should always be observed. The observance of Sabbaths is likewise a desire He has expressed for His children – a time He wants them to draw near to Him. Neither the moral code He established or the Sabbath observances (weekly and annual) which He cherishes should be viewed as a burden to us, but rather as a joy to uphold – if we truly want to please Father and draw near to His heart. We will cover the Sabbath aspect very shortly as well. It is only when we begin to see the Son as being separate from the Father and draw near to the Son to the exclusion of the Father that we would want to depart from keeping those things which we know the Father ordained – those things which we know would please Him.

Once the fulfillment of the Sabbaths has been totally enacted, the observance of these special times might change. However, they are only partially fulfilled at this time, with complete fulfillment being yet future. We believe that since the shadow-typing significance of God's Sabbaths (both weekly and annual) is treated as a whole, the entire scope of Sabbath should still be observed until the total fulfillment is realized. We will cover this more as we proceed.

The link of the earthly (physical) to the Heavenly (spiritual) is well established. We see for instance Y'shua's words in Matthew:

> [10] Thy kingdom come. Thy will be done in earth, as it is in heaven. - Matthew 6:10

The principal of physical and spiritual following one another is likewise evident:

> [46] Howbeit that was not first which is spiritual, but that which is natural; and afterward that which is spiritual. - 1 Corinthians 15:46

If we are to observe Father's dietary laws, we should consider both the physical and spiritual aspects of our food consumption. There is physical food and there is spiritual food. The spiritual food is to allow us to see, understand, embrace and conform to the more spiritual nature embodied in the Tree of Life. Again this tree and all which comes from it is a singularity of unity in essence – goodness and only goodness, cleanliness and purity, righteousness and holiness. When we partake of physical foods, they should be of the same nature, befitting our bodies to remain pure in Father's sight. Maintaining clean standards in our dining is also a sign and witness to others that we desire only what Father considers to be clean and acceptable for food. If we eat that which is unclean in His sight, it may imply to God and others that we don't care about having clean spiritual food either – the earthly is linked to the Heavenly. Of course, the unclean spiritual food gospel of duality from the Tree of Knowledge teaches that it is alright to consume unclean physical food. Those then who have internalized this instruction may well eat of the physically unclean as well, without thinking twice about it. When we physically eat unclean food we exhibit confusion to the world around us rather than a pure witness of the righteousness of Father and the unity and holiness of His ways. Note that we will get much more specific about the topic of what we should and shouldn't eat (as well as Paul's words about it) in the chapters ahead.

We should become more intimate with the full understanding of Father's intent as the physical and spiritual interact. Y'shua actually reinforced Father's moral code of conduct by amplifying it to a larger perspective for our spiritual walks. We don't need for Him to tell us why, we simply need to be obedient to His expressly stated will in these matters without trying to find ways to circumvent them:

> [4] Thou hast commanded us to <u>keep thy precepts diligently</u>. - Psalms 119:4

> [15] I will meditate in thy <u>precepts</u>, and <u>have respect unto thy ways</u>. - Psalms 119:15

> [159] Consider how <u>I love thy precepts</u>: quicken me, O LORD, according to thy lovingkindness. - Psalms 119:159

> [44] <u>So shall I keep thy law continually for ever and ever</u>.

> [45] And **I will walk at liberty**: <u>for I seek thy precepts</u>. - Psalms 119:44-45

You see, this last reference indicates to us that the concept of "liberty" as it relates to God's Law is totally misinterpreted by corporate Christendom today. Man's version has become that our liberty in Messiah is realized through no longer having to deal with the Law. Father's Word of Truth says otherwise. We are to find our liberty in seeking the Father's precepts. Liberty and seeking to follow Father's precepts are not opposed to one another. His precepts point us to His WAYS, and we are to honor those ways by keeping His precepts diligently. As we do so we please Him, and we bring health and well being to our inner man AND (especially as it relates to unclean foods) to our bodies as well. As the Spirit ministers through guiding us in these precepts we are spiritually liberated from our unclean state and brought into spotlessness.

Likewise, observing the Lord's Festivals cements the meaning of them as typologies of the work of our Savior for the benefit of mankind. While ceremonial Law is more relaxed at times, we believe adherence to Father's moral principles is still to be a basis for our walk, and the observations of Sabbath shadow-typing has a place in our belief system as well.

The Law and Bondage

The commonly perceived concept among today's tenets of the faith is that the "Law" is "bondage". Indeed Paul's writings seem to be somewhat a source of confusion in the church today, and have been largely misunderstood. When Paul was being tried in Acts, he said: "Neither against the law of the Jews … have I offended any thing at all":

> [8] While he answered for himself, Neither <u>against the law of the Jews</u>, neither against the temple, nor yet against Caesar, <u>have I offended any thing at all</u>. - Acts 25:8

By stating that he had not "offended" the law of the Jews, he is acknowledging his compliance to the Law. Paul took no issue with the Law, saying that it was good – even holy. His words of denigration regarding the subject of the Law were never directed toward the precepts of the Law:

> [12] Wherefore **the law is holy**, and <u>the commandment holy, and just, and good</u>.

> [13] **<u>Was then that which is good made death unto me? God forbid</u>**. But sin, that it might appear sin, working death in me by that which is good; that sin by the commandment might become exceeding sinful.

> [14] For we know that **the law is spiritual**: but I am carnal, sold under sin. - Romans 7:12-14

Though Paul's stance is often construed and taught to be against the "Law", this passage indicates that such teaching is invalid. Paul was not opposed to <u>the Law itself</u> at all, and <u>did NOT claim (per verse 13) that it was the Law that brings him death</u>. He then emphasizes this by saying: "God forbid"! Paul was professing that it is sin that brings one to death. His objective when criticizing the Law in relation to grace was to show that the Law serves to convict us of our inability to adhere to it totally, and points to the need for the provision of grace through a Savior.

Two Trees, Two Kingdoms, Two Kings

This passage also points to the need for Y'shua:

> [22] For <u>I delight in the law of God after the inward man</u>:

> [23] But I see another law in <u>my members</u>, <u>warring against the law of my mind</u>, and <u>bringing me into captivity to **the law of sin**</u> which is in my members.

> [24] O wretched man that I am! **who shall deliver me from the body of this death**?

> [25] I thank God through Jesus Christ our Lord. So then <u>with the mind I myself serve the law of God</u>; <u>but with the flesh the law of sin</u>. - Romans 7:22-25

Note here that <u>it isn't God's Law that caused his captivity or bondage</u>; the fault lies in his members, and it is <u>the law of sin that caused his bondage</u>. Paul's reference to the "law" is not always reference to Torah "Law", and when it is, it may be referencing the penalty of that Law, rather than the Law itself. Here he was trying to point out that while the Law of God itself is holy and good, the flesh of man is weak; so the Law of God alone could NEVER be able to provide for man's redemption. Our sin nature would prevent us from abiding perfectly within the Law of God, and would ultimately bind us under its penalty for failure.

Here the captivity of verse 23 relates to a "bondage" of sorts as being the "<u>law" in his members</u> which wars against the "<u>law" of his mind</u>. The "law" of his mind was the pure Law of God's Tree of Life, but the "law" in his members was not. Just as we have laws of nature which rule our 3-D realm, we feel there are also laws of Heaven that dictate Divine principle. As we understand it, the spiritual laws of Heaven imposed a consequence for sin. The consequence for disobedience in Eden would be the struggle of mankind with the temptations of sin for man's entire human existence. Thus the sin nature is operative within our physical bodies throughout time. It is this sin nature to which Paul then refers as the "<u>law" of sin</u> he sees in his members.

A second implied bondage (per verse 24) relates to the penalty imposed by failure to keep the Law totally and completely. That penalty was death, as shown earlier in Romans:

> [23] For <u>the wages of sin is death</u>; **but the gift of God is eternal life through Jesus Christ our Lord**. - Romans 6:23

Paul then credits Y'shua for deliverance from this death, but indicates that he still struggles with the "law of sin" in his flesh. Our justification after belief in Y'shua puts us in a <u>positional</u> state of purity before God, but we still have to deal with the sins of the flesh as long as we are yet human. Paul then acknowledges that Y'shua brings us into the Father's family and removes us from the "bondage" of fear:

> [15] For ye have not received the <u>spirit of **bondage** again to fear</u>; but ye have received the <u>Spirit of **adoption**</u>, whereby <u>we cry, **Abba, Father**</u>. - Romans 8:15

Thus the bondage and similar wording in Paul's teachings can relate to different things, but first and foremost it typically points to the need for a Savior. Likewise do many of his references to "law".

As we see it, Paul's overall message is somewhat like this: We have a sin nature that leads to death which is active within our being. We need a Savior. The Law cannot justify us as we cannot keep it properly. We need a Savior. We must be released from the bondage of sin and death and the bondage of fear from facing this death. We need a Savior. We must somehow find Life, and for this we need a Savior. Once we find our Savior, we must abide with Him and He with us. We must be conformed to His image and walk in His ways to find the fullness of that Life. Y'shua is that Savior. He alone has lived in perfect obedience to the Law, enabling Him to be our permanent sacrifice for sin. He shed His blood to atone for our sins and remove us from the bondage of the penalty of death which is bound to Father's pure and holy Law. To avail ourselves of this gift of grace which takes us from death to Life we must believe in <u>and follow</u> Y'shua:

> [8] Though he were a Son, yet learned he obedience by the things which he suffered;
>
> [9] And being made perfect, he became the author of <u>eternal salvation</u> **unto all them that obey him**; - Hebrews 5:8-9

<u>It is urgent that we realize that our eternal salvation is linked here to obedience.</u> <u>First</u> we must make Him our <u>Savior</u> through <u>belief</u> which provides for our <u>justification,</u> <u>then</u> we must make Him our <u>Lord</u> through <u>obedience</u> which provides for our <u>sanctification</u>. He was quickened and raised from death to everlasting Life to join His Father on the Heavenly Throne. He opens up to us the avenue of restoration with the Father. We must get to know our Father, as His ways are Y'shua's ways. We are given Father's Spirit to guide us in our walk. If we yield to the Spirit in our walk, it will be in obedience to the precepts Father established as upheld by His Spirit. Then we will be shown

the fullness of the Truth and understanding of Father's ways, and ultimately find the totality of Life we seek.

It is a message consistent with the entirety of the Biblical text through cyclical patterning. <u>If one enters into the readings of Paul with this understanding, all can be reconciled</u>.

Recalling that Paul's words may indeed be a test to mankind, the Holy Spirit which inspired them may have carefully chosen the words which Paul would use. This (coupled with the knowledge that his words were not originally written in English) means that there will be phrases used which on a stand-alone basis are easy to misunderstand. Peter acknowledges this in his second epistle:

> [15] And account that the longsuffering of our Lord is salvation; even as our beloved brother <u>Paul</u> also according to the wisdom given unto him hath written unto you;
>
> [16] As also <u>in all his epistles</u>, speaking in them of these things; in which are <u>some things hard to be understood</u>, which they that are unlearned and unstable <u>wrest</u>, <u>as they do also the other scriptures, unto their own destruction</u>. - 2 Peter 3:15-16

He admonishes that wrestling with Paul's epistles and the other Scriptures can lead one to destruction (the wide gate). Because Paul's words can be hard to understand (as Peter states), people who try to make them say something they weren't intended to convey can be led to the way of destruction. Those who are <u>learned</u> in Torah (rather than "unlearned" per verse 16) should not be fooled, as they will understand that agreement with Torah precepts is ALWAYS behind Paul's words. If his words seem alien to Torah instruction, then they must simply be examined more closely. Ultimately they must harmonize! If the interpretation cannot advance from that which preceded it (Torah) without conflict or contradiction of the primary essence, it is an invalid interpretation.

This little rabbit trail provides a foundation for insight to understanding New Testament text. It illustrates that Paul's use of the word "bondage" never relates to enslavement to Torah Law. This should become even more evident as we work through the chapters ahead. Keeping Father's Law is a privilege. Even when Paul uses the phrase "<u>under the law</u>" he is simply referring to being <u>"under" the penalty of death</u> which is linked to the Law unless we are coupled with Y'shua to be freed from it.

All of this is just to provide a foretaste of the things that lie ahead in our study of Paul's epistles. We must come to realize that Paul had a Torah mindset. Likewise he expected his audience to put his words within that same Torah framework. Once we have that understanding, it opens up the New Testament writings to a new perspective. This Torah mindset is a prerequisite to understanding his words and brings more comprehension and definition to his writings.

Returning to our Roman's 8 verse for a moment, we get a glimpse of this rationale:

> [15] For ye have not received the spirit of **bondage** again to fear;
> but ye have received the Spirit of **adoption**, whereby we cry,
> **Abba, Father**. - Romans 8:15

The "spirit of bondage" would refer to the contra spirit which brings us into bondage of sin. This then causes us to fear judgment by the Lord. Those in Y'shua instead receive the true Spirit of Adoption into the Father's family. The contra spirit leads to sin and death; the Holy Spirit leads to restitution and Life.

Through the Spirit of Adoption we cry Abba, **Father**. This verse shows us it is not Y'shua's family that we are adopted into, but that through Y'shua **we are adopted into the Father's family**. Should we not want a relationship with the Father of the house we are adopted into? Should we cry Abba, Father, then neglect the very things He has shown us that are near to His heart? Should we not want to do the same things the master of the house desires, performing them joyfully out of love, reverence and homage? Should we not exhibit gratitude for our adoption into the household of faith through obedience? While we are adopted into this family through the Son, **it is the FATHER'S family**, and it is our belief that His precepts are still intact within His family. Just as the earthly father maintains certain rules for those of his household, so will our Heavenly Father have such expectations of His adopted children.

Some say the Law was exempted per references in Acts 15 such as:

> [10] Now therefore why tempt ye God, to put a yoke upon the neck
> of the disciples, which neither our fathers nor we were able to
> bear? - Acts 15:10

Our view of this passage is based on the wider context. The preceding verses of this passage reference the insistence of the Pharisees that the keeping of the Law and circumcision were necessary to ENTER the household of faith.

Keeping all of the aspects of the Law was being touted as being necessary for justification. Because Paul understood that nobody could keep the Law to perfection, he was insisting that such standards must not be prerequisites for justification. He also understood that these newcomers to the faith were just leaving pagan practices and had no concept of the Torah Law. Paul was saying that they did not need to keep the whole Law <u>to come to</u> Y'shua. The rest would follow in good time as they listened to instruction. Paul had been a Pharisee and understood what these Pharisees were expecting of the new converts. The Pharisees had added all kinds of extra expectations to the God's Law. Paul was telling them to back off, as even he could not meet all of their Pharisaical expectations. To insist that these new converts must try to follow their lead was not at all appropriate.

Therefore a council of elders and apostles came together to ascertain what should be taught to new Gentile converts, and they determined that it was necessary to end the practices associated with their pagan religion in order to come to the faith, and the rest would follow. They determined that the new converts were simply to "abstain from pollutions of idols, and from fornication, and from things strangled, and from blood":

> [20] But that we write unto them, that they <u>abstain from pollutions of idols, and from fornication, and from things strangled, and from blood</u>. - Acts 15:20

It seems interesting to us that even these basic standards are not observed in our society today. Much of the chicken which appears on our tables has been strangled, and the meats of all types which we consume have not been drained of their blood. This protocol is repeated again in verse 29 of this chapter:

> [29] That ye abstain from meats offered to idols, and from blood, and from things strangled, and from fornication: from which if ye keep yourselves, ye shall do well. Fare ye well. - Acts 15:29

In the interim verse 28, we see it was perceived that the entire Law being laid on a new convert would initially be too great a burden:

> [28] For it seemed good to the Holy Ghost, and to us, <u>to lay upon you no greater burden</u> than these necessary things; - Acts 15:28

It would be too abrupt of an adjustment to expect for a new convert from paganism. The Holy Spirit was showing them to take it slowly and not to overwhelm them. They were first to come to terms with what their Savior was to mean to them and then be taught how to walk in His ways. If Paul was denigrating the Law itself as being an unreasonable yoke, it would not be consistent with the words of Y'shua, as Y'shua wants us to come under His yoke, and He taught that when we enter into His Life, we are to keep the commandments:

> [29] Take my yoke upon you, and learn of me; for I am meek and lowly in heart: and ye shall find rest unto your souls.
>
> [30] For my yoke is easy, and my burden is light. - Matthew 11:29-30
>
> [17] And he said unto him, Why callest thou me good? there is none good but one, that is, God: but if thou wilt enter into life, keep the commandments. - Matthew 19:17

John concurs:

> [3] For this is the love of God, that we keep his commandments: and his commandments are not grievous. - 1 John 5:3

Y'shua and John harmonize beautifully here: Y'shua's yoke is easy and His burden is light. This is then shown (just a few chapters later) to be keeping the commandments. John then says the commandments are not grievous. "Light" and "not grievous" are synonymous with one another. It is all part of the same process.

It is expected that after we come to Y'shua we should be yoked to Him as well as the Father. Y'shua purchased our redemption at a very high price so we could be adopted into our Father's house, and we are not to be under our own authority:

> [19] What? know ye not that your body is the temple of the Holy Ghost which is in you, which ye have of God, and **ye are not your own**?
>
> [20] For ye are bought with a price: therefore glorify God in your body, and in your spirit, which are God's. - 1 Corinthians 6:19-20
>
> [22] But now being made free from sin, and **become servants to God**, ye have your fruit unto holiness, and the end everlasting life. Romans 6:22

We are yoked to many in our lives through marriage, family, and work. Likewise (as we see in this Matthew 11 reference) we are to be yoked through gratitude, love, and affection to the One who delivered us from our death sentence. As we enter into the Father's household through the Son, we also become yoked to the Father and to the Law He has shown us which rules His household.

The yoke of love is always easy to carry and light to bear, because the heart lightens the load. How much better it is to carry than the yoke of fear and condemnation that one carries without our Savior. Condemnation will always follow such a one, as the inability to keep the Law looms heavily over him. When we are yoked to Y'shua though, His love, grace, mercy, and forgiveness make the yoke easy to bear. The awesome respect, admiration, and desire to please Him which He engenders in those who love Him, make His burden light. This makes all the difference in carrying out that which the heart of the Father desires. We no longer keep the "Law" because we have to attain to it in perfection in order to be saved. We desire to be attentive to Father's Law because we know it pleases our Father who has adopted us. We delight in keeping His Law to show our gratitude for the sacrifice of our Savior, and we know that when we slip and fall we have someone to help us up. The Holy Spirit within reminds us of the Father's precepts while showing us how to walk as Y'shua would have us to walk. We are guided to apply the spiritual Law to the physical while we live our daily lives. We are to do so in accordance with the perfect will of the Father as expressed in His Word and revealed to us by the Holy Spirit.

We understand that we will sometimes (perhaps often?) fall short of abiding by the precepts of the Father's Law. As we recognize our failures and confess them though, we find forgiveness, and our debt due to sin is absolved:

> [9] If we confess our sins, he is faithful and just to forgive us our sins, and to cleanse us from all unrighteousness. - 1 John 1:9

While we can find forgiveness through the atoning power of Y'shua's blood, that does not provide an escape from our responsibility to obedience. It is our reasonable service to obey God properly:

> [1] I beseech you therefore, brethren, by the mercies of God, that ye present your bodies a living sacrifice, holy, acceptable unto God, which is your reasonable service. - Romans 12:1

Again, Paul said "I delight in the Law of God after the inward man" (Romans 7:22). He understood that as Believers we should still desire to adhere to the moral principles of the Law which we know please our Father. We are shown by Y'shua Himself that we are not only to adhere to the commandments but we are to teach them as well:

[19] <u>Whosoever therefore shall break **one of these least** commandments, and shall teach men so</u>, he shall be called the <u>least
in the kingdom of heaven</u>: but whosoever shall do and **teach**
them, the same shall be called great in the kingdom of heaven. -
Matthew 5:19

Some would say that the two great commandments which Y'shua dictated
would be all that is necessary. However, Y'shua says here that we are not to
break even one of the least commandments. The two great commandments
mentioned by Y'shua are simply overview commandments on which all others hang:

[37] Jesus said unto him, Thou shalt love the Lord thy God with all
thy heart, and with all thy soul, and with all thy mind.

[38] This is the first and great commandment.

[39] And the second is like unto it, Thou shalt love thy neighbour
as thyself.

[40] On these two commandments hang all the law and the prophets. - Matthew 22:37-40

If we remove all of the "least" commandments from the picture, it leaves
nothing to "hang" on the two greatest commandments. While many today
believe that these two "greatest" commandments have replaced all of the
original Torah commandments, it seems obvious in Matthew 5:19 above that
Y'shua is promoting a far more detailed observance of the Law than merely
these two greatest composite commandments.

These least commandments are still in the picture. He tells us in this
Matthew 5:19 passage that we should not break any of them or teach others to do so. Teaching others that they are not for today (according to this
verse) DOES have consequences.

Y'shua's criticism of the Pharisees was not that they kept the Law; it was that
they were not addressing the spiritual aspects of it in addition to keeping it:

[23] Woe unto you, scribes and Pharisees, hypocrites! for ye pay
tithe of mint and anise and cummin, and have <u>omitted the weighti-
er</u> matters of the law, judgment, mercy, and faith: <u>these ought ye to
have done, and not to leave the other undone</u>. - Matthew 23:23

They were being shown that it was right to keep the Law ("these ought ye to
have done"). Rather His criticism of them was that they were not observing

spiritual aspects (the weightier matters) of the Law ("judgment, mercy, and faith") to which the physical Law points. Here we see that the physical Law was to be kept, but that the spiritual Law was "weightier" (having even more importance) and was not to be ignored as the physical Law was kept. It is not "either/or"; it is "both/and". It is for that reason we are told that our righteousness must <u>exceed</u> that of the Pharisees in order to enter into Heaven:

> [20] For I say unto you, That except your righteousness shall exceed the righteousness of the scribes and Pharisees, ye shall in no case enter into the kingdom of Heaven. - Matthew 5:20

Note that this verse follows directly after Matthew 5:19 above – the words of Y'shua that tell us to keep and teach the physical commandments. This brings strong implication that our Heavenly position is associated with the manner in which we keep and teach God's commandments. Striving to find the harmony of the physical and spiritual Law and showing this correlation to others with emphasis on judgment, mercy, and faith may be the Way Father designed for our righteousness to exceed that of the scribes and Pharisees.

God's Spirit exudes the essence of Truth brought forth from the beginning, and will always point us to the harmony of the Word - never pitting us against the physical Law, but always being in agreement with it. Paul says this Law is holy:

> [12] Wherefore <u>the law is holy</u>, and the commandment holy, and just, and good. - Romans 7:12

So much of the confusion regarding the word "law" as it is referenced in Paul's epistles derives from the fact that it relates to the pure Torah Law only a small fraction of the times it is used. The derogatory references to the "law" in Paul's epistles are typically loose references to the Pharisaical traditions which were taught as Law. Though these traditions are based on Torah, they have been so adulterated through modifications (adding here and deleting there) that the Pharisees make the pure Torah laws ineffective through their traditions:

> [4] For God commanded, saying, Honour thy father and mother: and, He that curseth father or mother, let him die the death.

> [5] But ye say, Whosoever shall say to his father or his mother, It is a gift, by whatsoever thou mightest be profited by me;

> [6] And honour not his father or his mother, he shall be free. Thus have **ye made the commandment of God of none effect by**

your tradition.

[7] Ye hypocrites, well did Esaias prophesy of you, saying,

[8] This people draweth nigh unto me with their mouth, and hono-
ureth me with their lips; but their heart is far from me.

[9] But in vain they do worship me, **teaching for doctrines the
commandments of men**. - Matthew 15:4-9

Thus Pharisaical "Law" had become merely doctrines of men, which Paul
soundly condemned:

[20] Wherefore if ye be dead with Christ from the rudiments of
the world, why, as though living in the world, are ye subject to
ordinances,

[21] (Touch not; taste not; handle not;

[22] Which all are to perish with the using;) **after the commandments and doctrines of men**? - Colossians 2:20-22

Likewise though are the teachings of man which denounce the singularity of
Truth. Doctrines built around this theology serve the same purpose, just moving in the opposite direction. Instead of adding to the Law, they subtract from
it. Either doctrine is intensely dangerous to the soul, as both are forbidden in
Torah:

[2] Ye shall not add unto the word which I command you, neither shall ye diminish ought from it, that ye may keep the commandments of the LORD your God which I command you. -
Deuteronomy 4:2

The moral fabric of Torah is pure, and observance of it is totally in line with
New Testament teaching when viewed from the proper perspective. What is
objectionable is the dutiful observance of it for the wrong reasons, looking to
it as a means of justification:

[16] Knowing that a <u>man is not justified by the works of the law,
but by the faith of Jesus Christ</u>, even we have believed in Jesus
Christ, that we might be justified by the faith of Christ, and not by
the works of the law: for by the works of the law shall no flesh be
justified. - Galatians 2:16

The Law was never intended to provide justification for man, but rather to
guide him. Man is to be blessed when he keeps it, and cursed (chastised) when

he rebels against it:

> [9] Know therefore that the LORD thy God, he is God, the faith-
> ful God, which keepeth covenant and **mercy** <u>with them that love
> him and keep his commandments</u> **to a thousand generations**; -
> Deuteronomy 7:9

This was established in Torah, and projected through the remainder of Scripture. It remains true yet today. Many of the chastisements on man in our era are due to our departure from its precepts.

By defining sin and pointing to our need for a Savior, the Law provides a great service to Believers. It assists us in our walk of sanctification by providing boundaries which guide our physical path of obedience. It works together with the power of the Holy Spirit within to draw us to the joy of God's stewardship and allow us to overcome the temptations of the world. Thus, rather than the Law (physical and/or spiritual) BEING a bondage, it actually serves to assist in removing us FROM the bondage of sin and death. It binds us to Life rather than death through Father's grace – Life brought to us by our Savior Y'shua. Then through the Holy Spirit (which Y'shua had the Father send us), the Tree of Life restoration process of God is manifested in the lives of man.

CHAPTER 6

FAITH AND LAW

We had often heard the term legalism applied to those who view the Law as still being somewhat valid today. Were our views legalistic? It seemed that the role of faith had a hand in determining what was and what was not legalistic, but how were we to get a grip on the way it all worked?

To Keep the Law Without Faith Is to Return to Bondage

Paul strictly condemns choosing the path of Law <u>instead of</u> the path of faith. The path of Law without faith leads to certain death. To choose this path is to be "under" the Law as Paul presents it. It is choosing to rely on the Law for justification. Since no man can be justified by the Law without faith, this puts such a one <u>under the penalty of death</u> which is linked to the Law. This is what Paul then means by being "under" the Law. This would fasten the Law on the person as a bondage which leads <u>to death</u> rather than looking on the Law as a mechanism of guidance for the walk of faith that can free one <u>from death</u>.

We read about Paul's concern when he relates being "under" the Law to the offspring of Hagar (called Agar in the New Testament):

> [21] Tell me, ye that desire to be under the law, do ye not hear the law?

> [22] For it is written, that Abraham had two sons, the one by a bondmaid, the other by a freewoman.

> [23] But he who was of the bondwoman was born after the flesh; but he of the freewoman was by promise.

> [24] Which things are an allegory: for these are the two covenants; the one from the mount Sinai, which gendereth to bondage, which is Agar.

[25] For this Agar is mount Sinai in Arabia, and answereth to Jerusalem which now is, and is in bondage with her children.

[26] But Jerusalem which is above is free, which is the mother of us all.

[27] For it is written, Rejoice, thou barren that bearest not; break forth and cry, thou that travailest not: for the desolate hath many more children than she which hath an husband.

[28] Now we, brethren, as Isaac was, are the <u>children of promise</u>.

[29] But as then he that was **born after the flesh** persecuted him that was **born after the Spirit**, even so it is now.

[30] Nevertheless what saith the scripture? Cast out the bond-woman and her son: for **the son of the bondwoman shall not be heir with the son of the freewoman**.

[31] So then, brethren, we are not children of the bondwoman, but of the free. - Galatians 4:21-31

As Paul contrasts the plight of Hagar with that of Sarah he points to their off-spring. Hagar's son Ishmael is equated to being "born after the flesh" while Sarah's son Isaac is seen as being "born after the Spirit". Indeed trying to keep the Law in order to be justified is trying to keep it in the flesh (the first covenant), and one simply will not attain to God's standards in that endeavor. It is a total impossibility due to man's sin nature. However, to look to the Law as our guiding Light while walking in the Spirit is to proceed down the walk of faith hand in hand with both Father and Son as a typological offspring of Sarah:

[23] For **the commandment is a lamp**; and **the law is light**; and reproofs of instruction are the way of life: - Proverbs 6:23

[24] Let that therefore abide in you, which ye have heard from the beginning. **If that which ye have heard from the beginning shall remain in you, ye also shall continue in the Son, and in the Father.** - 1 John 2:24

Paul wanted us to find freedom from the law of sin and death through looking to Y'shua. Without faith in Him, we cannot be free. Still there are those who reject such faith and choose the route of the Law alone. They try to attain to justification "after the flesh", and build their walk and works on their own soul's ambition. These are as the "bondwoman" and her children. Conversely, those who come to Y'shua in faith are as Isaac, the child of the "freewoman". They follow their belief with evidence of their faith as they produce works wrought by the Spirit within. They are children of promise, born "after the Spirit". They build their walk and works on true righteousness.

As seen in this passage, Paul rejected this obedience to the Law-without-faith system outright. He claims repeatedly that the works of the Law without faith in Y'shua can never justify man. This verse in Galatians which we referenced earlier is one such example:

> [16] Knowing that <u>a man is not justified by the works of the law</u>, <u>but by the faith of Jesus Christ</u>, even we have believed in Jesus Christ, <u>that we might be justified by the faith of Christ</u>, and not by the works of the law: <u>for by the works of the law shall no flesh be justified</u>. - Galatians 2:16

It is worthy of note here that while this justification is sometimes called "salvation" by Paul in other references, that is simply because it is the initial step of the salvation process. Any view of justification which appears to be the completed process of salvation is short-sighted. It should not be taken as a stand-alone promise. According to the balance of Scripture, justification merely points to the prospect of completed salvation at the conclusion of the walk of faith.

As we have indicated, much of the Biblical text points to "salvation" as being a progressive and interactive process of sanctification, rather than being an instantaneous gift which is bestowed at the moment of belief. This sanctification begins with justification when we first believe in the blood of Y'shua for our atonement. It concludes with our exit from this physical realm when salvation is fully realized. Justification is what restores our initial acceptance to Father so the balance of the restoration process can take place with Him. Y'shua's blood-stained cross has provided a bridge over the breach between the Father and man caused by man in the garden:

> [12] And they that shall be of thee shall build the old waste places: thou shalt raise up the foundations of many generations; and thou shalt be called, <u>The repairer of the breach</u>, <u>The restorer of paths to dwell in</u>. - Isaiah 58:12

Note that first the breach is repaired – justification. Then we are given the restored paths to dwell in - sanctification. Each of us has our own walk of sanctification, as we are called to yield to the voice of the Spirit within and walk in obedience without. Instructions of the Spirit will differ from one person to another, but all will come through with a unified Tree of Life essence which resounds the fullness of Truth. We must be justified to Father through Y'shua's blood before the journey (our walk of sanctification) can begin.

Justification is the first step in the process of alignment to the ways of God. At the end of our journey is glorification:

> [28] And we know that all things work together for good to them that love God, to them who are <u>the called according to his purpose</u>.
>
> [29] For whom he did foreknow, he also did predestinate to be **conformed to the image of his Son**, that he might be the first-born among many brethren.
>
> [30] Moreover whom he did predestinate, them he also called: and <u>whom he called</u>, them **he also justified**: and **whom he justified, them he also glorified**. - Romans 8:28-30

In between justification and glorification is sanctification – the conformity to the image of Y'shua (as seen in verse 29), which occurs during our walk of faith. Conforming to Y'shua's image occurs during the walk of sanctification through advancing faith. While the physical Law cannot bring justification, this same Law does become very important in the process of sanctification. The first step Paul designates in his epistles is to come to belief in Y'shua, which renders us justified. The keeping of the Law plays no part in this what-soever. We are then shown to develop a walk which will enable us to be sanctified. The physical Law DOES play a role in this process. Trying to be justified through the keeping of the Law rather than looking to Y'shua for justification is to put the Law in a role it was not meant to have. Even those who have come to Y'shua can put the Law in the wrong position in their lives. Let's look again at Isaiah's words:

> [12] And they that shall be of thee shall build the old waste places: thou shalt raise up the foundations of many generations; and thou shalt be called, **The repairer of the breach, The restorer of paths to dwell in**. - Isaiah 58:12

Y'shua is to restore the breach and put us on the paths to dwell in. The Law then provides the parameters for the paths we are to dwell in. It was never meant to be that which restores the breach! Yet, even some who find Y'shua revert to putting the Law in this capacity. Doing so could result in the removal of the true justification they had found in Y'shua, and falling from the grace which was meant to provide their route to salvation. Those who choose this path are seen as frustrating the grace they were given, and counting the sacrifice of Y'shua as vain:

[4] Christ is become of no effect unto you, <u>whosoever of you are</u> **<u>justified by the law</u>**; ye are fallen from grace. - Galatians 5:4

[21] I do not frustrate the grace of God: for <u>if righteousness come by the law, then Christ is dead in vain</u>. - Galatians 2:21

However, when we become justified through faith in Y'shua, then we are to maintain obedience to the Law because it is Father's guidelines to keeping the body blameless:

[12] Let not sin therefore reign in your mortal body, that ye should obey it in the lusts thereof.

[13] Neither yield ye your members as instruments of unrighteousness unto sin: but yield yourselves unto God, as those that are alive from the dead, and <u>your members as instruments of righteousness unto God</u>. - Romans 6:12-13

Thus we begin our walk of sanctification in alignment with His will. Through this walk we develop the understanding of the spiritual application of the Law as well. We then proceed to conform to the image of Y'shua (who kept the Law to perfection) by adhering to and harmonizing both the physical and spiritual aspects of the Law in one accord.

Y'shua did not remove our accountability to the Father through His victory at Calvary. He has told us that we are to take up our crosses to follow Him. Neither did Paul infer that there is no further accountability when he told us to become a living sacrifice. Y'shua made a very bold and profound statement in John:

[6] Jesus saith unto him, I am **the way**, **the truth**, and **the life**: <u>no man cometh unto the Father, but by me</u>. - John 14:6

He DIDN'T indicate that His BEING the "Way" was merely through simple belief on Him. He says here that He is three things, and these three are progressive in nature. He is first the Way, THEN the Truth, THEN the Life. He spoke more about this "Way" elsewhere in Matthew, saying that the "Way" to "Life" which He offers us is narrow and few will find it:

[13] Enter ye in at the strait gate: for wide is the gate, and broad is the way, that leadeth to destruction, and many there be which go in thereat:

> [14] Because strait is the gate, and **narrow is the way, which leadeth unto life, and few there be that find it**. - Matthew 7:13-14

He seems to be warning us that wide sweeping religious beliefs (which cause MANY [verse 13] to be seduced into error) can lead us astray. He may be showing us that we must adjust our minds and hearts to identify and reject these errant tenets of faith that open to the "broad way" and search diligently for the narrow way instead.

Next He states that He is also the Truth. Likewise Scripture tells us that the Law is Truth:

> [142] Thy righteousness is an everlasting righteousness, and **thy law is the truth**. - Psalms 119:142

As the living Word, Y'shua embodies the Law and He projects in every feasible way the Truth of this Law to mankind so we can understand both the physical and spiritual aspects of it and walk accordingly on the narrow way:

> [3] And many people shall go and say, Come ye, and let us go up to the mountain of the LORD, to the house of the God of Jacob; and he will teach us of his ways, and we will walk in his paths: for out of Zion shall go forth the **law**, and the **word** of the LORD from Jerusalem. - Isaiah 2:3

> [14] And **the Word was made flesh**, and dwelt among us, (and we beheld his glory, the glory as of the only begotten of the Father,) full of grace and **truth**. - John 1:14

Thus He is "Truth" by bringing us the Law of His Truth – being our living Word – our living Torah.

Then the third thing He claimed in John 14:6 is that He is "Life". We cannot find our way to the **Life** He offers without Him. Belief in Y'shua provides for our justification so the journey can begin:

> [25] Jesus said unto her, I am the resurrection, and the **life**: he that believeth in me, though he were dead, yet shall he live: - John 11:25

Likewise He tells us if we will enter into Life we are to keep the commandments:

> [17] And he said unto him, Why callest thou me good? there is none good but one, that is, God: **but if thou wilt enter into life, keep the commandments**. - Matthew 19:17

If we keep the commandments, then both He and the Father will abide with us:

> [23] Jesus answered and said unto him, <u>If a man love me, he will keep my words</u>: <u>and my Father will love him, and we will come unto him, and make our abode with him</u>. - John 14:23

This is hand in glove with walking in the narrow way to get to the Life Y'shua offers. If keeping the commandments is to abide with Y'shua, then it is integral to our bearing fruit of the Spirit:

> [4] <u>Abide in me, and I in you</u>. As the branch cannot bear fruit of itself, except it abide in the vine; no more can ye, <u>except ye abide in me</u>. - John 15:4

He opens up the Way through His sacrifice at Calvary. He shows us the Truth of Torah which He brings forth in a more spiritual level, and through following His Way and walking in His Truth, we find Life. We can't get to Life without first finding the Way He offers, then walking in the Truth He presents. Thus Y'shua is indeed the Way, which leads to the Truth, which leads to Life. They are presented to us progressively as we walk hand in hand with Him and the Father through the sanctification process.

The Old Testament has much the same message for us:

> [142] Thy righteousness is an everlasting righteousness, and **thy law is the truth**. - Psalms 119:142

> [23] For **the commandment is a lamp**; and the **law is light**; and **reproofs of instruction are the way of life**: - Proverbs 6:23

God's Law is Truth and Light. His commandments are the lamp, and the reproof of instructions they provide is the Way of Life. This was type and shadow of what Y'shua would bring to us as the living Torah, which amplified God's Law for our understanding. He opened the door to Life through His victory at Calvary. Now the penalty of the Law is abolished for those who believe on Him and follow His ways.

He offered us instruction regarding Torah through His words and His example. This instruction is intended as a means of reproof when we veer away from His Way of Life. It provides spiritual insights to bring us to Life. We are to abide within it while resting on the atonement He provided:

> [31] **The ear that heareth** the **reproof of life** abideth among the **wise**. - Proverbs 15:31

Two Trees, Two Kingdoms, Two Kings

We cannot look with any merit to the teaching that initial belief on Y'shua is all that is necessary to find Life. <u>Many</u> come to this initial belief on Him in the church today, but Y'shua Himself tells us that the Way to Life is narrow and <u>few</u> there be that find it. Many come to belief then proceed to live outside the Law of Father, but few come to belief, gravitate toward the Law of Father, and continue to abide within it:

> [14] For many are called, but few are chosen. - Matthew 22:14

If maintaining a respect for all of the parameters of God's Law is a crucial part of walking in the narrow way, and today's tenets of faith teach us that we don't need to abide within them, that would surely explain why so few find it. They choose instead the broad way which they are taught, as it does not place many expectations on their walk.

There are two gates that we may enter into after our justification by belief in Y'shua.

One gate is "strait" and opens to the "narrow way". This straight gate and narrow way leads to "Life". This is the Way of the Tree of Life.

The other gate is "wide" and opens to the "broad way". This wide gate and broad way leads to "destruction". This is the way of the Tree of Knowledge. It is this broad way that we are on prior to our belief. It is not the one we are to stay on after belief. Believing in Y'shua opens the straight gate up to us so we can make the transition we need to make through the power and direction of the indwelling Spirit.

Y'shua did not say the **GATE** that leads to Life is <u>narrow</u>. He said the **WAY** was <u>narrow</u>. What He said about the GATE that leads to Life is that it was **straight**. It is straight because it stays in perfect alignment with the rest of Scripture, and makes no digression from any other portions of Biblical text. The way is narrow because the Father's precepts are still intact. It is the Way of the Heavenly Kingdom under the Holy Spirit, and it leads to Life.

The gate of standard theological teaching regarding Paul's epistles is certainly not straight, and neither is the way narrow. The gate that is wide allows for deviation from the alignment of Shema. The unified essence of God's singularity is left behind when the wide gate is entered. It allows for the essence of the Almighty to be divided into opposing camps, where the Law can be pitted against grace and seen as defunct. The "way" this gate opens to is broad because the Father's precepts no longer need to be honored. It is the way of the earthly kingdom under the contra spirit and it leads to destruction (death).

Y'shua is the "Way" to the Father. We can't get there without Him. He also offers us the unified "Truth" of singularity that we need to get there and "Life" Eternal after we do. He opens up the Way to us through His death, crucifixion and resurrection. When we receive the atoning power of His blood, we are justified. As we begin our walk of faith, the Holy Spirit imparts the fullness of Truth to us. This is imparted to us progressively as we choose to walk in the "narrow" way and abide in Him. Doing so brings continual advances into the conformity to Y'shua's image. This ultimately leads to the conclusion of the salvation process when we exit this realm of 3-D reality and receive our new glorified bodies.

Law as an Extension of Love Rather Than a Bondage

When reading Paul's words, context is everything. We sense that is why Paul's words are so easily misunderstood. Much of what Paul criticized about the Law was actually the Pharisaical aspects tacked to it; Y'shua did likewise. Paul did proclaim emphatically that we are never to put ourselves back <u>under</u> the Law (as relying on it for our justification). Additionally he indicates that we are not to subject ourselves to all of the alterations made to it by the Pharisees. However, Paul would surely not have meant for his words about not being "under" the Law to be mistakenly construed as condoning violations of Father's originally ordained precepts.

We have indicated that the keeping of the physical Law is the first step to keeping the spiritual Law which is centered on the love of Father and mankind. It is then the combining of the physical and spiritual Law that brings about the love that fulfills the Law:

> [10] Love worketh no ill to his neighbour: therefore <u>love is the fulfilling of the law</u>. - Romans 13:10

As we walk in the Spirit, we are in constant contact with the moral precepts of the Law, as they are written by the Holy Spirit on our hearts:

> [3] Forasmuch as ye are manifestly declared to be the epistle of Christ ministered by us, <u>written</u> not with ink, but <u>with the Spirit of the living God</u>; not in tables of stone, but <u>in fleshy tables of the heart</u>. - 2 Corinthians 3:3

Thus we do not stray from its parameters and we show our love to the Lord and love our neighbor properly.

Regarding the physical Law:	Regarding the spiritual Law:
the Father gave the Law to Moses	the Father gave the Law to the Holy Spirit
who gave it to the people	who gave it to the people
written on tables of stone	written on tables of the heart
on Pentecost	on Pentecost
right after the exodus from Egypt.	right after the exodus of Y'shua from our earthly realm.

It is obvious that He wants us to see the parallel and understand that they are not alien to one another, but are very, very related! The spiritual will overlie the physical to add new perspective to the physical. We see the link between these two in Hebrews:

> [28] He that despised **Moses' law** died without mercy under two or three witnesses:

> [29] Of how much sorer punishment, suppose ye, shall he be thought worthy, who hath trodden under foot the Son of God, and hath <u>counted the blood of the covenant, wherewith he was sanctified, an unholy thing</u>, and hath <u>done despite unto the **Spirit of grace**</u>? - Hebrews 10:28-29

Those who despised (showed disregard for) the physical Law (which Moses brought to them) died without mercy. It is then shown to us that when Believers spite the Spirit of Grace that dwells within, it is considered to be even worse. The Holy Spirit provides us with more spiritual understanding of Father's physical precepts. Therefore, this spiting of the Spirit of Grace may be the disregarding of this more spiritual aspect of God's Law. Despising the spiritual (which is seen here as "worse") certainly does not negate the seriousness of despising the physical. Even that was worthy of death in times past. This seems to indicate that we should see that we do not despise either the physical or the spiritual application of the Law. The Spirit of Grace after Belief was given so we can align to and abide within God's precepts (both physical and spiritual) properly. As Believers, we are obligated to <u>choose</u> to do so.

While the physical Law deals with bringing the physical body into subjection, its spiritual expansion deals with subduing the wantonness of the human will and shows us how to apply a loving heart as we honor it. As we combine the two, we are shown how to abide within the confines of the physical, while developing more of a heart for working out our faith during our interaction with the world. Thus the Heavenly realm can overlie the physical realm properly in our personal lives:

> [10] Thy kingdom come. Thy will be done in earth, as it is in heaven. - Matthew 6:10

The physical no longer becomes rote obedience, but obedience with a purpose - an obedience that is an extension of love for God and man.

Seeing Law and Faith Work Together as One

Paul speaks of our walk of humanity by equating it to a race which not all will win. Here he links mastery with temperance in all things:

> [24] Know ye not that they which <u>run in a race</u> run all, but one receiveth the prize? So <u>run, that ye may obtain</u>.

> [25] And <u>every man that striveth for the **mastery** is **temperate in all things**</u>. Now they do it to obtain a corruptible crown; but we an incorruptible.

> [26] I therefore so run, <u>not as uncertainly</u>; so fight I, not as one that <u>beateth the air</u>:

> [27] But I **<u>keep under my body</u>**, and **<u>bring it into subjection</u>**: <u>lest</u> that by any means, when I have preached to others, <u>I myself should be a castaway</u>. - 1 Corinthians 9:24-27

Let's look at the words in verses 25 and 26 for a moment. They who strive for mastery should run or do so "<u>not as uncertainly</u>". "<u>Not as uncertainly</u>" could be "certainly", or with specific standards – God's precepts. The race is therefore to be run by upholding these precepts, and striving for mastery within their parameters. How do we run this race, and how is this mastery achieved? It can not be done in any "uncertain" fashion, where no such precepts provide restrictions for our behavior and character.

The physical Law relates to the body, and there is certainly no uncertainty about the physical Law. Its clear-cut and structured parameters **bring the body into subjection**. Those who beat against the air in this passage might be those who have bought into the teaching of the prince of the power of the air, and no longer have any "certain" boundaries to become temperate within. They go as they perceive the "Spirit" to be leading them, no matter how much they violate Father's boundaries in that process.

Two Trees, Two Kingdoms, Two Kings

They who strive for mastery "<u>keep under</u>" their bodies so they will be able to **bring them into subjection**. The phrase "keep under" is actually one Greek word, Strong's #G5299 ("hypōpiazō") - *like a boxer one buffets his body, handle it roughly, discipline by hardships*. We are NOT to pamper the body, even as an athlete trains for the championship game. Paul is instructing us here to be rigorous and exacting in curbing the carnal desires of the flesh. He understands the war of the flesh against the Spirit:

> [23] But I see another law in my members, warring against the law
> of my mind, and bringing me into captivity to the law of sin which is
> in my members. - Romans 7:23

James understands it as well:

> [1] From whence come wars and fightings among you? come
> they not hence, even of your lusts that war in your members? -
> James 4:1

Paul likewise understands that failure to bring the body "into subjection" might cause us to be castaways, and that even he was not exempt. If we toss aside the guidelines given to us by our Father in the written Word, then our boundaries become <u>uncertain</u>, and we can easily pamper the carnal desires of the flesh without realizing that we are undoing the system which is designed to render the body blameless:

> [23] And the very God of peace sanctify you wholly; and I pray
> God your whole spirit and soul and **body** <u>be preserved blameless
> unto the coming of our Lord Jesus Christ</u>. - 1 Thessalonians 5:23

This then applies to the physical body, but we have also seen that abiding in the Spirit brings the spiritual application of the Law to the forefront, enabling us to interact with others more properly as well. James refers to this application of the Law as being the "royal law":

> [8] If ye fulfil the **royal law** according to the scripture, Thou shalt
> love thy neighbour as thyself, ye do well: - James 2:8

James also references the "law of liberty" as relating to others. There is no implication in the wording of James regarding either the "royal law" or the "law of liberty" that the physical Law is a thing of the past. He does indicate though that judgment now will include the more spiritual "law of liberty" as well:

> [11] For he that said, Do not commit adultery, said also, Do not kill.

Now if thou commit no adultery, yet if thou kill, thou art become a transgressor of the law.

[12] So speak ye, and so do, as they that **shall be judged by the law of liberty**.

[13] **For he shall have judgment without mercy, that hath shewed no mercy; and mercy rejoiceth against judgment**.

[14] What doth it profit, my brethren, though a man say he hath faith, and have not works? **can faith save him**? - James 2:11-14

The strong implication in this last verse is that just as the Law alone cannot save one, neither can faith alone save him. The two must be knitted together as one throughout the salvation process! As we align to the Spirit of God within, we will be shown how to harmonize the two and bring judgment, mercy, and faith to the forefront of our walk as the weightier matters of the Law.

Y'shua likewise mentioned judgment and mercy and faith in Matthew. We recall that He did not render the physical Law obsolete, but rather indicated that it too should be addressed:

[23] Woe unto you, scribes and Pharisees, hypocrites! for ye pay tithe of mint and anise and cummin, and have omitted **the weightier matters of the law, judgment, mercy, and faith**: these ought ye to have done, **and not to leave the other undone**. - Matthew 23:23

When we come before the Throne, we will be judged. Will this judgment be coupled with mercy? The manner in which we relate to others is critical in this respect, per James in verse 13 above. Faith may enter the picture as well, as it is in our walk of faith that we learn to relate to others in mercy through the guidance of the Holy Spirit within. For every Believer will give account to Y'shua for the manner in which he has lived after receiving the blood atonement Y'shua provided for him:

[10] But why dost thou judge thy brother? or why dost thou set at nought thy brother? for **we shall all stand before the judgment seat of Christ**. - Romans 14:10

[36] But I say unto you, That every idle word that men shall speak, **they shall give account thereof in the day of judgment**. - Matthew 12:36

[10] For we must all appear before the judgment seat of Christ; **that every one may receive the things done in his body, according to that he hath done, whether it be good or bad**. - 2 Corinthians 5:10

Here we come full circle back to the physical Law. Everyone will receive judgment before the Throne regarding the "things done in his body" "whether they be good or bad". James concurs. He links the physical Law to the weightier matter of "faith" in the following text which indicates that works of the physical Law must accompany our faith as evidence of it:

[17] Even so faith, if it hath not works, is dead, being alone.

[18] Yea, a man may say, Thou hast faith, and I have works: shew me thy faith without thy works, and **I will shew thee my faith by my works**. - James 2:17-18

How will the weightier matters of faith, judgment and mercy be weighed before the Throne? How will our obedience to the physical Law enter into the picture? We see here that all are important, and pray that we will be found in good standing, leaving none of the above "undone".

Law, Faith, and Works

The spirit and soul of man are enclosed in human flesh, and will be until our redemption to the glorified state. While yet in this flesh, if we eat only of the spiritual food and ignore the physical, the physical body will ultimately die from starvation. As long as we have physical bodies, we must have physical sustenance to survive in this 3-D realm. Likewise our physical bodies need the framework of physical boundaries to keep them in proper alignment. We cannot focus on the spiritual to the exclusion of the physical. If the physical Law is removed from the role of the support system for the spiritual Law, the spiritual application is incomplete and will not properly nourish our being.

To try to abide in only the spiritual aspect of the Law while ignoring the physical is somewhat like trying to build a home by erecting the roof directly on the foundation with no walls to support it. The home would not be habitable. Faith is the beginning of the spiritual Law, and it must be founded on the understanding of a well-established structure of the physical Law:

[31] Do we then make void the law through faith? God forbid: yea, we establish the law. - Romans 3:31

Paul points here to a higher truth. It is a type of paradox. The physical Tabernacle was designed after the pattern of the Heavenly version. Likewise, the physical Law was patterned after the spiritual Law from which it was derived. Then our version of spiritual Law is in turn built on the physical Law, leading back again to the Heavenly version of it. It is Father's cyclical patterning. Both are necessary to form the cycle, and both are necessary as long as our spiritual being is confined in this physical wrapper - until our change in body when the physical is transcended.

While Paul says that the working of the Law without faith cannot save one, James indicates that neither can faith without the working of the Law save one:

> [16] Knowing that a **man is not justified by the works of the law, but by the faith of Jesus Christ**, even we have believed in Jesus Christ, that we might be justified by the faith of Christ, and <u>not by the works of the law</u>: for by the works of the law shall no flesh be justified. - Galatians 2:16

> [24] Ye see then how that **by works a man is justified, and not by faith <u>only</u>**. - James 2:24

Is there conflict between James and Paul in these verses? When we apply the entirety of the Word as our context, there is no conflict. Again it is not "either/or", but it is rather "both/and". Neither is wrong. They are both right. James is seeing the justification process extending on into sanctification.

Paul later says in Philippians:

> [12] Wherefore, my beloved, as ye have always obeyed, not as in my presence only, but now much more in my absence, **work out your own salvation with fear and trembling**. - Philippians 2:12

It takes the two together to "work out" and complete the salvation process. The physical and spiritual applications of the Law are designed to work together in harmony.

Paul sees that living by faith takes you from the initial step of faith to the end of our faith where the sanctification process concludes and we are ready to be glorified:

> [17] For therein is <u>the righteousness of God revealed from faith to faith</u>: as it is written, <u>The just shall live by faith</u>. - Romans 1:17

Only the just shall attain to this end, as they will walk "from faith to faith" (from justification at the beginning of faith through sanctification at the end of faith) in order to be fit for glorification. It is through the walk of faith that the righteousness of God is revealed. This is the process that befits our glorification:

> [30] Moreover whom he did predestinate, them he also called: and whom he called, them he also justified: and whom he justified, them he also glorified. - Romans 8:30

What Exactly Is Faith?

It is rather important to understand that faith is not only seen as a noun, but also seems at times to indicate action. The words "through faith" in Ephesians 2:8 advance this thought:

> [8] For <u>by grace are ye saved **through faith**</u>; and that not of your-selves: it is the gift of God:

> [9] <u>Not of works</u>, lest any man should boast. - Ephesians 2:8-9

Christendom often just teaches that we are saved by grace, and rarely gives equal emphasis to the importance of an active form of faith in the equation to salvation. The ordering of words makes it look like grace and faith are separate from one another. We do not believe this was Paul's intent. To keep the same words and put the order in a more fluid form, it would be to say: "for ye are saved by grace through faith". The important consideration here is that the two work together as one - **by: grace through faith**. Paul shows that our our entire salvation process is an act of grace which is accomplished through the walk of faith. Father did not have to allow for our justification or open the path for our return to Him. It was at great sacrifice that He sent His Son by an act of grace to allow for this to occur.

Even the walk of faith is a gift from Father, as He sent His Spirit to indwell man. Hebrews refers to the Holy Spirit within as the Spirit of Grace:

> [29] Of how much sorer punishment, suppose ye, shall he be thought worthy, who hath trodden under foot the Son of God, and hath counted the blood of the covenant, wherewith he was sanctified, an unholy thing, and hath done despite unto the Spirit of grace? - Hebrews 10:29

The Spirit then guides man in his walk to achieve the glorification that signifies our reconciliation with the holy essence of God. Walking "by grace through faith" is the key. <u>Our "faith" is actually the application of the gift of</u>

grace in our journey to glorification. It is a step by step progressive exercise
to: grow in the Spirit of Grace, through alignment with the Son, in obedience
to the Father. After the initial receipt of the gift of grace, it becomes our responsibility to develop the walk of faith:

> [5] By whom we have received grace and apostleship, for obedi-
> ence to the faith among all nations, for his name: - Romans 1:5

> [4] For whatsoever is born of God overcometh the world: and this is
> the victory that overcometh the world, even our faith. - 1 John 5:4

Y'shua stressed to the churches of Revelation that overcoming the things of
the world would allow them to attain good reward and avoid consequence.
This verse in 1 John tells us that it is through the walk of faith that this overcoming is accomplished.

Paul indicates in Ephesians 2:9 above that this salvation of grace through
faith is "not of works". The "works" he indicates here are works of the flesh
– those done in the flesh rather than through the Spirit. These works are built
somewhat on the foundation of Y'shua, yet they have little to do with yielding
to the Spirit in our walk of faith. They are enacted through fleshly motiva-
tion. They are wood, hay, and stubble which will be burned up during the
judgment:

> [11] For other foundation can no man lay than that is laid, which is
> Jesus Christ.

> [12] Now if any man build upon this foundation gold, silver, pre-
> cious stones, wood, hay, stubble;

> [13] Every man's work shall be made manifest: for the day shall
> declare it, because it shall be revealed by fire; and the fire shall try
> every man's work of what sort it is.

> [14] If any man's work abide which he hath built thereupon, he
> shall receive a reward. - 1 Corinthians 3:11-14

> [10] I the LORD search the heart, I try the reins, even to give every
> man according to his ways, and according to the fruit of his doings.
> - Jeremiah 17:10

James mentions works as being important to God. James builds here on our
initial justification which is accomplished by Y'shua, and indicates that progressive justification (or sanctification) includes the application of faith:

> [24] Ye see then how that **by works a man is justified, and not by faith <u>only</u>**. - James 2:24

The "works" spoken of by James are works that follow faith – works accomplished by the Spirit through us during our walk of sanctification – works that prove the validity of the progression of our faith. Speaking of the faith of Abraham, James says:

> [22] Seest thou how faith wrought with his works, and by works was faith made perfect? - James 2:22

Such works are Spirit-guided works (fruit of the Spirit) which fulfill our faith rather than working outside of the Spirit from fleshly origin. They are works of gold, silver, and precious stones, which will survive the revelation by fire of 1 Corinthians 3:11-13.

Obedience is the evidence of faith in action – the proof of our Love for God. We develop our faith as the Holy Spirit helps us to draw the application of the spiritual Law onto the keeping of the physical Law. It is this process that brings us through our journey of sanctification intact. It is the <u>work</u>ing out of our faith with fear and trembling that Paul references in Philippians:

> [12] Wherefore, my beloved, as ye have always obeyed, not as in my presence only, but now much more in my absence, **work out your own salvation with fear and trembling**. - Philippians 2:12

Faith is not a mere belief, or even a determined belief by which we expect to manifest a miraculous turn of events. Though the belief in Y'shua is the BEGINNING of faith, and the determined belief through which miracles occur can be a PART of faith as well, neither of these is the whole picture of faith. Faith is a commitment to conformity to the One in whom we believe, and choosing to walk out that commitment. It is a progressive walk in the narrow way. That is why we are told that faith without works is dead:

> [17] Even so <u>faith, if it hath not works, is dead</u>, being alone. - James 2:17

Faith is a progressive process, not a quick belief in what Y'shua accomplished on Calvary as the entire package:

> [17] The highway of the upright is to depart from evil: he that keepeth his way preserveth his soul. - Proverbs 16:17

Our souls are then saved at the END of our progressive walk of faith:

> [9] Receiving the **end of your faith**, even the **salvation of your souls**. - 1 Peter 1:9

> [11] And many **false prophets shall rise, and shall deceive many**.

> [12] And because **iniquity shall abound**, the love of many shall wax cold.

> **[13] But he that shall endure unto the end, the same shall be saved**. - Matthew 24:11-13

The word "iniquity" in verse 12 is Strong's #G458 ("anomia") - *the condition of being without law because of ignoring it or violating it, contempt and violation of law.*

Y'shua was warning here that due to false prophets many will be deceived into believing that the Law is now obsolete, and they will begin to violate it. It will become a widespread problem, with the deception of lawlessness abounding. As this type of activity curtails the walk of faith, many will fall away from the Truth of Father to the deception by the contra spirit, and those who continue their walk in faith until the end may become very few.

That is likely why Y'shua questioned whether He would even find faith when He comes:

> [8] I tell you that he will avenge them speedily. Nevertheless when the Son of man cometh, shall he find faith on the earth? - Luke 18:8

He knows that the closer we get to the time for His return, even many of those who understood His Truth will fall back into deception, and their walk of faith will fall away as they choose to leave the narrow path and walk on the broad path instead. The contra spirit operative within the serpent was extremely seductive in Eden, and has only improved the technique since then:

> [66] From that time many of his disciples went back, and walked no more with him. - John 6:66

We have to wonder if the chapter and verse number 6:66 here was not intentional, as the contra is the one who draws Y'shua's followers away. It was not limited to His day, but will continue through the end days:

> [3] Let no man deceive you by any means: for that day shall not

> come, except there come a **falling away** first, and that man of sin
> be revealed, the son of perdition; - 2 Thessalonians 2:3

The term "falling away" here is Strong's #G646 ("apostasia") - *a falling away, defection, apostasy*. Note that because it also can mean: *departure*, some teachers apply an entirely different meaning to this verse. One does not necessarily negate the other, as both can be meant by Father's intricate language. However, the one we are interested in here is the defection which is prophesied:

> [1] Now the Spirit speaketh expressly, that in the latter times some
> shall **depart from the faith**, giving heed to seducing spirits, and
> doctrines of devils; - 1 Timothy 4:1

> [38] Now the just **shall live by faith**: but if any man **draw back,
> my soul shall have no pleasure in him**. - Hebrews 10:38

Rather than drawing back into transgression which stymies faith, we must get on the right track. Faith endures and thrives only through works of true righteousness – those brought about through the Holy Spirit within. We walk in the Spirit, and progress forever forward. Glorification and Eternal Life through restoration of the soul with Father appear to be contingent on this process:

> [39] But we are not of them who draw back unto perdition; but of
> them that believe **to** the saving of the soul. - Hebrews 10:39

This "believe **to** the saving of the soul" is a progressive belief – the very walk of faith we have referenced. It is at the end of the walk that the soul is "saved":

> [9] Receiving the **end of your faith**, even the **salvation of your
> souls**. - 1 Peter 1:9

This faith begins with conviction to God's plan of salvation. This conviction must then be coupled to the commitment to uphold the precepts of Father while walking in the Spirit. The Spirit will bring forth the application of the amplified Law, the Law of the Spirit of Life in Y'shua:

> [2] For the law of the Spirit of life in Christ Jesus hath made me
> free from the law of sin and death. - Romans 8:2

The bearing of spiritual fruit is then the evidence that we have been walking in the Spirit. It is evidence that we have yielded to the Spirit. We have allowed the Spirit to align God's spiritual enhancement of the Law over His physical foundation of the Law in a way that glorifies God properly.

The physical Law brings the physical body into obedience to the confines of the Law. The spiritual Law helps the spiritual portion of our being align to the ways of Father, as the Holy Spirit amplifies the physical Law with new spiritual relevance. Together they allow us to relate more thoroughly to both God and our fellow man, and to bring the weightier aspects of the Law (judgment, mercy, and faith) into focus:

> [23] Woe unto you, scribes and Pharisees, hypocrites! for ye pay tithe of mint and anise and cummin, and have omitted <u>the weightier matters of the law, judgment, mercy, and faith</u>: these ought ye to have done, and not to leave the other undone. - Matthew 23:23

Just as the church does not REPLACE Israel, but is grafted into Israel (there will be more on this later), neither does the spiritual Law replace the physical. The application of both the physical and the spiritual components of the Law in our lives provides proof of our <u>love</u> to God and our fellow man. They are to be merged together in order that the Divine order for mankind can be realized and the entire sanctification process might be completed:

> [22] Seeing ye have purified your souls in <u>obeying the truth through the Spirit</u> unto unfeigned love of the brethren, see that ye love one another with a pure heart fervently: - 1 Peter 1:22

> [14] For all <u>the law is fulfilled in one word</u>, even in this; Thou shalt **love** thy neighbour as thyself. - Galatians 5:14

As we fulfill the Law in this manner, the sanctification process ensures that we will be found blameless on both a physical and a spiritual level:

> [23] And the very God of peace <u>sanctify you wholly</u>; and I pray God your whole spirit and soul and body be preserved blameless unto the coming of our Lord Jesus Christ. - 1 Thessalonians 5:23

CHAPTER 7

SPECIFICS OF THE LAW

We were getting a firmer grip on the generalities relative to the Law and its application today, but a few of the particulars on the matter seemed to require a bit more attention. What we found was an eye-opener. We began to see that the mainline teachings of Christendom were not addressing some things which were becoming increasingly obvious to us. How are some of the most basic moral precepts of the Law to be handled in the modern Christian era? One of the first topics that came to mind was Sabbaths. We could see that the Bible spoke of both weekly and annual Sabbaths. How were we to deal with them today?

Weekly Sabbaths

The weekly Sabbath of the seventh day is referenced first in Genesis where it receives a special blessing and is sanctified by God:

> [2] And on the seventh day God ended his work which he had made; and he rested on the seventh day from all his work which he had made.

> [3] And God blessed the seventh day, and sanctified it: because that in it he had rested from all his work which God created and made. - Genesis 2:2-3

Then it is first actually called a Sabbath in Exodus 16:23-26:

> [23] And he said unto them, This is that which the LORD hath said, <u>To morrow is the rest of the **holy sabbath unto the LORD**</u>: bake that which ye will bake to day, and seethe that ye will seethe; and that which remaineth over lay up for you to be kept until the morning.

> [24] And they laid it up till the morning, as Moses bade: and it did not stink, neither was there any worm therein.

[25] And Moses said, Eat that to day; for to day is <u>a sabbath **unto the LORD**</u>: to day ye shall not find it in the field.

[26] Six days ye shall gather it; but on <u>the seventh day, which is the sabbath</u>, in it there shall be none. - Exodus 16:23-26

Note that rather than being a "Sabbath unto the Jews" as we are often told, verse 25 specifies that it is a "Sabbath unto the Lord", our Father Yahweh. Thus it should be observed by all who are His. We will see a few chapters later that this is the fourth commandment of the famous ten commandments given to man by God Himself as He carved them with His finger into stone to be kept throughout time:

[10] And the LORD delivered unto me two tables of stone <u>written with the finger of God</u>; and on them was written according to all the words, which the LORD spake with you in the mount out of the midst of the fire in the day of the assembly. - Deuteronomy 9:10

[8] <u>Remember the **sabbath** day, to **keep it holy**</u>.

[9] <u>Six days shalt thou labour, and do all thy work</u>:

[10] But **the <u>seventh day</u> is the sabbath of the LORD thy God**: <u>in it thou shalt not do any work</u>, thou, nor thy son, nor thy daughter, thy manservant, nor thy maidservant, nor thy cattle, nor thy stranger that is within thy gates:

[11] For <u>in six days the LORD made heaven and earth, the sea, and all that in them is, and rested the seventh day</u>: wherefore **the LORD blessed the sabbath day, and <u>hallowed it</u>**. - Exodus 20:8-11

Here we see that He "hallowed it", as He had already told us in Exodus 16:23 above, that this specific day of the week was "holy".

The first tables of stone were broken, so God wrote them yet again. He was intent that the words written by His finger in stone would be carried forth. He then had Moses put these tables of stone in the Ark of the Covenant:

[1] At that time the LORD said unto me, Hew thee two tables of stone like unto the first, and come up unto me into the mount, and make thee an ark of wood.

[2] And I will write on the tables the words that were in the first tables which thou brakest, and thou shalt put them in the ark. - Deuteronomy 10:1-2

Two Trees, Two Kingdoms, Two Kings

Most churches still do teach that we should adhere to these basic ten commandments. However, in actual application, they keep only nine of the ten decrees that God recorded in stone with His finger and put into the ark for posterity. The fourth commandment is not kept. They teach that they are keeping it, but they have not upheld <u>that which was originally ordained</u>.

What we need to determine in order to keep this commandment properly is which day the weekly "Sabbath" is. It is clearly recorded in the fourth commandment above as being the seventh day and this is repeated throughout Torah:

> [2] And on <u>the seventh day God ended his work which he had made; and he rested on the seventh day</u> from all his work which he had made.
>
> [3] And <u>God blessed the **seventh day**, and **sanctified**</u> it: because that in it he had rested from all his work which God created and made. - Genesis 2:2-3
>
> [10] But **<u>the seventh day is the sabbath of the LORD thy God</u>**: in it thou shalt not do any work, thou, nor thy son, nor thy daughter, thy manservant, nor thy maidservant, nor thy cattle, nor thy stranger that is within thy gates:
>
> [11] For in six days the LORD made heaven and earth, the sea, and all that in them is, and rested <u>the seventh day</u>: wherefore **the LORD blessed the sabbath day, and hallowed it**. - Exodus 20:10-11
>
> [16] Wherefore <u>the children of Israel</u> shall keep the sabbath, to **observe the sabbath** throughout their generations, **for a perpetual covenant**. - Exodus 31:16

Combining these three references we see that the seventh day is the Father's Sabbath day, the day He sanctified and hallowed for observance as a perpetual covenant.

The dictionary definition of perpetual is: continuing without interruption, for an unlimited duration, throughout eternity. Father really couldn't make it much clearer that He never intended the disruption of His hallowed Sabbath day observance, then, now, or in the future. As long as time exists, He decreed that His Sabbath was to be observed perpetually, without end.

The church tends to excuse the clear wording of this commandment by saying it applies only to "Israel". When we read the entirety of the Word, we find out that we are grafted into Israel and are part of her. Paul says in Romans 11:

> [25] For I would not, brethren, that ye should be ignorant of this mystery, lest ye should be wise in your own conceits; that **blindness in part is happened to Israel, until the fulness of the Gentiles be come in**. - Romans 11:25

> [17] And if some of the branches be broken off, and **thou**, being a wild olive tree, **wert graffed in** among them, **and with them partakest of the root and fatness of the olive tree**; - Romans 11:17

This shows that we of the wild olive tree (the contra tree) are now accounted as being one with Israel, and are to partake along with them of the root and fatness of the cultivated olive tree (Tree of Life) as brought forward in Torah. There is a similar passage in Galatians which shows that we are Abraham's seed as a result of our Belief on Y'shua:

> [29] And if ye be Christ's, then are ye Abraham's seed, and heirs according to the promise. - Galatians 3:29

As we see it, if we do not claim to be a part of the children of Israel, then we are not of Y'shua, as those who ARE of Him are Abraham's seed according to the promise and were grafted into the cultivated olive tree (Tree of Life) with Israel to partake of the root and fatness of their heritage and Torah teaching.

If we become one with the children of Israel through grafting, then we too should observe the seventh day Sabbath (Saturday), perpetually (continuing throughout time without interruption).

When and how then did the church come to observe the first day of the week as their Holy Day rather than the seventh? How is this substitution of another day for God's ordained day justified?

We have heard many arguments as to why the New Testament Sabbath is supposed to be Sunday, but there is no argument that can stand against the clearly written words of Father Himself. As we see it, the seventh day is still the seventh day, hallowed is still hallowed, and perpetual is still perpetual. A main argument is that Y'shua was resurrected on Sunday, yet even this cannot be proven as when the tomb was visited "in the end of Sabbath" before dawn on Sunday morning (the first day of the week), it was already empty:

> [1] **In the end of the sabbath, as it began to dawn** toward the first day of the week, came Mary Magdalene and the other Mary to see the sepulchre.

> [2] And, behold, there was a great earthquake: for the angel of the Lord descended from heaven, and came and rolled back the stone from the door, and sat upon it.
>
> [3] His countenance was like lightning, and his raiment white as snow:
>
> [4] And for fear of him the keepers did shake, and became as dead men.
>
> [5] And the angel answered and said unto the women, Fear not ye: for I know that ye seek Jesus, which was crucified.
>
> [6] **He is not here: for he is risen**, as he said. Come, see the place where the Lord lay. - Matthew 28:1-6

Even if the resurrection had been on Sunday, that would not be a reason to abandon the clear instruction of the Father that was to be observed throughout time.

Another argument is that the church met on Sunday:

> [7] And <u>upon the first day of the week, when the disciples came together to break bread, Paul preached unto them</u>, <u>ready to depart on the morrow</u>; and continued his speech until midnight.
>
> [8] And <u>there were many lights</u> in the upper chamber, where they were gathered together. - Acts 20:7-8

We must remember that the first day of the week (according to Hebraic standards which were practiced in that day) would have begun at the sundown which ended the Sabbath. Thus there were many lights being in the upper chamber when they met and their meeting extended until midnight. It could easily have been right after the Sabbath teaching by Paul in the synagogues. Acts 18 refers to Paul when it says:

> [4] And he **reasoned in the synagogue every sabbath**, and per-suaded the Jews and the Greeks. - Acts 18:4

Obviously Paul could not be two places at the same time. Shortly following Paul's synagogue instruction each Sabbath would have been the natural time for the close-knit group of Believers to get together in their own meeting. Thus, this gathering just after the close of Sabbath would not provide a prototype for the worship on Sundays that we have in our current day. Likewise, even if this had been a Sunday morning meeting it would have in no way validated the <u>replacement of</u> Sunday for Father's perpetual mandate to keep the seventh day hallowed and holy.

There is actually a New Testament reference relative to Sabbath which implies that the seventh day still retains its former significance. We find it in Hebrews:

> [3] For we which have believed do <u>enter into rest</u>, as he said, As I have sworn in my wrath, if they shall enter into my rest: although the works were finished from the foundation of the world.

> [4] For he spake in a certain place of <u>the seventh day</u> on this wise, And <u>God did rest the **seventh day** from all his works</u>.

> [5] <u>And in this place again, If they shall enter into my rest</u>.

> [6] Seeing therefore it remaineth that some must enter therein, and they to whom it was first preached entered not in because of unbelief:

> [7] <u>Again, **he limiteth a certain day**, saying in David, To day, after so long a time; as it is said, To day if ye will hear his voice, **harden not your hearts**</u>.

> [8] <u>For if Jesus had given them rest, then would he not afterward have spoken of another day.</u>

> [9] There remaineth therefore a rest to the people of God.

> [10] For he that is entered into his rest, he also hath ceased from his own works, as God did from his.

> [11] <u>Let us labour therefore to enter into that rest, lest any man fall after the same example of unbelief</u>. - Hebrews 4:3-11

It is a spiraling typology which points to the rest which is ahead for the Believer in the prophetic Millennial Kingdom. This is the seventh millennial typological day (thousand year period of time):

> [8] But, beloved, be not ignorant of this one thing, that one day is with the Lord as a thousand years, and a thousand years as one day. - 2 Peter 3:8

This seventh millennium of rest is not yet here, so this typology has not yet been fulfilled. This is yet another reason that we should be honoring this seventh day each week.

Two Trees, Two Kingdoms, Two Kings

The conclusion of the Hebrews 4 passage above indicates that Y'shua is likewise our rest. As we abide in Him we cease our own labors and attain to His. However, we are shown in verse 8 of this Hebrews passage that Y'shua would have referenced another day if He had intended this rest to replace that which Father had referenced. The spiritual rest Y'shua offers us is a higher spiritual Truth or Law of sorts, but it does not negate the physical Law on which it is based. Again, the two must work together to attain to the intent of God. We are told which day the Sabbath is, and (though we do not mean to sound harsh) it simply is not the first day of the week. Father specifies without any ifs, ands or buts that it is the seventh day of the week. It will also remain the seventh day of the week throughout time.

Just as Father worked six days and rested on the seventh, we are to do likewise. It is not just any six days and rest on the following day, our rest is specified by God's finger in stone to be the Seventh day. We are to keep that specific day holy because Father has hallowed it:

> [11] For in six days the LORD made heaven and earth, the sea, and all that in them is, and <u>rested **the seventh day**</u>: wherefore **the LORD blessed the sabbath day, and hallowed it**. - Exodus 20:11

The word "hallowed" here is Strong's #H6942 ("qadash") - *to set apart as sacred, consecrate, sanctify, dedicate; to observe as holy, keep sacred; to honour as sacred*. Nowhere in the Word does it ever say He changed its status back to an unhallowed day and hallowed another in its place, so it is obviously still hallowed per His original intent:

> [15] Six days may work be done; but in **the seventh is the sabbath of rest, holy to the LORD**: whosoever doeth any work in the sabbath day, he shall surely be put to death.
>
> [16] Wherefore the children of Israel shall keep the sabbath, to observe the sabbath throughout their generations, for **a perpetual covenant**. - Exodus 31:15-16

While some measures of the ceremonial Law have been relaxed for a time due to one reason or another after the crucifixion and resurrection of Y'shua, the observation of Sabbath has not. The word "perpetual" in Exodus 31:16 above negates this potential. We will see this more as we proceed.

Our Heavenly Father was rather serious about this commandment. It was and still is one of the ten great commandments our churches SAY they uphold. We must not forget that Father had Moses put the book of Law (probably Torah) "in the side" of the Ark of the Covenant. He had it put there <u>as a witness</u>. While we are not sure what is meant by "in the side", they would have been placed near the Tables of the Law (including the fourth commandment), as these too were placed in the Ark:

> [26] Take this book of the law, and put it in the side of the ark of the covenant of the LORD your God, that it may be there for a witness against thee. - Deuteronomy 31:26

How will man explain away this "witness against them" when the ark is recovered some day and they stand before God?

He was so serious about the sanctity of the Sabbath in fact, that He had someone put to death who broke the portion of this commandment which specified not working on Sabbath:

> [32] And while the children of Israel were in the wilderness, <u>they found a man that gathered sticks upon the sabbath day</u>.
>
> [33] And they that found him gathering sticks brought him unto Moses and Aaron, and unto all the congregation.
>
> [34] And they put him in ward, because it was not declared what should be done to him.
>
> [35] And <u>the LORD said</u> unto Moses, <u>The man shall be surely put to death</u>: all the congregation shall stone him with stones without the camp.
>
> [36] And all the congregation brought him without the camp, and stoned him with stones, and he died; as the LORD commanded Moses. - Numbers 15:32-36

Since there was no atonement yet to deal with the penalty of this crime against God's command, Father had to uphold the application of its declared penalty. The mere severity of the penalty points to the importance of this Law in Father's eyes. The Pharisees have added all kinds of innuendos to this decree not to work, and we are not to look to their stipulations to determine what work is or is not. That is an area which the Spirit within can direct, as we consider our instructions in the Biblical text. This day is so holy to Father that He doesn't even want us to make our animals work, much less any other human. It is to be a day of rest for all:

> [12] <u>Keep the sabbath day to sanctify it</u>, as the LORD thy God hath commanded thee.

[13] Six days thou shalt labour, and do all thy work:

[14] But <u>the seventh day is the sabbath of the LORD thy God</u>: in it <u>thou shalt not do any work</u>, thou, <u>nor thy son, nor thy daughter, nor thy manservant, nor thy maidservant</u>, <u>nor thine ox, nor thine ass, nor any of thy cattle</u>, nor thy stranger that is within thy gates; that thy manservant and thy maidservant may rest as well as thou. - Deuteronomy 5:12-14

We thought it might be good to provide a general idea of what we have personally been prompted to do in order to observe Sabbath. We have been led to abstain from labor and basically separate ourselves from the world on Father's Holy Day. There is no shopping, eating out, or anything of that nature on Father's Sabbaths, as that would be to have others work for us. It is our practice to have all of our cooking, housework and chores done in advance so so we can enjoy the day (from sundown Friday through sundown Saturday) with Father. Typically we meet in worship, study, and fellowship with like-minded Believers on Saturday. What a blessing it has been to us to find the joys of His rest on this special day of the week. Isaiah indicated that it will be a blessing throughout the Millennial Kingdom as well:

[23] And it shall come to pass, that from one new moon to another, and from one sabbath to another, shall all flesh come to worship before me, saith the LORD. - Isaiah 66:23

Annual Sabbaths

We mentioned earlier that there were annual Sabbaths as well. The weekly Sabbath and the annual Sabbaths are all designated as Sabbaths by Father and to be observed. We would note the plurality of the word "Sabbaths" in Leviticus 19:

[30] Ye shall keep my sabbaths, and reverence my sanctuary: I am the LORD. - Leviticus 19:30

Father expects us to honor His Sabbaths (plural – both weekly and annual) in order to reverence His sanctuary.

The annual Sabbaths are found in Leviticus 23. Not all feast days are Sabbaths, but the ones that Father designated as Sabbaths are to be honored without working. So we will be certain to understand this, it is spelled out specifically in the surrounding text of each Sabbath. These annual Sabbaths are Holy Days – Sabbath days of rest ordained by Father, just as the weekly

Sabbaths are. An example is found in verse 39 which refers to the Feast of Tabernacles:

> [39] Also in the fifteenth day of the seventh month, when ye have gathered in the fruit of the land, ye shall keep a feast unto the LORD seven days: <u>on the first day shall be a **sabbath**, and on the eighth day shall be a **sabbath**</u>. - Leviticus 23:39

> [35] On the <u>first day shall be an holy convocation: ye shall do **no servile work**</u> therein.

> [36] Seven days ye shall offer an offering made by fire unto the LORD: <u>on the eighth day shall be an holy convocation</u> unto you; and ye shall offer an offering made by fire unto the LORD: it is a solemn assembly; and <u>ye shall do **no servile work**</u> therein. - Leviticus 23:35-36

If Father hallowed His weekly Sabbath and He calls these Sabbaths as well, then it makes sense to us that these too are hallowed days in His sight. There are seven annual Sabbaths. We will cover them in more detail momentarily. Many would say these are Jewish feast days. Our Bibles say otherwise:

> [2] Speak unto the children of Israel, and say unto them, Concerning **the feasts of the LORD**, which ye shall proclaim to be holy convocations, <u>even these are **my** feasts</u>. - Leviticus 23:2

Again we are clearly shown in this passage that they are Yahweh's (the LORD's) feast days, and it appears that all of His people should observe them. As Believers we were adopted into the Father's house so that would include us as well.

We do understand that Y'shua said He is Lord of the Sabbath:

> [8] For the Son of man is Lord even of the sabbath day. - Matthew 12:8

Being of the Father, He can allow for relaxation of the legal system that comes from Heaven, but that would be for a higher purpose, such as healing or instruction:

> [14] And the ruler of the synagogue answered with indignation, because that <u>Jesus had healed on the sabbath day</u>, and said unto the people, There are six days in which men ought to work: in them therefore come and be healed, and not on the sabbath day. - Luke 13:14

Two Trees, Two Kingdoms, Two Kings

There is no evidence of Y'shua encouraging anyone to discount the observance of Sabbath. The closest we get to that is found in the book of John:

> [16] And therefore did the Jews persecute Jesus, and sought to slay him, because he had done these things on the sabbath day.
>
> [17] But Jesus answered them, My Father worketh hitherto, and I work. - John 5:16-17

Genesis says the Father rested "from all his work which He had made" on the seventh day:

> [2] And on the seventh day God ended his work which he had made; and he rested on the seventh day from all his work which he had made. - Genesis 2:2

Even our New Testament reference in Hebrews reminded us that the Father rested from His work on this day:

> [4] For he spake in a certain place of the seventh day on this wise, And God did rest the **seventh day** from all his works. - Hebrews 4:4

Yet Y'shua says in the above John reference that Father worked on the seventh day:

> [17] But Jesus answered them, My Father worketh hitherto, and I work. - John 5:17

Evidently the words "worketh" and "work" in this verse have a slightly different connotation than those in Genesis and Hebrews, and Y'shua was pointing to a higher spiritual Truth. Both the words "worketh" and "work" in this John passage are Strong's #G2038 ("ergazomai"). The meaning encompasses a variety of types of work, but the obvious intent by Y'shua was more along the lines of being active in the sense of working miracles and such righteous tasks rather than working at manual labor. This type of work was to benefit others who were under affliction or in need of spiritual instruction rather than working in the carpentry shop. He was trying to show the Pharisees the spiritual application of Sabbath. Even priests are innocent after speaking on Sabbath:

> [5] Or have ye not read in the law, how that on the sabbath days the priests in the temple profane the sabbath, and are blameless? - Matthew 12:5

Y'shua also said that Sabbath was for man:

> [27] And he said unto them, <u>The sabbath was made for man, and not man for the sabbath</u>: - Mark 2:27

This indicates that the human body needs rest, and we are to observe it as a day of rest not only to honor Father who hallowed it, but to give our bodies the weekly rest they need. During this physical rest, we are to draw nearer to Father so our inner man rests as well, being undistracted by the things of the world. This is the keeping it "holy" aspect of our Sabbath rest. It is likewise to be a time of growth and closeness as we spend this day with Him – a benefit for us.

Paul shows us in Colossians that we were not to judge one another IN RESPECT to sabbath days because they are a shadow of things to come, but Y'shua is the embodiment of these shadows:

> [16] <u>Let no man therefore judge you</u> in meat, or in drink, or **in respect** of an holyday, or of the new moon, or of the sabbath days:

> [17] Which are a <u>shadow of things to come</u>; but <u>the body is of Christ</u>. - Colossians 2:16-17

The word "respect" here is Strong's #G3313 ("meros") and has considerable latitude in meaning, which includes: *part due or assigned to one.* Paul may have simply been indicating that we were not to judge one another <u>in the RESPECT by which</u> the Sabbath days ARE TO BE observed. We are not to look to all of the ways of the Pharisees in our keeping of Sabbath, but to allow the Holy Spirit to direct us in the manner in which to observe these Holy Days of rest.

While Y'shua's ministry does imply some extra flexibility regarding assisting others on Sabbath for the right reasons, He does not insinuate that we now have license to ignore Father's desire that we should rest on that day and keep it holy. Neither did He or any portion of Scripture indicate that the weekly Sabbath day was ever changed from the seventh day of the week to the first day.

This change was brought into effect by the Roman Catholic Church, and initiated originally by Constantine in AD 321:

> Unquestionably the first law, either ecclesiastical or civil, by which the sabbatical observance of Sunday is known to have been ordained is the sabbatical edict of Constantine, A.D. 321. - Chamber's Encyclopaedia, Article "Sunday."

Two Trees, Two Kingdoms, Two Kings

The Catholic church never claims any Biblical grounds for this change, and acknowledges that the day they are proclaiming as the new day of rest is the "Venerable Day of the Sun" or the "sacred day of the Sun". In substance this lends a sacredness to the sun and establishes a mandate to honor that day, making it akin to worship of the sun or the sun god Ra (a pagan entity of worship):

> On the Venerable Day of the Sun ["venerabili die Solis"--the sacred day of the Sun] let the magistrates and people residing in cities rest, and let all workshops be closed. In the country, however, persons engaged in agriculture may freely and lawfully continue their pursuits; because it often happens that another day is not so suitable for grain-sowing or for vine-planting; lest by neglecting the proper moment for such operations the bounty of heaven should be lost--Given the 7th day of March, [A.D. 321], Crispus and Constantine being consuls each of them for the second time. - The First Sunday Law of Constantine 1, in "Codex Justinianus," lib. 3, tit. 12, 3; trans. in Phillip Schaff "History of the Christian Church," Vol. 3, p. 380.

We might also note that this consent to work on this supposed "Holy Day" of the week is in direct contradiction to the directive in Exodus about resting on Sabbath during harvest:

> [21] Six days thou shalt work, but on the seventh day thou shalt rest: in earing time and in **harvest** thou shalt rest. - Exodus 34:21

Not only did the Catholic church enact Sunday as their "Sabbath" of rest, but they forbade resting on the seventh day as well. In ecclesiastical legislation they referred to those who kept the Biblical Sabbath as Judaizing, and forbade the keeping of God's ordained Sabbath:

> The Council of Laodicea ... forbids Christians from judaizing and resting on the Sabbath day, preferring the Lord's day, and so far as possible resting as Christians. - Encyclopaedia Britannica, 1899 Edition, Vol. XXIII, page 654.

> Christians shall not Judaize and be idle on Saturday [in the original: "sabbato" shall not be idle on the Sabbath], but shall work on that day; but the Lord's day they shall especially honour, and as being Christians, shall, if possible, do no work on that day. If, however, they are found Judaizing, they shall be shut out ["anathema,"--excommunicated] from Christ. - Council of Laodicea, c. A.D. 337, Canon 29, quoted in C.J. Hefele, "A History of the Councils of the Church," Vol. 2, p. 316.

We will be commenting momentarily on the term "the Lord's day" as it is used here. In the meantime though, we will focus on man's switch from God's Sabbath to the Venerable Day of the Sun. Such transition to Sunday was NEVER Biblically ordained, and none of the reasoning to observe the first day of the week rather than the seventh can stand up against Biblical scrutiny. It becomes obvious that there is considerable dissension regarding the true Sabbath when man's religious leaders go to the extreme to forbid observance of it <u>even in conjunction with</u> Sunday observance. They are not merely showing preference to Sunday, but totally deleting potential observance of seventh day Sabbath in any way. The Roman Catholics say they have complete authority over the interpretation of Scripture and the doctrinal direction it takes them:

> The task of interpreting the Word of God authentically has been entrusted solely to the Magisterium of the Church, that is, to the Pope and to the bishops in communion with him. - Chatechism of the Catholic Church Paragraph 100

Thus their interpretations are to be the manner in which the Bible is viewed by those who fall under their banner, and these interpretations are to override the actual Biblical instruction to the individual. One such instance might be their interpretation of the "Lord's Day", which they view as being Sunday. This specific term is mentioned only one time in the King James version of our Bibles (as well as 12 other major versions we checked). This single reference is in the book of Revelation, and there is no Biblical indication whatsoever that this "Lord's Day" is Sunday rather than Sabbath:

> [10] I was in the Spirit <u>on the Lord's day</u>, and heard behind me a great voice, as of a trumpet, - Revelation 1:10

John knew, believed, and taught Torah principles; and Torah says: "the <u>seventh day</u> is the sabbath of the LORD thy God". Torah also indicates that the seventh day is the day the Lord hallowed. Therefore, John would likely be indicating the seventh day when he references the "Lord's Day" here. Apparently the Catholic Church's presumption that Y'shua's resurrection was on Sunday is their basis for seeing Sunday as the "Lord's Day", and (following that line of thinking) they then observe it as Sabbath:

> Sunday, the "Lord's Day," is the principal day for the celebration of the Eucharist because it is the day of the Resurrection. It is the pre-eminent day of the liturgical assembly, the day of the Christian family, and the day of joy and rest from work. Sunday is "the foundation and kernel of the whole liturgical year" (SC 106). - Chatechism of the Catholic Church Paragraph 1193

Two Trees, Two Kingdoms, Two Kings

As we have shown, this is a potentially errant view from the onset, as the tomb was empty when it was found <u>prior to</u> dawn on Sunday morning.

They are therefore taking a potentially errant interpretation and building a doctrinal stance around that interpretation, then using that derived stance to override the specific written mandate of God. We must also recall that this mandate was recorded by God's finger in stone tablets which yet reside in the Ark of the Covenant. God's perpetual commandment was never meant to be breached by man, yet man's religious order has done so. Ezekiel's prophetic words reveal that God looked forward in time to see that this would happen:

> [8] Thou hast despised mine holy things, and hast profaned my sabbaths. - Ezekiel 22:8

The resurrection is indisputably the single most emotionally inspiring event in Biblical history. By pointing to this event as the reason to establish Sunday as the new day of rest, it strikes a chord with our hearts and becomes acceptable to the mind. We must be objective though to see it for what it is – man's ordained substitution of the "Venerable (sacred) Day of the Sun" for God's mandated observance of His hallowed seventh day Sabbath:

> The celebration of Sunday observes the moral commandment inscribed by nature in the human heart to render to God an outward, visible, public, and regular worship "as a sign of his universal beneficence to all."109 Sunday worship fulfills the moral command of the Old Covenant, taking up its rhythm and spirit in the weekly celebration of the Creator and Redeemer of his people. - Chatechism of the Catholic Church Paragraph 2176

The words "Sunday worship fulfills the moral command of the Old Covenant..." is simply man's justification for his substitution and has absolutely no footing in Biblical context.

The Eucharist (Catholic version of communion) is given and received on their substituted Sabbath which is simply and only ordained by man:

> The Sunday celebration of the Lord's Day and his Eucharist is at the heart of the Church's life. "Sunday is the day on which the paschal mystery is celebrated in light of the apostolic tradition and is to be observed as the foremost holy day of obligation in the universal Church."110 (1167, 2043) - Chatechism of the Catholic Church Paragraph 2177

Even this sacred remembrance of Y'shua's crucifixion and resurrection (the paschal mystery) is referenced here as being observed "in light of the apostolic tradition". It is not our purpose to address how their tradition overshadows the simple instructions for communion in the Biblical text, but merely to show that the "traditions" established by the papal authority are given supremacy over the clearly written words of our Biblical text. As evidenced in Chatechism of the Catholic Church Paragraph 100 above, they do not intend for individuals to discern the Biblical text and determine their own doctrinal beliefs, but for all to subscribe to the traditions they establish in light of their corporate interpretation. This overrides the New Testament mandate that each individual Believer is to study to show <u>thyself</u> approved:

> [15] <u>Study to shew thyself approved</u> unto God, a workman that needeth not to be ashamed, rightly dividing the word of truth. - 2 Timothy 2:15

We take strong issue with the supremacy of church tradition (no matter how well-meaning) over the clearly written words of the Biblical text. In our view, NOTHING should be put above God's Word – the Holy Writ of Scripture. To do so is very dangerous indeed. Scripture in and of itself says we do not need to depend on man to determine our belief system:

> [27] But the anointing which ye have received of him abideth in you, and **ye need not that any man teach you**: but as <u>the same anointing teacheth you of all things</u>, and is truth, and is no lie, and even as it hath taught you, ye shall abide in him. - 1 John 2:27

The Protestant denominations have failed to break from this tradition, and still observe the "Venerable Day of the Sun" which was authorized so long ago. In a similar vein they have attributed their doctrinal stance that excuses keeping the mandated Sabbath to the words of Paul, which have been interpreted using the dutiful contra mode of thought. The following verse in Romans is often used to justify no longer keeping weekly or annual Sabbaths:

> [5] One man esteemeth one day above another: another esteemeth every day alike. Let every man be fully persuaded in his own mind.

> [6] He that regardeth the day, regardeth it unto the Lord; and he that regardeth not the day, to the Lord he doth not regard it. <u>He that eateth, eateth to the Lord</u>, for he giveth God thanks; and <u>he that eateth not, to the Lord he eateth not, and giveth God thanks</u>. - Romans 14:5-6

Two Trees, Two Kingdoms, Two Kings

Is negating the need to keep Sabbath really the intent of this passage? The word "eateth" in verse 6 is Strong's #G2068 ("esthiō") - *eat, consume, to take food, eat a meal*. Paul is not specific in his statement of verses five and six, but he is likely discussing the concept of fasting on certain days which were never mandated by Scripture. These would be such days as Av 9, and the fasts of the fourth, fifth, seventh, and tenth months which are mentioned in Zechariah 8:19 without being mandated by Father. These special days of our Romans passage being fast days would seem to be validated by the reference in verse 6 of those who choose to eat (as on any other day) and those who choose not to eat. What Paul seems to be pointing out is that the man who eats on such days is giving God thanks for what he is eating, just as the one who is fasting is giving God thanks for his fasting. It appears that he is indicating that one is not to be judged for fasting or choosing not to fast. To try to make these "days" into something which Paul almost certainly did NOT mean (such as whether or not to honor Sabbath) can easily lead to error. When we view the entirety of the Biblical text, we can see that keeping Sabbath was important to Paul.

While it is obviously not our intent to endorse the broader scope of Wesleyan instruction, a specific quote by Wilber T. Dayton is very apropos here, as well as in a number of other Biblical discussions. He shows here that it is failure to be Berean (to refer back to the Torah instruction of the Father Himself) which leads to errant interpretation and doctrinal teaching. He stresses that relative to matters of moral consideration, when God has spoken there is no other legitimate side to the issue:

> "… No such questions can be conscientiously raised concerning the fundamental moral issues that are clarified in the Decalogue, the Sermon on the Mount, or in any other plain statement of Scripture. **When God has spoken there is no other legitimate side to the issue**." - Wesleyan Bible Commentary – Wilber T. Dayton

Let's recall again what Father has to say regarding the common manner in which His people have chosen to disregard His Sabbath:

> [8] Thou hast despised mine holy things, and hast **profaned my sabbaths**. - Ezekiel 22:8

It appears that when we fall in line behind the Roman stance, or justify by any other means the removal of Father's ordained perpetual Sabbaths from our lives, we might inadvertently pit ourselves against the Father and profane Him. In a similar reference we find:

[26] Her priests have violated my law, and have profaned mine
holy things: they have put no difference between the holy and
profane, neither have they shewed difference between the unclean
and the clean, and have **hid their eyes from my sabbaths**, and I
am profaned among them. - Ezekiel 22:26

He is referring in this passage to the "house" of Israel (which has spiritual figurative implications of being the Church). Indeed much of the church does not understand His holy things, or His Law, and has put no difference between the holy and the profane or the clean and the unclean, and they do hide their eyes from the seventh day Sabbath which profanes Father. Oh that it were not so!

We are sorry about the severity of this passage, but the words in our Biblical text speak for themselves in this matter. The words are not of our choosing. They were ordained by Father. Likewise this will probably be one of the most difficult portions of the book for some to read, and we apologize that it was necessary to be so blunt in some portions of it. It seems there is no way to soften the message, as the contra message must be exposed in all of its distortion in order to establish why it is invalid. We also understand the gravity from Father's perspective regarding the mandate He gave His people, and it is our most earnest desire for all to come to HIS understanding on the matter before having to stand before Him. We realize that if you have been drawn into the Sunday Sabbath mindset, this reading has not been easy, but we pray it will be taken to heart.

We would note that in both Ezekiel 22:8 and 22:26 above, the word "sabbaths" is plural. We will see how this then might relate to both the weekly and annual Sabbaths of the our Father.

Festival Observance – Holy Days Vs. Holidays

[30] Ye shall keep my sabbaths, and reverence my sanctuary: I am
the LORD. - Leviticus 19:30

Again, we would emphasize that the word "sabbaths" in this Leviticus text is plural, potentially implying annual Sabbaths as well as weekly ones. The wording of the introduction to the Feast of Trumpets on the first day of the seventh month in Leviticus points to these annual Holy Days as being Sabbaths:

[24] Speak unto the children of Israel, saying, In the seventh
month, in the first day of the month, shall ye have a sabbath,
a memorial of blowing of trumpets, an holy convocation. -
Leviticus 23:24

Two Trees, Two Kingdoms, Two Kings

It seems to us that Father would not have called these annual Holy Days "Sabbaths" if He had not intended them to carry the same significance as His hallowed weekly Sabbaths. Indeed they too are designated as days of rest. This is shown in the following verse:

> [25] Ye <u>shall do no servile work therein</u>: but ye shall offer an offering made by fire unto the LORD. - Leviticus 23:25

We also want to bear in mind that such days are not just for our rest, they are "holy" to the Father:

> [7] In the first day ye shall have an <u>holy</u> convocation: <u>ye shall do no servile work therein</u>. - Leviticus 23:7

These days are special to Him, so they should be special to His children. Are we not His children? We are told that we don't need to honor such observances today, but what did Father mean when He spoke of all observing one Law?:

> [49] <u>One law</u> shall be to him that is homeborn, and unto the stranger that sojourneth among you. - Exodus 12:49

He was referring here to the ones who would be added to their number during ancient times, but there might be even greater significance to those who would be added to the Hebraic people in Romans 11 as well. We are to be of the same Law, observing the same Torah, the root and fatness (Torah Truth) of the cultivated olive tree (Tree of Life) into which we were grafted:

> [16] For if the firstfruit be holy, the lump is also holy: and if the root be holy, so are the branches.
>
> [17] And if some of the branches be broken off, and thou, being a wild olive tree, wert graffed in among them, and with them partakest of the root and fatness of the olive tree; - Romans 11:16-17

Those of Hebraic descent are already to observe Torah, but this indicates that those who come to sojourn with them are to observe it in like manner. When we who are from the wild olive tree (Tree of Knowledge) are grafted into the cultivated olive tree of the Hebraic faith through belief on Y'shua, we are to tap into the nutrition of the roots and fatness (Torah) of this tree (the Tree of Life). We are to likewise look to the Law this tree provides and observe it in like manner as the Hebraic people.

Many say Paul has excused the observance of the festivals and the keeping of annual Sabbaths, but did Paul ever say NOT to observe them? If he did we have not found it.

The book of Acts records the following in reference to Paul:

> [21] But bade them farewell, saying, **I must by all means keep this feast that cometh in Jerusalem**: but I will return again unto you, if God will. And he sailed from Ephesus. - Acts 18:21

It is obvious that Paul saw the importance of keeping the feast at hand. Then two chapters later Paul was again determined to be in Jerusalem for Pentecost:

> [16] For Paul had determined to sail by Ephesus, because he would not spend the time in Asia: for he hasted, if it were possible for him, **to be at Jerusalem the day of Pentecost**. - Acts 20:16

In his own epistle of 1 Corinthians, Paul addresses the Passover festivities (specifically Unleavened Bread), when he actually stated:

> [8] Therefore **let us keep** the feast, not with old leaven, neither with the leaven of malice and wickedness; but <u>with the unleavened bread of sincerity and truth</u>. - 1 Corinthians 5:8

He was advising the Body of Messiah to <u>keep</u> or observe the Holy Day of Unleavened Bread, but to do so with new spiritual insight as to what the day means. He wanted them to draw near to the Father with sincerity and truth on that day.

While we see (as Paul sees) that the festivals are a shadow of that which Y'shua fulfills, we also understand that some of this fulfillment (particularly aspects of the fall Festivals) has not yet happened. Because the yearly festival cycle is a composite unit, it is a portion of the Father's Law which remains partially unfulfilled. The festival sequence is a rehearsal for the acts of the Divine play which is still being enacted through its repeated cycles until the play is concluded in Heaven. It seems, therefore, that the entire festival cycle should be observed until its total Divine fulfillment is accomplished.

Paul also said not to judge one another in "respect" of Holy Days:

> [15] And having spoiled principalities and powers, he made a shew of them openly, triumphing over them in it.

> [16] <u>Let no man therefore judge you</u> in meat, or in drink, or <u>in respect of an holyday, or of the new moon, or of the sabbath days</u>:

Two Trees, Two Kingdoms, Two Kings

> [17] Which are a shadow of things to come; but the body is of
> Christ. - Colossians 2:15-17

As we indicated relative to this verse when discussing the weekly Sabbath above, the word "respect" may be the key to understanding what Paul was actually saying here. Whether or not annual Holy Days and Sabbaths are to be kept is not likely Paul's objective here. He seems instead to be saying to stop judging one another regarding the respect (manner) in which they are observed. This would retain the harmony of Scripture by keeping intact Father's command to observe the Holy Days found in Torah.

As children of the Father, Believers also are to observe all of the days which are special to Him, particularly when His Words as recorded in the Biblical text of Torah are emphatic about such observance. However, since the festivals are mere shadows of Y'shua's role to mankind, there are few absolutes to dictate the <u>means</u> by which we are to observe them. There are a few items regarding observance criteria in Torah, but there are also many traditions attached within Judaism, which are often Pharisaical. Obviously, such traditions need not be observed.

The Festivals reveal the plan of God's redemption for His children. They were designed to bring revelation to His children regarding the accomplishment of Y'shua as their Savior through the cyclical patterns which rehearse His role as Redeemer:

> [4] These are <u>the feasts of the LORD</u>, even <u>holy convocations</u>,
> which ye shall proclaim in their seasons. - Leviticus 23:4

The Hebrew word for both "feasts" and "seasons" is Strong's #H4150 ("mow`ed") - *rehearsal, appointed time, sacred season, set feast, appointed season, appointed meeting, appointed sign or signal.*

The feasts are rehearsals of the cyclical play in which Y'shua is depicted as the Redeemer for mankind. The various appointed times show how this is accomplished in the complete plan of the Father. Those who have Torah but don't yet know Y'shua are shown annually in shadow form the picture of Y'shua as mankind's Redeemer, so they can ultimately be drawn to Him. Those who know Him already will be reliving His accomplishment and bringing Him glory through their remembrance of His victory. They will likewise be looking to the final acts of the play when He will complete their fulfillment as well.

Since we (as Believers) are to have this understanding already, it may allow for more flexibility in the manner that the festivals are observed. In one such instance Torah differentiates:

> [42] Ye shall dwell in booths seven days; <u>all that are Israelites born</u> shall dwell in booths: - Leviticus 23:42

This particular manner of observance (dwelling in booths) is shown here by Father to be specifically for those who were born in Israel. Many believe that when we are grafted into the natural olive tree it is akin to being born in Israel. However, the word used in the Hebrew text does not indicate this. The word "born" here is Strong's #H249 ("'ezrach") - *a native (one rising from the soil); of man, native Israelites; of tree, native (to Israel)*.

While we acknowledge <u>identity with</u> Israel after being grafted into the cultivated olive tree, we do not necessarily see it as being the same here as being born an Israelite. Romans is clear that we are adopted children, so we would fall more under the category of the Old Testament "stranger" who "sojourns" with Israel. In many ways the two are treated the same, but when there is a distinction as we find here, we believe it is meaningful.

While it may not be NECESSARY for the Believer who was not physically born in Israel to dwell in booths throughout this festival period, it is certainly desirable to do so, and fits with the symbolism and mores of the Festival occasion. It presents a wonderful opportunity to tabernacle with others in a literal observance and fellowship that can be very fulfilling. In such an instance, there are not as many specifications for us (as Believers who were adopted into the Father's household of Israel through Y'shua). Yet, it is our understanding that we are still to observe such Holy Days with our Father by abstaining from work. It is an opportunity to draw nearer to Him, reflecting spiritually on the meaning of His special days.

At other times, Torah includes both those who are Israel born and those who are grafted in:

> [19] Seven days shall there be no leaven found in your houses: for whosoever eateth that which is leavened, even that soul shall be cut off from the congregation of Israel, <u>whether he be a stranger, or born in the land</u>. - Exodus 12:19

The word "stranger" here is Strong's #H1616 ("ger") - *a newcomer lacking inherited rights*. Thus all (both those who are Israel born and those who are adopted or grafted into Israel) should observe the "no leaven" aspect of this festival as well as abstaining from work on the days which Father designated as Sabbaths of rest.

Because Y'shua has proven His identity with the patterning of the Festival typologies, we (as Brethren) can now rejoice as we celebrate what He has done and is doing. We can delight to observe these days in the presence of the Father and the Son. Just as the Father set aside the weekly Sabbath as a symbol of the coming Millennial "Day" (1000 year period) of rest, so He set aside the annual Festival Sabbaths as special days of rest for mankind so we could reflect on what they signify to us today. They are special days where we are to set aside the world and commerce and separate ourselves to Him. Then we can draw nearer in worship to Him as we consider what He has done for us. These are the "Holy Days" which should be observed INSTEAD OF the "holidays" the world has put in place.

How did we become so severed from our Hebrew roots? In 70 AD, the Jewish worshipers had to go underground due to intense persecution by the Roman religious system. As the Jews fled from the heavy hand of the Romans, this Roman religious/political system began to banish anything even loosely associated with the Jewish ideology. The removal of this ideology which had been embraced and taught by the early church fathers (who had known Y'shua personally and understood His message clearly) resulted in a warped version of Christendom. Then it got worse.

When Constantine came to power, he embraced Christianity, but proceeded to force everyone else to become Christian as well. In an attempt to draw in the pagans, he adopted their religious days, and he used them to replace the Holy Days established by Father. This not only attracted the pagan people who could continue to celebrate their festivities unchecked, but it further alienated the Hebraic people, as well as the early Christians who understood the importance of their Jewish roots. Consequently the Hebraic people began to reject the Savior (Y'shua), whom they associated with this new-found religious distortion. Constantine therefore effectively curtailed the salvation of the Hebrew people at that time. Likewise, the Hebraic roots of our Judaeo-Christian faith were then successfully severed, and a rather twisted and contaminated version of Christendom emerged where God's key directives and observances were abandoned and replaced with more pagan alternatives.

In keeping with Constantine's alterations, the world around us today keeps Christmas to celebrate the birth of Y'shua and Easter to celebrate His resurrection from the dead. Constantine not only sabotaged observance of the weekly Sabbath, but derailed Father's sacred Holy Days as well. These holiday traditions which uprooted and replaced Father's Biblical Holy Days came about almost 300 years after the resurrection of Y'shua beginning in about 325 AD. The early church (right after Y'shua's time on earth) celebrated the Holy Days (even as Y'shua had done) rather than the replacement holidays which came into being much later. Constantine wanted to draw the pagans into Christendom, so he adapted their celebrations into Christianity, and wrapped Christian meaning around them. Such is the reason for Christmas falling on December 25. It is the birthday of Mithra, whom this pagan festival date honors. Easter is likewise a pagan celebration – the pagan worship of Ishtar (or Astarte). The pagan fertility symbols of rabbits and eggs associated with Ishtar are a part of our Easter festivities to this very day.

With just a little study, we can show the likelihood of Y'shua's birth being in the vicinity of the fall festivals. It is derived by using the timing of the course of Zachariah's Temple service (the #8 course of Abia or Abijah) to determine the approximate time of Elizabeth's conception:

> [5] There was in the days of Herod, the king of Judaea, a certain priest named <u>Zacharias, of the course of Abia</u>: and his wife was of the daughters of Aaron, and her name was Elisabeth. - Luke 1:5

Abia is the New Testament spelling for Abijah in the Old Testament. The 1 Chronicles text then tells us which course of Temple service Zacharias would have been performing:

> [10] The seventh to Hakkoz, <u>the eighth to Abijah</u>, - 1 Chronicles 24:10

Without listing all of the courses, we see that Abijah was the eighth course, and that this was his placement in the ordering of Temple service:

> [19] <u>These were the orderings of them in their service to come into the house of the LORD</u>, according to their manner, under Aaron their father, as the LORD God of Israel had commanded him. - 1 Chronicles 24:19

Luke 1 implies that Elizabeth conceived right after Zechariah returned home. Judging from the manner in which the courses of Temple service were played out (per Alfred Edersheim's book <u>The Temple</u>), it is therefore likely that Elizabeth's conception was on or very near Pentecost. This would put the beginning of Elizabeth's pregnancy in early Sivan (the third month of the religious year).

When the angel appeared to Mary, he told her that Elizabeth was in her sixth month of pregnancy:

> [36] And, behold, <u>thy cousin Elisabeth, she hath also conceived a son</u> in her old age: and <u>this is the sixth month with her</u>, who was called barren. - Luke 1:36

Adding six months to the third month (Sivan) we come to the ninth month (Kislev). Thus we can loosely calculate and surmise that the approximate timing of Y'shua's conception might fall on or near Chanukkah (Kislev 24), which was during the sixth month of Elizabeth's pregnancy.

The conception of Y'shua on Chanukkah might actually be seen when we compare New Testament words of 1 Corinthians to those of Haggai:

> [11] For other foundation can no man lay than that is laid, which is Jesus Christ. - 1 Corinthians 3:11

We know that Y'shua is the foundation for our spiritual Temple. Accordingly, we see some very prophetic wording in Haggai. It shows that the foundation of the Temple was laid on Kislev 24, the eve of the first day of Chanukkah:

> [18] Consider now from this day and upward, from <u>the four and twentieth day of the ninth month</u>, even from t<u>he day that the foundation of the LORD's temple was laid</u>, consider it. - Haggai 2:18

Could there be a cryptic message there? In conjunction with this laying of the foundation of the Temple is the very next verse which asks a hypothetical question. "Is the seed yet in the barn?"

> [19] <u>Is the seed yet in the barn?</u> yea, as yet <u>the vine</u>, and the fig tree, and the pomegranate, and the olive tree, hath not brought forth: <u>from this day will I bless you</u>. - Haggai 2:19

The word "barn" here is Strong's #H4034 ("mĕguwrah") - *storehouse*. Its root is Strong's #H1481 ("guwr") - *to sojourn, abide, dwell in, dwell with, remain, inhabit, be a stranger; dwell temporarily*. Could Haggai have been prophesying the virgin birth, when the seed which would produce Y'shua was miraculously conceived within Mary to be born in human flesh and abide with man for a time? We believe these two verses were strung together for a reason, and that Haggai's next words relative to "the <u>vine</u>" may be a slight implication to Y'shua as well:

> [5] <u>I am the vine</u>, ye are the branches: He that abideth in me, and I in him, the same bringeth forth much fruit: for without me ye can do nothing. - John 15:5

We are told in Haggai 2:18-19 that there is a blessing linked with Kislev 24, and we believe this blessing was fulfilled with the conception of Y'shua as Chanukkah began – that the seed was planted in Mary's womb right as it commenced. Chanukkah is also widely known as the feast of lights, and Mary was bringing forth the Light of the world, Y'shua:

> [12] Then spake Jesus again unto them, saying, <u>I am the light of the world</u>: he that followeth me shall not walk in darkness, but shall have the light of life. - John 8:12

It is also called the Feast of Dedication, and associated with the cleansing and restoration of the Temple. We are to be dedicated to the Father through Y'shua, and it is Y'shua who will bring about the cleansing and restoration of our body Temples when we are transformed.

If indeed the conception was on Kislev 24, then 270 days later (the period of human gestation) would be the Feast of Trumpets (Tishri 1). This day is usually considered to have been the first day of the year prior to Father changing it in the book of Exodus. It is also thought by many that this might be when the first Adam was brought into being. Might it not, therefore, be a likely Heavenly pattern to orchestrate the birth of the last Adam (Y'shua) on the same Hebrew calendar day?:

> [45] And so it is written, The first man Adam was made a living soul; the last Adam was made a quickening spirit. - 1 Corinthians 15:45

The trumpet blew loud and long when God descended to Mt. Sinai during the wilderness journey:

> [16] And it came to pass on the third day in the morning, that there were thunders and lightnings, and a thick cloud upon the mount, and <u>the voice of the trumpet</u> exceeding loud; so that all the people that was in the camp trembled.

> [17] And Moses brought forth the people out of the camp to meet with God; and they stood at the nether part of the mount.

> [18] And mount Sinai was altogether on a smoke, because <u>the LORD descended</u> upon it in fire: and the smoke thereof ascended as the smoke of a furnace, and the whole mount quaked greatly.

> [19] And when the voice of <u>the trumpet sounded long, and waxed louder and louder,</u> Moses spake, and God answered him by a voice. - Exodus 19:16-19

Two Trees, Two Kingdoms, Two Kings

The trumpet will sound again when Y'shua descends from Heaven to receive His people:

> [16] For the Lord himself shall <u>descend from heaven</u> with a shout, with the voice of the archangel, and <u>with the trump of God</u>: and the dead in Christ shall rise first: - 1 Thessalonians 4:16

Each arrival of the Divine into the earthly realm seems to be announced by a trumpet. Thus it might be very appropriate that the sound of trumpets would announce the arrival of <u>God in the flesh</u> as well when Y'shua was born in Bethlehem:

> [14] And <u>the Word was made flesh</u>, and dwelt among us, (and we beheld his glory, the glory as of the only begotten of the Father,) full of grace and truth. - John 1:14

The first day of the seventh month was the Feast of Trumpets, a day of blowing the trumpets:

> [1] And in the seventh month, on the first day of the month, ye shall have an holy convocation; ye shall do no servile work: it is a_ <u>day of blowing the trumpets</u> unto you. - Numbers 29:1

What a glorious tribute to the arrival of the Redeemer!

Being near Jerusalem, the inns in Bethlehem were likely full with people traveling to Jerusalem for Feast of Tabernacles which would start some two weeks later. This was a feast that lasted for a whole week, also known as the Feast of Ingathering. It was one of three feasts when <u>all males of the faith were required to meet in Jerusalem</u>.:

> [17] Three times in the year all thy males shall appear before the Lord GOD. - Exodus 23:17

They were to be there sleeping in their sukkot (tents) <u>for the entire week</u>.:

> [42] <u>Ye shall dwell in booths seven days</u>; all that are Israelites born shall dwell in booths: - Leviticus 23:42

All righteous Jews were careful to journey to Jerusalem and be there prior to the onset of the week-long festival. The Hebrew word "sukkot" is the plural form of "sukkah", and means: *booths*. It is the festival which mandated the sleeping in booths per our Leviticus 23:42 text above. Thus travelers would have to arrive in time to secure the materials for their sukkot and construct them prior to the first day of the festival. Joseph too (being a righteous Jew) would have been trying to coincide his trip to Bethlehem with the observance of this festival. He would need time to get to Jerusalem, secure the necessary materials and set up his sukkah prior to the first day of the weekly celebration, and there would be travel time between Bethlehem and Jerusalem. The trek would be slow and tedious as they were probably on foot or donkey and Mary was in a very tender condition. This makes the timing for his being in Bethlehem for the birth of Y'shua on Tishri 1 (two weeks prior to day one of the festival) very appropriate.

Although we believe the criteria above builds a good case for Y'shua's birth being on Feast of Trumpets, it is usually agreed by those who have studied the evidence that His birth would have occurred at least in the vicinity of the fall festivals. Winters can be harsh and cold with intervals of snow almost every year, so it is not likely that shepherds would be in the fields with their flocks during in the cold of night in the winter months:

> [8] And there were in the same country shepherds abiding in the field, keeping watch over their flock by night. - Luke 2:8

Even natural thinking would indicate that Caesar Augustus would not have sent people to their homelands for taxation purposes in the severity of winter when roads might be impassable to the average person on foot or beast and the bitter cold might endanger life.

Since Y'shua's birth was almost certainly not on December 25, why would we celebrate it on Mithra's birthday? Mithra is the antithesis of His purpose for being here. How do we think Y'shua feels when we put the celebration of His birth on the birthday of a counter type figure – a god the people were supposed to leave behind when coming to the faith? We are never told to celebrate Y'shua's birth at all, nor any birthday for that matter. There is actually no record of such a practice at all in the Biblical text. Perhaps that is why the exact timing of His birth is not revealed to us. However, if we choose to do so, we suggest that it should not be observed on Mithra's birthday!

It can also easily be seen by studying the Festival days that Y'shua was the fulfillment of the typology of the Passover lamb. He was slain on Passover and raised back to life for First Fruits. Why then would we celebrate His resurrection on any other day than First Fruits - especially on a day so heavily linked with Ishtar as Easter?

There is one mention of Easter in the KJV version of our Bible:

> [4] And when he had apprehended him, he put him in prison, and

> delivered him to four quaternions of soldiers to keep him; intending after <u>Easter</u> to bring him forth to the people. - Acts 12:4

The word "Easter" in this verse is actually Strong's #G3957 ("pascha") - *the paschal sacrifice, the paschal lamb, the lamb the Israelites were accustomed to slay and eat on the fourteenth day of the month of Nisan (the first month of their year) ..., the paschal feast, <u>the feast of the Passover</u>*. In our post-Constantine era, the word "Easter" is unfortunately man's traditional word of choice in our English translations to replace God's "pasca" or Passover of the Greek text. It mixes the pagan roots of Ishtar with the sacred resurrection of God's pure Pascal Lamb. Our Father doesn't take kindly to such mixing!

> [26] Her priests have violated my law, and have <u>profaned mine holy things</u>: they have <u>put no difference between the holy and profane</u>, neither have they shewed difference between the unclean and the clean, and have <u>hid their eyes from my sabbaths</u>, and <u>I am profaned among them</u>. - Ezekiel 22:26

The contra strikes again! We are sorry to be so blunt, but there is no easy way to reveal the extent of this deception except to state it as it is and how it came to pass. If you are observing the holidays instead of the Holy Days, maybe now is the time to take a close look at the evidence and decide if a change might not be in order. Maybe it is time for us as Believers to learn about Yahweh's designated Festival days and make them a part of our lives. It is not easy, but it can be done. We have been through it, as have many others. Even the world stops their worldly pursuits to observe the false. Why should not the Father's children do so to observe the true?

As with the weekly Sabbath, we also understand that Y'shua being Lord of Sabbath would apply to the annual Sabbaths as well, and if there is a higher pursuit (such as the healing performed by Y'shua) which occurs on a Sabbath (weekly or annual), we are likewise obliged to observe that. The danger is that we will abuse this type of higher pursuit, viewing it as carte blanche to say such observation is no longer important, and begin to take such precious times for granted. Since Father clearly indicates that they are important to Him, maybe they should be important to us as well.

We mentioned in the first chapter of this book the concept of linear thinking as contrasted to cyclical thinking. Father's Festival seasons are an example of the cyclical. They begin in the spring and conclude in the fall. The next spring they begin once again, starting a new cycle. The word "path" is often used in the books of Psalms and Proverbs, with one of the more well-known instances being the Psalms 23:3:

> [3] He restoreth my soul: he leadeth me in the <u>paths</u> of righteousness for his name's sake. - Psalms 23:3

Again, we think of long linear paths, but the word for "paths" in this verse is Strong's #H4570 ("ma`gal") which indicates a more circular rendering. It is actually from Strong's #H5696 ("agol") - *round*. In fact the related Hebrew word "gilgal" is the word typically translated as "wheel" in our English language. The two consonants "gimel" (G) and "lamed" (L) in succession typically express the concept of wheel or rotation in many Hebrew words and names. For instance, the hub of Y'shua's ministry was Galilee, and He was crucified in Golgotha, both pertaining to the relativity of the "wheel" (G L "gimel" "lamed"). This was likely intentional to show the accelerating spiral of Father's cyclical patterning. The completion of Y'shua's earthly ministry and the eternal Life it provides is superimposed in cyclical style over the composite Torah Festival instructions given by Father in our Old Testament texts.

This does not mean that a path can never be linear, but the concept usually associated with the Hebrew word for path ("ma`gal") is that of a cyclical pattern, one which circles back to cover the same terrain yet again, making another circuit above that which came before.

In our Festival allocation we see a repeat of the cycle each year. We are to review the meaning of the festivals as we observe them. While there will likely be a great deal of similarity in the observance each year, no two such observances will be identical. We will be one year older, and things around us will inevitably have changed during that year. Therefore, rather than being a flat circle, the circle will spiral ever upward as we observe these annual events. Each year will overlie the one which preceded it. Cycles are so very integral to the understanding of God's ways. We have the daily cycle (moonrise, moonset, sunrise, and sunset), the monthly cycle (changes in the moon turning from new to full and back to new again), the yearly cycle (changes in the sun through solstice and equinox stages, as well as related harvest and festival celebrations), etc. Father wants us to acknowledge the beauty of the sequence of events He has orchestrated in the Heavens, and to be aware of their significance. He did not just put them there to decorate our sky. They are intricately linked to His plan for us, and we are well advised to develop a thirst to understand their relevance to our lives:

> [9] Then shalt thou understand righteousness, and judgment, and
> equity; yea, every good <u>path</u>. - Proverbs 2:9

The word for path in this verse is again "magal". In this we see that the cyclical patterning of God reveals His righteousness, judgment and equity. Indeed this is exactly what we see when we follow the observance of His festivals and dwell on the meaning of each. The phrase "<u>every</u> good path" in this verse is interesting as well, as it may point to the multiple cycles we have mentioned.

We now use a calendar (the Gregorian) which starts the year on January 1. The Gentile calendar new year had previously been in the spring, but Roman influence secured this change in 46BC under Julius Caesar. The month January is named after the Roman mythological goddess Janus. The Latin spelling of Janus is "Ianuarius". The Latin word for door is "ianua", so Janus is the Roman goddess of the door, and January 1 became the doorway to our new year. Father told us back in Exodus when to start our new year. Speaking of the month Abib or Aviv (also known as Nisan in other Scriptural references) He said:

> [2] This month shall be unto you the beginning of months: it shall
> be the first month of the year to you. - Exodus 12:2

Nothing has changed since then relative to the way Father sees time, but again man has seen fit to change what God ordained, basing the opening of our year on Roman mythology. Virtually everything ordained of Father to show us His sacred cycles of time has been derailed and reconfigured to meet the standards of paganism. It is a travesty that causes us much grief. Yet these days are celebrated with high spirits by many today who have come to view the traditions of men as sacred:

> [9] And he said unto them, Full well ye reject the commandment of
> God, that ye may keep your own tradition. - Mark 7:9

We too had personally been partakers of these pagan-rooted festivities until we awakened to God's true picture, so we can surely point no fingers. However, it is important to awaken and depart from them. When we substitute holidays for Father's intended Holy Days, we step out of the paths of righteousness He established and enter the paths of man's tradition which fall far short of the rich understanding we were meant to have. Not only do we observe them at a time which may be very offensive to Father due to the false deities who are acknowledged on those days, but we fail to see the beauty of His plan on the days He intended for our observance.

Regarding His festivals, He has revealed His special days to us in His Word so we can track them and even see in advance when we are to observe them. This allows us to plan ahead so we can make the time to separate from the world and spend those days with Him. Praise You, Father!

A Brief Summation of Festival Significance

The following is a very brief overview of our perceptions regarding the manner in which the Festivals of the Lord have been, are being, and will be totally fulfilled by the interaction of Y'shua with His own. They are listed in the chronological order of Leviticus 23.

Passover

The destroyer passed over those who had applied the blood of the Passover lamb to the doors of their homes:

> [23] For the LORD will pass through to smite the Egyptians; and when he seeth the blood upon the lintel, and on the two side posts, the LORD will pass over the door, and will not suffer the destroyer to come in unto your houses to smite you. - Exodus 12:23

Y'shua is our Passover Lamb:

> [7] Purge out therefore the old leaven, that ye may be a new lump, as ye are unleavened. For even Christ our passover is sacrificed for us: - 1 Corinthians 5:7

> [29] The next day John seeth Jesus coming unto him, and saith, Behold the Lamb of God, which taketh away the sin of the world. - John 1:29

His blood is applied to His own through their belief and walk of faith, in order that those who come to Him might be spared the death for payment of sin which each of us would otherwise face:

> [23] For the wages of sin is death; but the gift of God is eternal life through Jesus Christ our Lord. - Romans 6:23

> [11] For the life of the flesh is in the blood: and I have given it to you upon the altar to make an atonement for your souls: for it is the blood that maketh an atonement for the soul. - Leviticus 17:11

> [22] And almost all things are by the law purged with blood; and without shedding of blood is no remission. - Hebrews 9:22

> [7] In whom we have <u>redemption through his blood</u>, the <u>forgiveness of sins</u>, according to the riches of his grace; - Ephesians 1:7
>
> [9] Much more then, being now <u>justified by his blood</u>, we shall be <u>saved from wrath</u> through him. - Romans 5:9

More references to Passover can be found in: Leviticus 23:5, Numbers 28:16, and Deuteronomy 16:1-6.

Fulfillment of this Festival was the death of Y'shua as our Passover Lamb. It brought forth the blood (wine) portion of our communion today which provides for our atonement before the Father.

Unleavened Bread

During this time the eating of leavened food (bread) is forbidden for seven days:

> [15] <u>Seven days shall ye eat unleavened bread</u>; even the first day ye shall put away leaven out of your houses: for whosoever eateth leavened bread from the first day until the seventh day, that soul shall be cut off from Israel. - Exodus 12:15

Other Old Testament references are: Deuteronomy 16:1-8, Leviticus 23:4-8, Numbers 28:17-25

Leaven is symbolic of sin:

> [6] Your glorying is not good. Know ye not that <u>a little leaven leaveneth the whole lump</u>?
>
> [7] <u>Purge out therefore the old leaven</u>, that ye may be a new lump, as ye are unleavened. <u>For even Christ our passover is sacrificed for us</u>:
>
> [8] Therefore let us keep the feast, not with old leaven, neither with the <u>leaven of malice and wickedness</u>; but with the <u>unleavened bread of sincerity and truth</u>. - 1 Corinthians 5:6-8

Seven days is the duration of the creation process, and might indicate that we were created to be without sin throughout time. Since that is impossible in our human state, it points to the need of a savior. After finding Him we are then enabled to and expected to turn from the old leavened lifestyle of malice and wickedness and walk in the the new unleavened character of sincerity and truth. Y'shua had never sinned, but because He willingly took on our sins,

He had to pay the price of sin which was death. He suffered physical death as our surrogate so we would not have to endure spiritual death in order that the Law be satisfied. He became our righteousness so that we might inherit that righteousness from Him:

> [4] Therefore we are buried with him by baptism into death: that like as Christ was raised up from the dead by the glory of the Father, even so we also should walk in newness of life. - Romans 6:4

> [21] For he hath made him to be sin for us, who knew no sin; that we might be made the righteousness of God in him. - 2 Corinthians 5:21

Fulfillment of this Festival was the burial of Y'shua. His body was broken and buried to deal with our sin. This brought forth the broken body (bread) portion of our communion today which enables healing of our bodies and souls to begin. When we partake of the blood (cup) and body (bread) in communion today, the bread should be unleavened to represent the sinlessness of Y'shua:

> [25] Thou shalt not offer the blood of my sacrifice with leaven; neither shall the sacrifice of the feast of the passover be left unto the morning. - Exodus 34:25

First Fruits

Sheaves of the first fruits of the barley harvest were to be waved on Feast of First Fruits as an offering to God:

> [10] Speak unto the children of Israel, and say unto them, When ye be come into the land which I give unto you, and shall reap the harvest thereof, then ye shall bring a sheaf of the firstfruits of your harvest unto the priest:

> [11] And he shall wave the sheaf before the LORD, to be accepted for you: on the morrow after the sabbath the priest shall wave it. - Leviticus 23:10-11

First Fruits references can be found in: Leviticus 23:9-14, Numbers 28:26-31.

Other passages indicate that what is waved is barley, and the timing is the day of First Fruits.

The New Testament provides us with the spiritual correlation of the human resurrection to the harvest season. Y'shua was a type of first fruits for the human harvest, the first fruits offering to the Father on Feast of First Fruits, after He arose from the dead:

> [20] But now is Christ risen from the dead, and become <u>the first-fruits of them that slept</u>.

> [21] For since by man came death, by man came also the resurrection of the dead.

> [22] For as in Adam all die, even so in Christ shall all be made alive.

> [23] But every man in his own order: Christ the firstfruits; afterward they that are Christ's at his coming. - 1 Corinthians 15:20-23

As indicated above, it is important to note that the date of First Fruits when this occurred does not concur with the dating of Easter on our calendars today, since Easter is derived from Roman Catholic tradition rather than Hebraic means.

Fulfillment of this Festival by Y'shua came through His being the first to be resurrected from death to new Life, enabling us to find the promise of resurrection in our lives as we seek to live them through Him.

Feast of Weeks

> [22] And thou shalt observe the feast of weeks, of the firstfruits of wheat harvest, and the feast of ingathering at the year's end. - Exodus 34:22

> [15] And ye shall count unto you from the morrow after the sabbath, from the day that ye brought the sheaf of the wave offering; seven sabbaths shall be complete:

> [16] Even unto the morrow after the seventh sabbath shall ye number fifty days; and ye shall offer a new meat offering unto the LORD. - Leviticus 23:15-16

This festival (also known as Pentecost) is 50 days from Feast of First Fruits. The Hebrew people were freed from slavery and then bound in covenantal relationship with God at Mt. Sinai 50 days later at Pentecost when they received the Law.

Another reference can be found in: Deuteronomy 16:9-10.

Likewise those who would come to follow Y'shua were released from the slavery of their sin through His death and resurrection, then come into a new relationship with God 50 days later at Pentecost (Acts 2:1-4) as the Law was written on the hearts of His Believers at the coming of the Holy Spirit to indwell man:

> [3] Forasmuch as ye are manifestly declared to be the epistle of Christ ministered by us, written not with ink, but with the Spirit of the living God; not in tables of stone, but in fleshy tables of the heart. - 2 Corinthians 3:3

Fulfillment of this Festival by Y'shua was to provide the impartation of the Holy Spirit for a new relationship to His own through forgiveness of sin:

> [38] Then Peter said unto them, Repent, and be baptized every one of you in the name of Jesus Christ for the remission of sins, and ye shall receive the gift of the Holy Ghost. - Acts 2:38

Feast of Trumpets

This is a Feast that is celebrated with the blowing of trumpets:

> [1] And in the seventh month, on the first day of the month, ye shall have an holy convocation; ye shall do no servile work: it is a day of blowing the trumpets unto you. - Numbers 29:1

Another reference can be found in: Leviticus 23:23-25.

It is typically correlated with the sound of the trumpet in New Testament texts such as Matthew 24:31, 1 Corinthians 15:52, Revelation 1:10, Revelation 4:1, etc.

The most famous of these is the 1 Corinthians 15:52 passage:

> [52] In a moment, in the twinkling of an eye, at the last trump: for the trumpet shall sound, and the dead shall be raised incorruptible, and we shall be changed. - 1 Corinthians 15:52

This is associated with the change of man from a terrestrial body form to that of a celestial version per 1 Corinthians 15:40-44 a few verses before. It is the time when Y'shua will call us forth in new bodies to be with Him, as indicated in John:

> [1] Let not your heart be troubled: ye believe in God, believe also in me.

Two Trees, Two Kingdoms, Two Kings

> [2] In my Father's house are many mansions: if it were not so, I would have told you. I go to prepare a place for you.
>
> [3] And if I go and prepare a place for you, <u>I will come again</u>, and <u>receive you unto myself</u>; <u>that where I am, there ye may be also</u>. - John 14:1-3

It is thought that creation of mankind via Adam and Eve was on this day, so some surmise that the transition of corruptible man to his new incorruptible form might be on this day as well.:

> [53] For this corruptible must put on incorruption, and this mortal must put on immortality. - 1 Corinthians 15:53

Fulfillment of this Festival is yet future when Y'shua will return at the sound of the trumpet.

Day of Atonement

This is a day of judgment – a time when people are convicted of their sins, and seek atonement for them, afflicting their souls as they repent and seek God:

> [27] Also on the tenth day of this seventh month there shall be a day of atonement: it shall be an holy convocation unto you; and <u>ye shall afflict your souls</u>, and offer an offering made by fire unto the LORD.
>
> [28] And ye shall do no work in that same day: for it is a day of atonement, to make an atonement for you before the LORD your God.
>
> [29] For whatsoever soul it be that shall not be afflicted in that same day, he shall be cut off from among his people. - Leviticus 23:27-29

In surrogate fashion, the Old Testament text says a goat was slain at this time so sin could be absolved, while a second goat was let go into the wilderness:

> [7] And he shall take the two goats, and present them before the LORD at the door of the tabernacle of the congregation.
>
> [8] And Aaron shall cast lots upon the two goats; one lot for the LORD, and the other lot for the scapegoat.
>
> [9] And Aaron shall bring the goat upon which the LORD's lot fell, and offer him for a sin offering.

[10] But the goat, on which the lot fell to be the scapegoat, shall be presented alive before the LORD, to make an atonement with him, and to let him go for a scapegoat into the wilderness.

[11] And Aaron shall bring the bullock of the sin offering, which is for himself, and shall make an atonement for himself, and for his house, and shall kill the bullock of the sin offering which is for himself: - Leviticus 16:7-11

This may have been to depict the crucifixion of Y'shua to atone for the sins of man and the letting go of Barabbas. (This will be explained at length in a later chapter of the book.)

When He comes back, Y'shua will judge the nations, as many will still not know Him. That judgment may well be at this particular time, and it will be a somber occasion:

[31] When the Son of man shall come in his glory, and all the holy angels with him, then shall he sit upon the throne of his glory:

[32] <u>And before him shall be gathered all nations</u>: and he shall separate them one from another, as a shepherd divideth his sheep from the goats: - Matthew 25:31-32

Other references are: Leviticus 16:29-31, Numbers 29:7.

Fulfillment of this Festival is yet future when Y'shua will judge humanity at His return.

Feast of Tabernacles

This is a feast that lasts 7 days, then a transitional day to conclude the festivities on day 8 is celebrated as well. During the initial 7 days, the people were to dwell in tabernacles (temporary abodes). Then on day 8 they were to leave them:

[42] Ye shall dwell in booths seven days; all that are Israelites born shall dwell in booths:

[43] That your generations may know that I made the children of Israel to dwell in booths, when I brought them out of the land of Egypt: I am the LORD your God. - Leviticus 23:42-43

This would represent the seven thousand years we are to live in a temporal state in this fallen world - a wilderness of sorts. It is the span of time before entering into the realm which awaits us after the Millennial reign of Y'shua. Biblically seven is construed to be a the number representing completion, and eight is the number of new beginning.

Some other references are: Leviticus 23:33-43, Numbers 29:12, Deuteronomy 16:13-16.

Fulfillment of this Festival is yet future when we will complete time in this realm during the Millennial reign with Y'shua, then exit time to enter the new beginning on the other side of time with Y'shua and the Father.

Please note that this chapter of the book was not meant to provide all of the richness associated with these special days to Father, but is merely introductory in nature. There is so much more to learn about them, and we encourage individual study on the topic. Many interesting articles are available today on the internet, and many fabulous books have been written to help us as Believers to become familiar with the treasures to be found in connection with these special days.

CHAPTER 8

TO EAT OR NOT TO EAT

We had tackled a difficult topic, but there was one more that would test our resolve to do God's bidding. We had become pretty acclimated to eating whatever our hearts desired. However, we had to confront a haunting question: Was this what Father desired for us?

Can We Eat Whatever We Want Today?

The church often teaches that because the dietary guidelines of Leviticus and Deuteronomy are a part of the "Law", we are in bondage if we adhere to them. As we see it, we are not to abuse our liberty from the penalty of the Law by using it as freedom to violate Father's Law and eat whatever we want. Redemption through Y'shua was never designed to enable us to walk in disobedience to Father's Law. Y'shua did not save us from our sin in order to give us license to continue in it. We do violence to the Word when we cut away sections of it and look only to the remainder to form our doctrinal beliefs. This in turn does violence to the One who gave it to us. May it not be so:

> [15] What then? shall we sin, because we are not under the law,
> but under grace? God forbid. - Romans 6:15

Sin is the transgression of the Law:

> [4] Whosoever committeth sin transgresseth also the law: for <u>sin is
> the transgression of the law</u>. - 1 John 3:4

Simply because of our fallen state, the carnal portion of our being naturally craves those things which are forbidden by Father. In Mark 8 Y'shua lashed out at Peter, referencing the role of Satan in his life at that time and indicated that the reason for the rebuke was because Peter was savoring the things of man over the things of God:

> [33] But when he had turned about and looked on his disciples, he rebuked Peter, saying, Get thee behind me, Satan: **for thou savourest not the things that be of God, but the things that be of men**. - Mark 8:33

A HUGE majority of the church is under the deception that comes through the improper use of Paul's words, to overthrow the will of the Father as expressed in Torah. They can then align to the things of man. It appears that Peter learned from Y'shua's rebuke, as Peter turned around and warned the church. He cautions Believers not to turn from God's ways back to lawlessness:

> [21] For it had been better for them not to have known the way of righteousness, than, after they have known it, to turn from the holy commandment delivered unto them.

> [22] But it is happened unto them according to the true proverb, The dog is turned to his own vomit again; and the sow that was washed to her wallowing in the mire. - 2 Peter 2:21-22

He warns us not to wrestle with Paul's words in order to create loopholes to endorse iniquity by aligning with the doctrines of man rather than the Law of God. Instead we need to align Paul's words to "the other Scriptures" (the entirety of the Biblical text) in order to properly interpret them:

> [16] As also in all his epistles, speaking in them of these things; in which are some things hard to be understood, which they that are unlearned and unstable wrest, as they do also the other scriptures, unto their own destruction. - 2 Peter 3:16

The word "unlearned" is Strong's #G261 ("amathēs") - *unlearned, ignorant*.

The word "unstable" is Strong's #G793 ("astēriktos") - *unstable, unsteadfast*.

The word "wrest" in this verse is Strong's #G4761 ("strebloō") - *twist, turn awry, pervert*.

Note that it is supposed to be those who are unlearned and unstable in Torah instruction who twist, turn awry, and pervert the words of Paul to their own destruction. It is understandable that those who have been in nothing but New Testament churches might fall easily into this error, but this is a wake up call. Please heed Peter's warning and be faithful to harmonize all Scripture as a congruent package to form any understanding. It is so much sadder when those who are learned in Scripture still manage to fall prey to this error. Oh that they might come to the Truth of this Scriptural harmony, gain a more complete understanding and begin to teach it while there is yet time. Peter shows us here that Paul's writings are not easily understood, and that to twist and disengage them from the unity of Scriptural integrity brings destruction. While Paul's writings might at first glance <u>appear</u> to sanction turning from the Law, they do not, and that interpretation leads to destruction. Again Hebrews 10:26-31 comes to mind.

It is important to understand what the Spirit of Grace is in this passage and what it is not!:

> [29] Of how much sorer punishment, suppose ye, shall he be thought worthy, who hath trodden under foot the Son of God, and hath counted <u>the blood of the covenant, wherewith he was sancti-fied</u>, an unholy thing, and **hath done despite unto the Spirit of grace**? - Hebrews 10:29

Note that the ones being criticized here are those who have received the blood covenant of Y'shua. This would indicate that the justification portion of the sanctification process was accomplished, and the sanctification process had begun. However, it was derailed prior to completion when the Believer departed from the way in which he was to walk. Again we would stress that the grace provided by the death and resurrection of Y'shua is to provide for our redemption. It is not a permission slip to abuse our liberty under this grace, to turn against precepts of the Father and violate them. To do so after being shown by His Word to refrain might well be seen as insulting the Holy Spirit. This Spirit of Grace is to guide us through the sanctification process. We are not to quench the Spirit by rejecting the singularity of Torah Truth the Spirit brings us:

> [19] Quench not the Spirit. - 1 Thessalonians 5:19

We know Father is patient with our little slip-ups, but when He sees a pattern developing, He is faithful to send out an alarm message. We pray this book will serve as one such message. A walk which shows a pattern of turning from the precepts spelled out by the Father should be a major concern!

Thus it is that we have chosen to abstain from unclean meats out of love for the Father, respect for the restraints He ordained in Torah for our best interest, AND a desire to NOT disrespect the Spirit He sent with His measure of grace. His restraints are never imposed just for the fun of it and to cause His children undue frustrations. They are always for a purpose.

A simple analogy would be a young couple with a young child. They want to allow the child to play safely in the back yard. Therefore they fence in the yard so the child will not stray into a dangerous situation. The child may hate the fence and the boundary it imposes on his existence. His parents, on the other hand, love the fence because they can rest assured that if their child stays behind it he is not likely to be injured. If someone comes along and cuts a hole in the fence and the child goes through it, the potential dangers to the child become dramatically increased.

Likewise Father has erected a hedge of moral Law for us, and as we abide within its parameters, we live in relative safety. We have come to love the hedge (fencing) our loving Father has provided, as we realize it is for our protection, and He loves us. We believe it was for our own good that some things are forbidden to us. If we breach His hedge by sinning against His Law, we are more prone to injury. One such hedge is His mandate to refrain from eating things which He has deemed to be unclean:

> [47] To make a difference between the unclean and the clean, and between the beast that may be eaten and the **beast that may not be eaten**. - Leviticus 11:47

Again, relative to matters of moral consideration, when God has spoken, there is no other legitimate side to the issue. There should be no controversy in the interpretation of New Testament text, as every New Testament directive must maintain a root from its underlying Torah foundation, and should be harmonized to it. This is the protocol of Pardes, the essence of Shema, and the sod revelation of Tree of Life which Paul obtained through the Spirit. The words of Paul which are thought to condone eating the unclean are greatly misunderstood. When Paul says we can eat freely, he is indicating only that which falls in the Torah parameters of what God sees as being edible. If it is not edible in Father's book of instruction, it should never have been made edible in our lives. The "beast that may not be eaten" (in Leviticus 11:47 above) is obviously not even considered to be food in God's eyes, and remains inedible in Paul's Torah root-based teachings. Paul would not intend that such "beast that may not be eaten" products even come into consideration as his words are heard or read.

The passage in Acts which relates Peter's vision actually helps to clarify this. Ironically though, it is this same passage which is often used as a green light to justify consumption of the unclean. This is due to the assumption that animals which had been deemed unclean by God have now been cleansed. However, is that what the passage in Acts really says? Here it is for your reference:

[9] On the morrow, as they went on their journey, and drew nigh
unto the city, Peter went up upon the housetop to pray about the
sixth hour:

[10] And he became very hungry, and would have eaten: but while
they made ready, he fell into a trance,

[11] And saw heaven opened, and a certain vessel descending
unto him, as it had been a great sheet knit at the four corners, and
let down to the earth:

[12] Wherein were all manner of fourfooted beasts of the earth,
and wild beasts, and creeping things, and fowls of the air.

[13] And there came a voice to him, <u>Rise, Peter; kill, and eat</u>.

[14] But Peter said, Not so, Lord; for <u>I have never eaten any thing
that is common or unclean</u>.

[15] And the voice spake unto him again the second time, <u>What
God hath cleansed, that call not thou common</u>.

[16] This was done thrice: and the vessel was received up again
into heaven. - Acts 10:9-16

It seems Peter's vision was simply a matter of being shown a PHYSICAL application of a SPIRITUAL concept. <u>There is absolutely no Scriptural indication that Peter ever did consume the unclean animals after he had his vision,
or that he ever taught others to do so</u>. Actually, the next verse indicates that he
did not even consider doing so as an option, as it says he doubted in himself
what the vision should mean:

[17] Now while **Peter doubted in himself what this vision which
he had seen should mean**, behold, the men which were sent
from Cornelius had made inquiry for Simon's house, and stood
before the gate, - Acts 10:17

Peter KNEW that God did not mean that these animals were suddenly made
clean and edible, so he was absorbed with trying to figure out what it actually
DID mean.

We are shown as the passage proceeds that the vision was in reference to that
which the Lord had made SPIRITUALLY clean, indicating the SPIRITUAL
cleansing of some previously SPIRITUALLY polluted people. Those who
were Torah observant could not fathom that the people who had no such background could be acceptable to their God. They viewed them as unclean and

would have no contact with them. God simply used the tangible physical aspect of unclean creatures to point to the intangible spiritual aspect of the unclean man in need of salvation. By using this visual aid, God simply showed Peter how Y'shua's victory at Calvary provided for the spiritual cleansing (justification) of the heathen.

If unclean animals had been PHYSICALLY cleansed at that time, then we would not be seeing what we do today as the ramifications from consuming them. It is estimated that at least one hog out of every ten has worms of some type, and still others are infested with the very dangerous trichina. Because this deadly organism is not visible to the naked eye, one would not know that the meat was infected unless a sample of the meat was viewed under a microscope before eating. This hearty little worm lives in the cells of the meat in a tiny cyst, making it very hard to kill when cooking. When the meat is consumed, the cyst is dissolved by the gastric juices during the digestive process. The tiny deadly parasite then leaves its prison to penetrate the muscular walls of the stomach. From there it can invade the muscular system at large and continue to propagate until it affects the entire body of its host. At this point trichinosis or trichina poisoning is full blown and can bring about excruciating death.

The number of deaths each year due to tainted pork is hard to calculate. Misdiagnosis occurs routinely because symptoms of trichinosis closely resemble certain stages of other diseases. However it is thought that possibly hundreds of people die of the disease. The deadly pork they had eaten being long forgotten, it is unknown how many actually suffer and die without ever understanding what has caused their agony and death. How sad this is, as it is totally preventable if we would stick to the guidelines established by the Father for our own good. It _is not_ our intent to curl your hair, but this is the reality of pork today, and it _is_ our intent to help our readers see the physical dangers it poses. If Peter's vision actually meant that God had made the PHYSICAL pork clean at the time of his vision, why would this parasite issue still be in our world today?

While we certainly do not recommend the eating of raw fish, it should be noted that _most_ sushi can normally be eaten without consequence. This is largely because _most_ sushi is prepared with seafood that is "clean" by the Father's standards. Conversely, consumption of raw shellfish is associated with diseases such as typhoid and hepatitis. Oysters can carry a bacterium called vibrio vulnificus. The freshness of the oysters is no guarantee of their safety relative to vibrio vulnificus, and contamination cannot be detected by sight or smell which means that one's choice to consume raw oysters entails his willingness to gamble on his health and possibly even his life. If the waters where the oysters feed have this bacterium, the oysters will be contaminated and pass this dangerous organism to the host, potentially causing serious illness or death. Symptoms usually occur within one to two days after consumption and can include sudden chills, fever, nausea, vomiting, diarrhea, shock and even skin lesions. If the victim has a weakened immune system due to other causes, this bacterium can be fatal, bringing about death two days later.

According to author Rex Russell, MD, shellfish can be placed in a body of water that is contaminated with cholera bacteria, and they will actually purify the water. Where does the cholera go? We'll give you two guesses and the first one doesn't count. Even cooked shellfish can be very unhealthy to the human body. Some toxins from the pollutants the shellfish take in can linger even after cooking and still manage to poison the consumer. Mercury, heavy metals, and industrial contaminants are among such hazardous potentials for consumption, and the consequences of the ingestion of these contaminants are now beginning to come to light.

By tuning in to the words of our Creator, we will find that He did not create pigs and shellfish to be food for humans. Those things rendered as "unclean" by the Father were never intended to be "food" to us at all in the first place. He tagged them as "unclean" (instructing that they were inappropriate for human consumption) for a good reason.

The creatures which the Father has listed as being unclean were probably so designated because He designed them to be garbage cleaners. Generally speaking, their digestive systems are simply not capable of filtering out the contaminants and toxins of the rotting carcass tissues and feces they consume. While wild hogs, vultures and other assorted unclean animals were designed to clean up the surface of visible land, shellfish are designed to clean up the garbage on the sea bottom. When we eat these unclean creatures, we are taking into our bodies (in a second hand manner) all of the feces and other rubbish they continually consume. The One who created these creatures for such purpose has deemed them to be unfit for human consumption for our own protection. For that reason alone, it is really difficult for us to understand why anyone who has come to know Father's dietary Laws would be so resolute about consuming what He says is unclean. Yet some choose to override His caution and violate His expressly stated Word in order to do so.

Two Trees, Two Kingdoms, Two Kings

How Are We to View 1 Timothy 4:1-5?

Possibly the text quoted most often by those who believe that there are no longer any food boundaries is verse 4 of the following 1 Timothy passage:

> [1] Now the Spirit speaketh expressly, that in the latter times some shall depart from the faith, giving heed to seducing spirits, and doctrines of devils;

> [2] Speaking lies in hypocrisy; having their conscience seared with a hot iron;

> [3] Forbidding to marry, and commanding to abstain from meats, which God hath created to be received with thanksgiving of them which believe and know the truth.

> [4] For every creature of God is good, and nothing to be refused, if it be received with thanksgiving:

> [5] For it is sanctified by the word of God and prayer. - 1 Timothy 4:1-5

The common teaching regarding verse 4 today is that through prayer (verse 5) God will now sanctify even those creatures He had created as being unclean. If prayer is required for the unclean food source to be sanctified, what if one forgets to pray? Is his ham sandwich then unsanctified?

Is Paul really telling us that we now have permission to eat everything that God created? We must acknowledge that such interpretation directly contradicts the unclean dietary guidelines of Leviticus. It would be instituting the removal of the restrictions God Himself has set in place. In order to interpret 1 Timothy 4:4 as allowing for consumption of unclean creatures, we must come to the belief that it is now alright to reject the clean and unclean Laws of God – and be free to eat any creature of God's creation. If we rest on this interpretation, then Paul is now endorsing the eating of poisonous snakes, slugs, rats, buzzards, bats, lizards, skunks, and even cannibalism. Yes, people are His creation too. Can we not see how off-track this interpretation is? It simply does not harmonize with the balance of Scripture.

The consistency of God's Truth is our guarantee so we can discern properly and avoid deception. Therefore, when one Scripture <u>appears</u> to contradict another, there must be a reconciliation. Total DISHARMONY of the Word would be the case if we were to view Paul's words with the interpretation that all things are now edible to us. The intrinsic meaning of an apostolic passage must maintain harmony with that which God Himself has already clearly spoken on the matter in our Scriptural text. Again, when God has spoken there is no other legitimate side to the issue.

The proper dividing of the Word brings consistency and provides continuity. Therefore, 1 Timothy 4:4 (which many use to oppose and override the clear teaching of the Father) must have an interpretation which <u>is</u> consistent with the clean and unclean dietary guidelines the Father explicitly provided earlier in our Bibles.

If we are faithful to be Berean and harmonize the Scriptures of Paul to the instructions of the Father, we will see that Paul did not bother to differentiate between clean and unclean creatures in verse 4, because he had just clarified this differentiation in verse 3. Recall that Paul presumed that his audience was learned in Torah. The preliminary identification with the Levitical guidelines of Torah would be presupposed by Paul. He expected that his words would automatically be understood in the context of Torah, so he did not need to clarify further. Furthermore, there would be no need to specify again in verse 4 that he meant all creatures <u>which align to these guidelines,</u> as he had already said in verse 3: "<u>which God hath created to be received with thanksgiving of</u> <u>them</u> **which believe and know the truth**". The Truth that he understood they would know is found in Psalms:

> [142] Thy righteousness is an everlasting righteousness, and <u>thy</u> <u>law is the truth</u>. - Psalms 119:142

Paul was a Hebrew scholar. He knew the Law inside and out, as well as the Scripture that professed this Law to be Truth. He knew his audience already understood the Levitical ordinances and would not even THINK to apply his words to anything other than those ordinances. His words "<u>which God hath</u> <u>created to be received</u>" actually excludes those which God had created for other reasons and told us <u>NOT to receive</u> as food. Those who believe and know the Truth will understand that pork and shellfish aren't even considered to be food to begin with and never would be intended to be food.

The first few verses we have shown as context here play a part as well:

> [1] Now the Spirit speaketh expressly, that in the latter times some shall depart from the faith, <u>giving heed to seducing spirits</u>, and doctrines of devils;

> [2] Speaking lies in hypocrisy; having their conscience seared with a hot iron; - 1 Timothy 4:1-2

Two Trees, Two Kingdoms, Two Kings

Paul speaks here of seducing spirits, while John speaks of the spirit of error:

> 6] We are of God: he that knoweth God heareth us; he that is not of God heareth not us. Hereby know we <u>the spirit of truth</u>, and <u>the spirit of error</u>. - 1 John 4:6

The Spirit of Truth and the spirit of error are the two spirits of the two trees in the garden. It is the spirit of error's "false doctrine" issue of verses 1-3 that prompted Paul's words in the first place. Vegetarianism was being professed in Paul's day, and had become pervasive in the teachings of God's people. <u>The people were being told they could eat no meat at all</u>:

> [3] Forbidding to marry, and **<u>commanding</u> <u>to abstain from meats, which God hath created to be received with thanksgiving</u> <u>of them which believe and know the truth</u>**. - 1 Timothy 4:3

Paul was simply confirming to the people that those meats which were deemed edible in Torah were still alright to eat if received with thanksgiving. He knew these guidelines would be understood without question by his listeners, as they would know the Law. Paul was simply saying that the prohibition of clean meat was derived by the spirit of error. He was not condemning vegetarianism, but was saying that it should not be taught as doctrine and commanded of the people. God's standards professed in Leviticus were still and always would remain intact. He is further stressing that they should be able to see that this teaching was of the spirit of error simply by looking to the Law (which aligns to the the Spirit of TRUTH) to prove it right or wrong. Therefore, what many stand on in verse 4 to indicate that ALL creatures are now edible was actually delineated in verse 3 to specify only creatures that were authorized as clean by Father's dietary Laws of Leviticus. Paul is exhorting Believers to look to the Law for guidance so we will not be falsely dissuaded from eating those things which God DID tell us we could eat. He was not authorizing abuse of the Levitical guidelines.

Then Paul concludes his comments on what we can eat by saying:

> [5] <u>For IT is **sanctified**</u> by the **word** of God and **prayer**.
> - 1 Timothy 4:5

This word "sanctified" here is Strong's #G37 ("hagiazo") - *to separate from profane things AND to dedicate to God.*

The word "IT" in verse 5 is coupled with the word "hagiazo" (**sanctified**). This specifies then that this "it" can refer only to sanctified creatures - those edible creatures that are "**<u>separated from profane things</u>**" (unclean creatures). This same verse gives us the criteria by which this separation is derived - <u>by the Word of God</u>. The portions of the Word of God which details this separation of that which is clean from that which is unclean and unfit for consumption is the entire chapter of Leviticus 11, as well as Deuteronomy 14:3-21. Thus clean meats are shown by the Word of God to be set apart from those which are profane, and these clean meats can be received with prayer.

The **prayer** of verse 5 then completes the "hagiazo" meaning (shown above) by being the portion of the process that **dedicates** that which God has sanctified to Him.

Instead of saying that God somehow chooses to now sanctify through prayer what He has deemed to be unclean and inedible for our consumption, Paul is merely saying that we do not have to be vegetarians. He is assuring us that the mandate to abstain from the clean meat which God ordained is from the spirit of error. We can freely eat any and all creatures which God has created to be sanctified (set apart for consumption) as dictated by His Word. We are then to dedicate them back to Him in prayer before consuming them.

Far from being a license for unclean dining, this short five verse passage actually confirms that the consumption of meats which are seen as objectionable to God is NOT God's intent, nor is it Paul's. Again, it is so important that we avoid falling prey to the false doctrine propagated by the "spirit of error". We can steer clear of this error by choosing to rely on the <u>harmony</u> of ALL Scripture as our final authority. The chief component of Biblical harmony for any moral consideration must be the clear Word on that matter as delineated by Father in Torah – from the beginning:

> [24] Let that therefore abide in you, which ye have heard <u>from the beginning</u>. If that which ye have heard from the beginning shall remain in you, ye also shall continue in the Son, and in the Father.
> - 1 John 2:24

Other References and Considerations Regarding Our Food

In 1 Corinthians chapters 8 and 10 Paul addresses whether one should reject meat which has been offered to an idol:

> [25] Whatsoever is sold in the shambles, that eat, asking no question for conscience sake:

> [26] For the earth is the Lord's, and the fulness thereof.

> [27] If any of them that believe not bid you to a feast, and ye be disposed to go; whatsoever is set before you, eat, asking no question for conscience sake.
>
> [28] But if any man say unto you, This is offered in sacrifice unto idols, eat not for his sake that shewed it, and for conscience sake: for the earth is the Lord's, and the fulness thereof: - 1 Corinthians 10:25-28

When we look to the culture of Paul's day, the meat which was sold in the "shambles" (the marketplace) came from questionable spiritual sources, some having been offered to idols before it was sold. Again Paul was addressing here only meats that were considered to be clean by God's dietary Laws, as all that falls outside of these guidelines was not to be considered edible in the first place. Because Paul understood that the idols are nothing to God, they were as nothing to him either. He said not to question whether the meat in the marketplace might have been offered to idols; but if confronted with the information that it HAD been offered to idols, he advised to abstain if it would be a stumbling block to others. Thus Paul was not teaching people to eat things offered to idols (as Revelation 2:14 speaks against), he was saying that one need not question the origin of every piece of clean meat (by Biblical standards) which one consumes.

Though it was not Biblically sound, the mandate that no meat should be consumed at all might well have stemmed from the fear of consuming such meat which had been spiritually defiled due to idol sacrifice. Accordingly, some had come to believe that being vegetarian was the only righteous path. The teaching that one must be vegetarian was then exposed by Paul in the 1 Timothy passage above as being from the spirit of error. It appears that Paul was once again battling this ideology in Romans 14:

> [13] Let us not therefore judge one another any more: but judge this rather, that no man put a stumblingblock or an occasion to fall in his brother's way.
>
> [14] I know, and am persuaded by the Lord Jesus, that there is nothing unclean of itself: but to him that esteemeth any thing to be unclean, to him it is unclean.
>
> [20] <u>For meat destroy not the work of God</u>. All things indeed are pure; but it is evil for that man who eateth with offence.
>
> [21] <u>It is good neither to eat flesh</u>, nor to drink wine, nor any thing whereby thy brother stumbleth, or is offended, or is made weak. - Romans 14:13-14, 20-21

If viewed as a stand alone passage, it might sound as though Paul was endorsing the eating of things Father had said not to consume. When put into the total context of Paul's writings, we can see that he was again addressing the vegetarian and idol sacrifice conflict. This is clear from verse 2 of this chapter:

> [2] For one believeth that he may eat <u>all things</u>: **another, who is weak, eateth <u>herbs</u>**. - Romans 14:2

Again, Paul ALWAYS taught within the scope and boundaries of Torah Law. Therefore, he expected his audience to understand this and to automatically apply those parameters. Accordingly, Paul was assuredly <u>not</u> insinuating by the term "all things" that all creatures which God had created were now alright to eat. Instead, verse 2 indicates that the term "all things" would be <u>both God's clean meat AND herbs,</u> as contrasted to "herbs" only. Paul is merely denouncing vegetarianism as a command yet again, and clarifying that God's clean animals may be consumed as well as herbs. He then shows us in verse 20 that the controversy over meat should not be allowed to destroy the work of God by causing dissension within the body. Paul is insisting in verse 14 that the meat from animals which the Father had ordained as edible was clean "of itself" when God created it, and will remain clean in His eyes. This again addresses the idea that they need not worry about the shambles and any supposed spiritual defilement to the meat that is sold there. He repeats his insistence of its purity in verse 20, but advises that some of the brethren may still view such meat as unclean, and to respect their views. At such times, he stresses that it should not be eaten so it will not be a stumbling block to them. In verse 21 he again confirms that Biblically clean meat ("flesh") can be consumed unless a brother in the faith would be offended. This again stresses that unity of the Body is paramount. Division over such matters as whether one can eat <u>both God's acceptable meat AND herbs</u> or be limited to eating <u>just herbs</u> is unacceptable.

Some have also used the words of Y'shua in Matthew as justification to eat whatever they desire:

> [11] Not that which goeth into the mouth defileth a man; but that which cometh out of the mouth, this defileth a man. - Matthew 15:11

By looking back to verses 1-2 of this passage we see that Y'shua was speaking to the Scribes and Pharisees. He was simply addressing the Pharisaical extensive ritual of hand washing before food consumption. Again, Y'shua knew they understood the Levitical written Torah restrictions regarding unclean foods, and they would not presume that He was authorizing the eating of such. Y'shua was simply indicating that they needed to look instead at their speech as being the potential to defile them rather than some dirt or germ that would enter the mouth due to the absence of their ritualistic hand washing practice. Neither was Y'shua saying that washing the hands before eating was wicked. It was simply their adamant requirement of this ritual of hand washing that He was addressing. Such wording by Matthew should not be contorted to indicate the authorization of Y'shua to violate His Father's specific instruction regarding dietary Laws in our written Torah text. This type of invalid interpretation destroys the Shema essence of Father and Son.

Deuteronomy mentions the "abominable thing":

> [3] Thou shalt not eat any **abominable thing**. - Deuteronomy 14:3

The word "abominable thing" is a single Hebrew word, Strong's #H8441 ("tow`ebah") - *disgusting thing, unclean meat*. If Father sees the consumption of the flesh of unclean animals as disgusting, then why should we not view it as He does? Per its broader definition this same Hebrew word is also loosely affiliated with sexual perversity, idolatry and even child sacrifice. Maybe He sees it as being a much greater issue than we do!

As stated earlier, it is obvious from the reality of the condition of pork in our present world that pork was **never made clean** by God. Nor will it be in the future.

Again the prophetic words of Ezekiel ring in our ears. It looks as though they have our day in view, at least as a secondary prophetic fulfillment. Ezekiel laments as he records the words of the Lord that the priests have mislead the people into sinful behavior to violate His Laws, profane His holy things, and disregard the clean and unclean standards He had established:

> [26] Her priests have **violated my law**, and have profaned mine holy things: they have put no difference between the holy and profane, **neither have they shewed difference between the unclean and the clean**, and have hid their eyes from my sabbaths, and **I am profaned among them**. - Ezekiel 22:26

Father speaks here of Israel's religious leaders. We personally assert that today's church relates figuratively to the spiritual House of Joseph, and (by extension) it is also referenced as the house of Israel. We will cover this more a bit later. Judah has by and large stayed within the confines of Torah directives. However, the theological instructions of "Israel" (the corporate church system) have come to the conclusion that the dietary Laws of clean and un-clean are no longer applicable. This should prompt us to sit up and take no-tice, and look to our Heavenly Father to see if what we are eating is proper in HIS eyes. He says clearly here that they have shown no difference between the unclean and the clean.

The summation at the beginning of the verse for the details that follow empha-sizes that the violation of the Law profanes the Father. Do we really believe that Paul through the Holy Spirit would condone the abolishing of Father's Law so we could violate it freely and profane the Father? We will discuss later how the Houses of Joseph, Ephraim, and Israel are all spiritually aligned to today's church. Likewise there is importance to the meaning of names in the Hebraic language. We would note that the meaning of Egypt is: *oppressors*, and the meaning of Assyria is: *exalted*. Sometimes proper place names are used in a figurative sense to project their meaning to the subject at hand, rather than to indicate their actual geographical location. Accordingly, this Hosea passage may be very meaningful to us today:

> [3] They shall not dwell in the LORD's land; but **Ephraim** shall return to Egypt, and they **shall eat unclean things** in Assyria.

> [4] They shall not offer wine *offerings* to the LORD, **neither shall they be pleasing unto him**: their sacrifices shall be unto them as the bread of mourners; **all that eat thereof shall be polluted**: for **their bread for their soul shall not come into the house of the LORD**. - Hosea 9:3-4

If indeed Ephraim is equated to today's church, verse 3 may be indicative of their acceptance of the unclean as a food option. It may imply that they will return to oppression – eating that which is forbidden, and will do so in an exalted state – thinking they are in good standing with God.

Contrary to God's approval for this offense, verse 4 is sobering. The word "sacrifice" in verse 4 is Strong's #H2077 ("zebach"). It does not necessarily imply an animal sacrifice, but rather can mean: *thank offering*. It could there-fore indicate the prayer of thanks offered for the consumption of the unclean. Both times the word "bread" is used, it is Strong's #H3899 ("lechem") - *food in general (literally or figuratively [spiritually speaking])*. The word "mourn-ers" is Strong's #H205 ("'aven") - *idolatry, wickedness*.

Note that these two verses are linked. It is the physical eating of unclean things in verse 3 that is linked to a less than desirable spiritual condition in verse 4. Potentially this passage could be linking the consumption of unclean foods in verse 3 to what is viewed by God in verse 4 as the spiritual condition of "aven" above, idolatry and wickedness. Verse 4 indicates that this "bread of their soul" (the unclean creatures that they have consumed due to the carnality of their soul) might actually even prevent them from being able to enter the house of the Lord. How tragic would that be!

We grieve when we think of how often this is enacted in the lives of Christians today (pastors and parishioners alike) who love Y'shua but are unwittingly being led into iniquity. We especially extend an arm of compassion and encouragement to our brothers and sisters who feel offended by these Biblical passages and our stance regarding them. Please understand that we wish to express our support rather than condemnation – our love rather than judgment.

However, we earnestly appeal to all who read these words to consider them soberly. If we still need further proof that the creatures Father addressed in Torah as being unclean are still unclean today, we might want to look to the future. The words in Isaiah are enough to wake us up that the flesh of pigs wasn't suddenly made clean in early New Testament days. Otherwise how does one explain that the flesh of pigs is still abominable as the Millennial Kingdom opens? This text relates prophetically to the onset of the Millennial Kingdom:

> [17] <u>They that sanctify themselves</u>, and <u>purify themselves in the gardens behind one tree in the midst</u>, <u>eating swine's flesh, and the abomination, and the mouse, shall be consumed together</u>, saith the LORD. - Isaiah 66:17

The word "behind" here is Strong's #H310 ("'achar") - *after, from behind, following*. This verse indicates to us that some will think of themselves as sanctified and purified, but that this deception comes from following after the tree in the midst of the garden (the Tree of Knowledge of Good and Evil). The thorny contra fruit message of this tree has convinced them that the consumption of unclean meats is acceptable. The "spirit of error" of this tree stands in direct contrast to the real "Spirit of Truth" from the Tree of Life which upholds the continuity of Torah teaching in today's world.

The Tree of Knowledge caused our downfall, yet this verse shows us that some are still following after it and being seduced to believe that they are already sanctified when this is not yet so. The words "that sanctify themselves, and purify themselves" are very troubling. We know Biblically that we cannot sanctify and purify ourselves, so this indicates that either they believe they can and have, or they view themselves as sanctified when they are not, because they are convinced that they have been sanctified at the time of belief. Either way they have followed after the Tree of Knowledge in the midst of the garden.

As a result of common instruction today, people have come to believe they are still walking in sanctification while eating swine's flesh. Many well educated pastors have had an unflinching trust in the tenets derived from their seminary or other instructors, and have unwittingly passed along such spirit of error teaching to their congregations. Likewise as unsuspecting Believers who have confidence in their pastors, many have been swayed by this spirit of error teaching. When we read God's Word in its entirety, it indicates that this may be a costly error. This book is being written as a wake up call.

This Isaiah passage rather ruins any appetite we personally might otherwise think we still have for pork or any of the other "unclean" creatures referenced in Torah. Please know we don't mean this to be harsh, but there is so little latitude for softening this message. It is simple to see that Father would not forbid the eating of unclean things then have Y'shua clean them, only to declare them abominable yet again as the Millennial Kingdom begins. Two plus two does not equal five.

Paul claims to be inspired in his writings by God's Spirit. If we interpret his writings to say that it is now alright to eat that which Father deemed as unclean, then we are pitting the inspiration of God's Spirit against the instruction God initially gave us. This would totally shatter Biblical harmony and the platform it provides for our discernment. When the Old Testament falls away in disuse, there is no means to illustrate the error of incorrect interpretation. Such it is with common teaching today. The congruency of Father's dietary Laws relative to the words of Paul fails to come through, and error becomes prominent.

There is harmony in the understanding that things which were created as unclean and pronounced as being inedible were never made edible, and are still unclean during the Millennial reign. Unfortunately, the message seems quite harsh, but that is because it is so important that we understand it. The understanding that to eat unclean things is equated with bread of the soul was a real eye opener to us, and the consequence in Hosea 9:4 above that some may not be able to come into the house of the Lord as a result is very unsettling!

This Isaiah passage should make it very clear that Father's view of the abomination associated with these unclean foods has NEVER changed – nor will it change in the future, so such interpretation of Paul's words simply cannot be valid. Father's standards were never obliterated by the New Covenant, but rather they are maintained THROUGHOUT the New Covenant, and continue on into the Millennial reign.

Thankfully, it appears that eventually during the Millennial Kingdom all of this will be sorted out:

> [23] And they shall teach my people the difference between the holy and profane, and cause them to discern between the unclean and the clean. - Ezekiel 44:23

Paul says in 2 Corinthians:

> [2] For I am jealous over you with godly jealousy: for I have espoused you to one husband, that I may present you as a chaste virgin to Christ.
>
> [3] But I fear, lest by any means, as the serpent beguiled Eve through his subtilty, so your minds should be corrupted from the simplicity that is in Christ.
>
> [4] For if he that cometh preacheth another Jesus, whom we have not preached, or if ye receive another spirit, which ye have not received, or another gospel, which ye have not accepted, ye might well bear with him. - 2 Corinthians 11:2-4

The influence of the contra spirit is still strong. Eve was the first Adam's wife, and we are the last Adam's wife. Will we make the same mistake again? Eve was seduced to fall prey to deception which cost her greatly. The same seducer is active in the church today. We are to learn from her mistakes and overcome, but unfortunately many appear to be falling prey yet again to this deadly seduction.

Remember that what Y'shua spoke came from the Father:

> [24] He that loveth me not keepeth not my sayings: and the word which ye hear is not mine, but the Father's which sent me. - John 14:24

To say we are in Y'shua while continuing to choose violation of the Father's Law might well be viewed by Father as hypocrisy. Paul says in the 2 Corinthians passage above that such a lifestyle is not what he is teaching, which is further verification that his words have been misconstrued over time. He seemed to understand what would happen in the end of days and was warning against it here.

We are told in Ephesians that Y'shua is looking for a HOLY church:

[25] ... Christ also loved the church, and gave himself for it;

[26] That he might **sanctify** and cleanse it with the washing of water by the word,

[27] That he might present it to himself a glorious church, not having spot, or wrinkle, or any such thing; but that it should be **holy and without blemish**. - Ephesians 5:25-27

[23] And the very **God** of peace **sanctify you wholly**; and I pray God your whole **spirit** and **soul** and **body** be preserved **blameless** unto the coming of our Lord Jesus Christ. - 1 Thessalonians 5:23

Paul says here that we are to be sanctified "**WHOLLY**" which relates to holiness. The culmination of the sanctification process occurs after all has been accomplished within us. It is obvious here that this is not an automatic thing, or Paul would not have been asking Father to help his brethren with it.

Y'shua wants to be able to present to Himself a glorious church that is blameless and HOLY, yet many within His church are still eating the things that do not align with holiness in the least. We really do need to be careful with our dietary choices, as we are to glorify God with our bodies:

[19] What? know ye not that your body is the temple of the Holy Ghost which is in you, which ye have of God, and **ye are not your own**?

[20] For ye are bought with a price: therefore **glorify God in your body, and in your spirit, which are God's**. - 1 Corinthians 6:19-20

In our quest to become holy to God, should we not seek to cleanse ourselves from defilement both spiritually AND physically? Father has clearly stated what profanes Him in Ezekiel 22:26. Shouldn't we align our dietary choices with what pleases Him and exclude those things which we know do not in order to glorify Him and strive for physical blamelessness?

CHAPTER 9

CALVARY AND THE LAW

Then there was another consideration as we began to deal with this issue of Law. Where did the cross fit in? Indeed the mantra of the Christian faith was that the cross was a game changer. While we fully acknowledged that this was so, we began to look into just how it changed the game. Exactly what effect does the cross of Calvary have on the keeping of the Law in our age?

Atonement

Passion runs deep when a Believer perceives that the sufficiency of the sacrifice and atonement provided by Y'shua is being questioned. However, could there be a bit of confusion regarding the word "atonement" as it is referenced in our Bibles? The key to understanding it might be found as we see how it was originally used in our Old Testament:

> [28] And ye shall do no work in that same day: for it is a day of atonement, to make an atonement for you before the LORD your God. - Leviticus 23:28

The first use of the word "atonement" in this verse is Strong's #H3725 ("kippur") - *expiation, atonement*. This word is the noun which is *the end product*. It is derived from the root word in its verb form, which is the second use of the word "atonement" in this verse. This verb form is typically translated in our English text as "make atonement". It is Strong's #H3722 ("kaphar") - *to cover, purge, make an atonement, make reconciliation, pacify, propitiate; expiate, condone, placate, cancel; appease, disannul, cleanse, forgive, be merciful, pardon, purge away, put off, reconcile, atone for sin and persons by legal rites*.

We find "kippur" again in reference to sin offerings. Exodus tells us sin offerings are for atonement and they cleanse the altar:

> [36] And thou shalt offer every day a bullock for a <u>sin offering for atonement</u>: and thou shalt <u>cleanse the altar</u>, when thou hast made an atonement for <u>it</u>, and thou shalt anoint it, to <u>sanctify it</u>. - Exodus 29:36

It is important to note that **after the altar is cleansed it must still be be anointed to sanctify it**. Apparently, the sin offering brings atonement which cleanses the altar. However this cleansing of the altar is only the beginning of the process.

This Old Testament process of cleansing the physical altar with the blood of animals is to point to the process of man's spiritual justification through the blood of Y'shua. The word "atonement" is found in our New Testament text as well:

> [11] And not only so, but we also joy in God through our Lord Jesus Christ, by whom we have now received the <u>atonement</u>. - Romans 5:11

This is actually the ONLY reference to any form of the word "atonement" in the English text of our New Testament (KJV). It is Strong's #G2643 ("katallagē") - <u>*exchange*</u>*; of the business of money changers, exchanging equivalent values; adjustment of a difference,* <u>*reconciliation*</u>*,* <u>*restoration to favor*</u>*; in the NT of the restoration of the favor of God to sinners that repent and put their trust in the expiatory death of Christ.* It is the <u>exchange</u> of our sins for the life of our Savior – Y'shua's death on the cross as payment for the IOU of death which hung over the head of man. This atonement provides cleansing for an individual's spiritual altar, initiating restoration to favor with Father. It is the spiritual counterpart to the cleansing of the physical corporate altar in Old Testament days. Then (even as we saw in the Old Testament), the New Testament process of spiritual cleansing (justification) must be followed by anointing (receiving the Holy Spirit) and walking out our new-found faith hand in hand with God (sanctification).

This base foundation for the physical atonement of the Old Testament was followed by the more profound spiritual application through the victory of Y'shua at Calvary in the New. We will compare and contrast each step of the two below.

1 - The Old Testament cleansing of the altar was relative to the <u>physical</u> portion of man.

2 - This version of atonement was derived through cleansing the <u>physical</u> altar (which symbolizes the <u>outer physical</u> self) with the spilling of blood by the sacrifice of an <u>animal</u>.

Two Trees, Two Kingdoms, Two Kings

3 - It would provide the means for <u>temporal</u> restitution to Father.

4 - This enabled people in their <u>corruptible physical</u> form to be <u>temporarily</u> in the sacred space of the <u>physical</u> Tabernacle/Temple and the Divine Glory.

Now for the contrast:

1 - The New Testament cleansing of the altar was relative to the <u>spiritual</u> portion of man.

2 - This version of atonement was derived through cleansing the <u>spiritual</u> altar (which symbolizes the <u>inner spiritual</u> self) with the spilling of blood by the sacrifice of <u>Y'shua</u>.

3 - It would provide the means for <u>eternal</u> restitution to Father.

4 - This enables people in their <u>incorruptible spiritual</u> form to be <u>eternally</u> in the sacred space of the <u>spiritual</u> Temple, and the Father Himself.

The New Testament version of atonement through Y'shua's sacrifice would provide eternal restitution to Father through cleansing of the spiritual altar of man's inner spiritual self. The key to understanding this is to realize the extent of defilement of the human state. As long as we have the flesh and blood of the human anatomy, the sin nature and the senses prevent us from being pure enough to be in Father's presence. To be in His presence requires that our corruptible bodies be changed.

Without Y'shua's sacrifice, there would be no opportunity to be changed to our incorruptible spiritual state. The sacrifice of animals was repeated because there was no lasting measure of restitution available for the corruptible physical form. Only when the spiritual altar within is cleansed can man finally proceed through sanctification to find eternal restitution in an incorruptible spiritual body:

> [28] So Christ was once offered to bear the sins of many; and unto them that look for him shall he appear the second time without sin unto salvation. - Hebrews 9:28

While this is a fantastic blessing, it also provides a serious consideration. Y'shua's sacrifice was the final means of restitution. If we receive Him and then turn our back on Him to oblige our lusts in a continuous, wanton, sinful lifestyle, there is no further sacrifice to cover that sin:

> [26] For if we sin wilfully after that we have received the

knowledge of the truth, there remaineth no more sacrifice for sins,
- Hebrews 10:26

We will cover this in much more detail in a later portion of the book, but for now we will see how the atonement wrought by Y'shua begins the process which is culminated in the transition to our new bodies. Y'shua's blood brings us to the threshold of eternity, which no animal's blood could ever do. However, in the same manner in which the physical altar must be anointed and sanctified after its cleansing, so must our spiritual altar be anointed and sanctified:

[36] And thou shalt offer every day a bullock for a <u>sin offering for atonement</u>: and thou shalt <u>cleanse the altar</u>, when thou hast made an atonement for <u>it,</u> and thou shalt anoint it, to <u>sanctify it</u>.
- Exodus 29:36

Our New Testament atonement provides for our justification, the cleansing of our spiritual altar, when we receive Y'shua as our Savior. Then "thou shalt anoint it, to sanctify it". This anointing equates to our receipt of the Holy Spirit to provide for sanctification. We receive the Spirit to indwell us immediately after our justification, and the Spirit guides us through our sanctification, the walk of faith. To recap this process: our spiritual altar is cleansed through belief on the atoning blood of Y'shua, is anointed by the indwelling Holy Spirit, and is sanctified through our yielding to the direction of the Holy Spirit as we walk in obedience to God's ways.

The atonement provided by Y'shua does not have to be repeated, as it unequivocally accomplished a surrogate atonement for man. It is an atonement by proxy, which successfully absolves the death penalty of sin for those who repent and follow Y'shua, which the temporal cleansing on the physical level could never accomplish.

Though the Greek word "katallagē" appears only this once with the translation "atonement", this same Greek word is used three other times in our New Testament text as forms of the word "reconcile". An example is found in 2 Corinthians:

[19] To wit, that God was in Christ, <u>reconciling</u> the world unto himself, not imputing their trespasses unto them; and hath committed unto us the word of <u>reconciliation</u>. - 2 Corinthians 5:19

The thought is also carried through with other New Testament words which have parallel meaning and intent:

> [10] Herein is love, not that we loved God, but that he loved us, and sent his Son to be the <u>propitiation</u> for our sins. - 1 John 4:10

The word "propitiation" here is Strong's #G2434 ("hilasmos") - *atonement, expiation (amends or reparation)*. The thought continues in Hebrews:

> [14] How much more shall <u>the blood of Christ</u>, who through the eternal Spirit offered himself without spot to God, <u>purge</u> your <u>conscience</u> from dead works to serve the living God? - Hebrews 9:14

The word "purge" here is Strong's #G2511 ("katharizō") - *to make clean, cleanse; in a moral sense to free from defilement of sin and from faults; to purify from wickedness; to free from guilt of sin, to purify; to consecrate by cleansing or purifying; to consecrate, dedicate; to pronounce clean in a Levitical sense*. This verse tells us that it cleanses and revitalizes the <u>conscience</u> or the spiritual portion of our being. This word "conscience" is Strong's #G4893 ("syneidēsis") - *<u>the soul</u> as distinguishing between what is morally good and bad, prompting to do the former and shun the latter, commending one, condemning the other*. The conscience is somewhat a **<u>spiritual</u>** <u>altar</u> within us, where the wickedness of our desires and deeds are to be realized and burned up through confession. Once we are spiritually cleansed by the propitiation of Y'shua, we are to retain that cleansing through adapting our walk to the guidance of the Spirit, and adhering to Father's standards.

Some want to disregard the literal meaning of Ezekiel's Temple, yet far too much detail is offered regarding its construction for it to be merely figurative – detail such as:

> [13] And these are the measures of the altar after the cubits: The cubit is a cubit and an hand breadth; even the bottom shall be a cubit, and the breadth a cubit, and the border thereof by the edge thereof round about shall be a span: and this shall be the higher place of the altar. - Ezekiel 43:13

Ezekiel's yet future Temple is very real, and the sacrifices which are offered in it are also very real. They are likewise sin offerings to cleanse the **<u>physical</u>** <u>altar</u> of this yet future **physical** Temple:

> [21] Thou shalt take the bullock also of the **sin offering**, and he shall burn it in the appointed place of the house, without the sanctuary.
>
> [22] And on the second day thou shalt offer a kid of the goats

> without blemish for a **sin offering**; and they shall **cleanse the altar**, as they did cleanse it with the bullock. - Ezekiel 43:21-22

This correlates hand and glove back to what we found in Exodus when the altar was cleansed through sacrifice of sin offerings in the Old Testament:

> [36] And thou shalt offer every day a bullock for a **sin offering** for atonement: and thou shalt **cleanse the altar**, when thou hast made an atonement for it, and thou shalt anoint it, to sanctify it. - Exodus 29:36

Notice the similarity in the wording. The same provision of atonement through the cleansing of the altar with animal sacrifice will be happening yet again in the Millennial Kingdom. It is obvious that the purpose for the atonement wrought by Y'shua was slightly different, or such animal sacrifice would no longer be needed in the yet future Temple. Ezekiel assures us that this resumption of the sacrificial system will NOT be offensive to God. Rather it will be compulsory, and directed by God Himself. His Glory will fill the newly erected Temple even as this sacrificial system is instituted once again:

> [4] And the glory of the LORD came into the house by the way of the gate whose prospect is toward the east.
>
> [5] So the spirit took me up, and brought me into the inner court; and, behold, **the glory of the LORD filled the house**. - Ezekiel 43:4-5

His Glory abiding within the Temple signifies acceptance of this sacrificial system, and we must realize that it serves a distinct purpose or He would not have reinstituted it. We know then that the sacrifices which take place there <u>**cannot** be abhorrent to God OR in any way contradict, diminish, or invalidate that which Y'shua accomplished on Calvary</u>.

Until the physical was conquered by Y'shua's perfect life, the spiritual could not be fully addressed. Calvary was the exact point in time that the physical emphasis moved to a more spiritual level. Y'shua's perfection in the physical realm to the physical Law completed the physical mandates, and allowed re-mission of sin to move to a spiritual level. Y'shua became our high priest after conquering the flesh, so our <u>spiritual</u> atonement can now be accomplished through belief on Y'shua. We can now come before Father spiritually because Y'shua paved the way for that relationship to be restored:

> [15] For we have not an high priest which cannot be touched with the feeling of our infirmities; but was in all points tempted like as we are, yet without sin.

Two Trees, Two Kingdoms, Two Kings

> [16] Let us therefore come boldly unto the throne of grace, that
> we may obtain mercy, and find grace to help in time of need. -
> Hebrews 4:15-16

Until perfection was achieved by Y'shua on a physical level, our spiritual atonement could not occur. The Passover lamb had to be without spot or blemish to be an appropriate sacrifice. The human Lamb of God (Y'shua) had to be perfect as well – sinless – in order to be our surrogate sacrifice. Only then could the offering accomplish this cleansing of the spiritual part (spirit and soul) of man's being. Animals could not attain to the Law perfectly to provide for this spiritual cleansing. It took Y'shua putting on human flesh to provide absolution for the penalty of sin that extends to the very depths of the human soul.

Belief on Y'shua now brings atonement to our inner spiritual man. We manifest this atonement through our sanctification, as we walk in obedience to Father's precepts and become a living <u>spiritual</u> sacrifice to Him. It brings one into reconciliation with Father which would not be possible without Y'shua's sacrifice. Y'shua's sinless life rendered Him to be pure on both a physical AND a spiritual basis, which enabled the transition from the physical to the spiritual atonement. Such transition could be accomplished in no other way. That is where the following Hebrews passage comes in:

> [11] But Christ being come an high priest of good things to come,
> by a greater and more perfect tabernacle, not made with hands,
> that is to say, not of this building;
>
> [12] Neither by the blood of goats and calves, but by his own blood
> he entered in once into the holy place, having obtained eternal
> redemption for us.
>
> [13] <u>For if the blood of bulls and of goats, and the ashes of an
> heifer sprinkling the unclean, sanctifieth to the **purifying of the
> flesh**</u>:
>
> [14] How much more shall <u>the blood of Christ</u>, who through the
> eternal Spirit offered himself without spot to God, **purge your
> conscience from dead works to serve the living God**? -
> Hebrews 9:11-14
>
> [4] For it is not possible that the blood of bulls and of goats should
> take away sins. - Hebrews 10:4

These Hebrews passages actually tell us that though the blood of bulls and goats was a sin offering, it was limited in its scope. It provided the "purifying of the flesh" (verse 13). This was necessary as a temporal measure in order to make the corruptible flesh of physical mortal man acceptable before God when he approached the physical Tabernacle/Temple. Otherwise man could never have <u>physically</u> approached the Tabernacle/Temple where the Glory of God covered the mercy seat.

A key to understanding the purpose of the sacrificial system is to understand the three types of sacrifices in Old Testament days – burnt offerings, sin offerings, and trespass offerings.

As we understand it, the burnt offering was not associated with sin. It was a voluntary offering of worship which provided a sweet savor to God. It was likely a physical picture of the spiritual activity of the sanctification process. It would point to the voluntary process of burning off the old man, in worship and adoration to Father, as we commit to serving Him fully.

The other two - offerings for sins and trespasses - are often and easily confused. To begin to sort it out, we would say that all trespasses are sin, though not all sins are trespasses.

When we have unwarranted anger toward our brother, Y'shua tells us that we are in danger of judgment - almost as though we had murdered. In such a case, not a hair on the head of the victim would have been harmed by our internal anger, so no physical transgression would have occurred. Yet the very anger within would be sin in the more spiritual application of the Law:

> [21] Ye have heard that it was said by them of old time, Thou shalt not kill; and whosoever shall kill shall be in danger of the judgment:
>
> [22] But I say unto you, That whosoever is angry with his brother without a cause shall be in danger of the judgment: and whosoever shall say to his brother, Raca, shall be in danger of the council: but whosoever shall say, Thou fool, shall be in danger of hell fire.
> - Matthew 5:21-22
>
> [21] For from within, <u>out of the heart of men</u>, proceed evil thoughts, adulteries, fornications, murders,
>
> [22] Thefts, covetousness, wickedness, deceit, lasciviousness, an evil eye, blasphemy, pride, foolishness:
>
> [23] All these evil things come from within, <u>and defile the man</u>. - Mark 7:21-23

Two Trees, Two Kingdoms, Two Kings

We concur with what seems to be a fairly common consensus that the sin offering is to deal with the continual sin nature that inhabits the human flesh. The sin nature of man is always within him, and pours forth from the heart to pollute him. "For from within, out of the heart of men, proceed evil thoughts ...". These inner intents of the heart can then "defile the man". This would seem to be the type of sins for which the sin offering is meant. Conversely, the trespass offering would deal with the expressed sin of transgressing the more literal commandments of God.

As long as we have the human flesh, complete with its sin nature, this type of sin will ALWAYS be a part of the human condition, even after coming to Y'shua. This would preclude our physical entrance into the physical presence of God. Even if there was no covert or blatant trespass in our lives, there would be impure thoughts and intents at times. Sin will never be in short supply to the human being in mortal form.

Therefore we see that sins which are harbored in the heart are addressed by the sin offerings, while sins of the transgression of Father's explicit Laws are addressed by the trespass offerings.

Even in this future Temple, the shedding of the blood of animals (being similar to the human blood which carries the sin nature) is required for temporal acceptability of defiled human flesh so man can to come before God in the Temple. This then is the temporal cleansing of <u>the mortal external body</u> (the flesh of Hebrews 9:13 above). It will enable man in his fallen state to come for a brief time into the sanctity of the physical Temple.

However, only the blood of our perfect sacrifice Y'shua can deal with the spiritual consequence of our sin on an eternal basis by cleansing the inner man. The blood of Y'shua alone can provide atonement for the spiritual part of man which is eternal in nature – purging the conscience to serve the living God as a living (spiritual) sacrifice through an obedient walk in the Spirit:

> [16] This is the covenant that I will make with them after those days, saith the Lord, I will put my laws into their hearts, and in their minds will I write them;
>
> [17] And their sins and iniquities will I remember no more.
>
> [18] Now **where remission of these is, there is no more offering for sin**. - Hebrews 10:16-18

We will discuss the timing for the fullness of this covenant a bit later, but for the continuity of the subject at hand, we would say that as long as we remain in human flesh, such remission of sin is ongoing, and is contingent on our walk in the Spirit:

> [1] There is therefore now **no condemnation to them** which are in Christ Jesus, **who walk** not after the flesh, but **after the Spirit**. - Romans 8:1

> [9] **If** we **confess** our sins, he is faithful and just to forgive us our sins, and to **cleanse** us **from all unrighteousness**. - 1 John 1:9

Paul and John explain that it is through this walk that we have remission of sins.

Then only as we commit to a walk in the Spirit subsequent to Y'shua's resurrection can the Law be fulfilled in us as it was in Him:

> [4] That the righteousness of the law might be fulfilled in us, who walk not after the flesh, but after the Spirit. - Romans 8:4

The temporal atonement of the animal sacrifice can only avail the temporal portion of our being – that of the flesh which is mortal in nature. It took the pure and holy sacrifice of Y'shua which would reach into eternity to atone for the spiritual portion of man which is eternal in nature. The temporal measure of the sacrifice of the blood of beasts deals with the temporal mortality of the flesh of man, while the eternal nature of the sacrifice of the blood of Y'shua deals with the eternal nature of the spiritual portion of man's being. He then had the Father send us the Spirit after He departed so we would have the guidance we need to become a living sacrifice – the means for the Law to be fulfilled within us.

The Hebrew word for atonement relative to animal sacrifice ("kaphar") is all about purging and cleansing that which is physical, where the Greek word for atonement relative to Y'shua's sacrifice ("katallage") is about cleansing AND restoration on a spiritual level. The first pertains to acceptability through temporal purification of the physical flesh relative to the holiness of the physical Temple, while the latter pertains to acceptability through eternal restoration of the spiritual part of our being to the holiness of the spiritual Temple and the spiritual personage of Father Himself:

> [24] **God is a Spirit**: and they that worship him must worship him in spirit and in truth. - John 4:24

Physical relates to physical and is temporal in nature; spiritual relates to spiritual, and is eternal in its scope. This does not mean that there is not over-lap between the two. Even the physical will ultimately be restored eternally when the physical body is made spiritual:

> [53] For this corruptible must put on incorruption, and this mortal must put on immortality. - 1 Corinthians 15:53

However, we are not there yet, and a large portion of understanding God's Laws while we are in the 3-D realm of "space and time" is relative to this differentiation of physical and spiritual.

When the new physical Temple of Ezekiel's vision is manifested, there will still be many inhabitants of Earth who are in their fleshly mortal bodies. The flesh will still be ceremonially impure to attain to the physical presence of Father due to the sin nature in their human blood. Of those, some may be on track with their sanctification process, and may be seen as positionally (spiritually) clean before God. However, even then the ongoing defilement associated with the physical flesh (which houses their spiritual beings) will still create a barrier to their physical presence with the Divine:

> [10] And if Christ be in you, <u>the body is dead because of sin</u>; but the Spirit is life because of righteousness. - Romans 8:10

Though the spiritual aspect is seen as righteous through the Spirit, the body is still seen as dead (defiled) on a ceremonial basis. Yet, they will need to come to the Temple for worship. Thus, the physical sacrifices of animal flesh on the altar will still perform the ceremonial cleansing in order to allow for the physical presence of man in his mortal flesh with God:

> [3] And he shall sit as a refiner and purifer of silver: and he shall purify the sons of Levi, and purge them as gold and silver, that they may offer unto the LORD an offering in righteousness.
>
> **[4] Then shall the offering of Judah and Jerusalem be pleasant unto the LORD, as in the days of old, and as in former years.** - Malachi 3:3-4
>
> [7] Even them will I bring to my holy mountain, and make them joyful in my house of prayer: <u>their burnt offerings and their sacrifices shall be accepted upon mine altar</u>; for mine house shall be called an house of prayer for all people. - Isaiah 56:7

This type of sacrifice during the Millennial reign does not contradict that which was accomplished for the saving of the soul by Y'shua on Calvary's cross. It will merely be an immediate temporal measure to make possible the approach of the carnal physical flesh of mortal man to the holiness of this physical Temple. It will deem man's physical being acceptable to God for a moment in time so that he might enter into the holy ground of the Temple complex:

> [23] And it shall come to pass, that from one new moon to another, and from one sabbath to another, shall all flesh come to worship before me, saith the LORD. - Isaiah 66:23

These animal sacrifices (unlike the one-time sacrifice of Y'shua) will have to be repeated over and again as <u>temporal</u> physical measures of purification for the flesh:

> [25] Seven days shalt thou prepare every day a goat for a sin offering: they shall also prepare a young bullock, and a ram out of the flock, without blemish.

> [26] Seven days shall they purge the altar and purify it; and they shall consecrate themselves.

> [27] And when these days are expired, it shall be, that upon the eighth day, **and so forward**, the priests shall make your burnt offerings upon the altar, and your peace offerings; and I will accept you, saith the Lord GOD. - Ezekiel 43:25-27

Referring to the Millennial Kingdom in the preceding verses, chapter 13 of Jeremiah also speaks of Temple sacrifices. Note that the word "want" here simply means: *lack*; so the Levites will never lack a man to offer sacrifices continually:

> [18] Neither shall the priests the Levites <u>want</u> a man before me to offer burnt offerings, and to kindle meat offerings, and <u>to do sacrifice **continually**</u>. - Jeremiah 33:18

Zechariah follows through with more words about the Millennial Temple:

> [20] In that day shall there be upon the bells of the horses, HOLINESS UNTO THE LORD; and the pots in the LORD's house shall be like the bowls <u>before the altar</u>.

> [21] Yea, every pot in Jerusalem and in Judah shall be holiness unto the LORD of hosts: and all <u>they that sacrifice</u> shall come and take of them, and seethe therein: and in that day there shall be no more the Canaanite in the house of the LORD of hosts. - Zechariah 14:20-21

Two Trees, Two Kingdoms, Two Kings

Therefore we see that there will still be temporal sin sacrifices for cleansing during at least a portion of the Millennial Kingdom.

Change of Body

How will things be different when there is no longer any physical flesh and everyone has a spiritual body?

It would seem that the Heavenly spiritual Law would thoroughly incorporate all which under girded it, and the aspects of the Law which relate to the fleshly body will no longer be operative when mankind has departed from his fallen physical form:

> [44] It is sown a <u>natural body</u>; it is raised a <u>spiritual body</u>. There is a natural body, and there is a spiritual body.
>
> [45] And so it is written, The first man Adam was made a living soul; the last Adam was made a quickening spirit.
>
> [46] Howbeit that was not first which is spiritual, but that which is natural; and afterward that which is spiritual. - 1 Corinthians 15:44-46

The physical body is our terrestrial version, and the spiritual body is our celestial composition:

> [40] There are also celestial bodies, and bodies <u>terrestrial</u>: but the glory of the <u>celestial</u> is one, and the glory of the terrestrial is another. - 1 Corinthians 15:40

The word "celestial" here is Strong's #G2032 ("epouranios") - *of Heavenly origin or nature*.

We suspect that the celestial body will be able to transition to some degree or other between the physical and the spiritual state. This is Biblically derived, as we correlate the text in Philippians with that of 1 John and the Gospels of John and Luke:

> [20] For our conversation is in heaven; from whence also we look for the Saviour, the Lord Jesus Christ:
>
> [21] Who shall <u>change our vile body, that it may be fashioned like unto his glorious body</u>, according to the working whereby he is able even to subdue all things unto himself. - Philippians 3:20-21

[2] Beloved, now are we the sons of God, and it doth not yet appear what we shall be: but we know that, when he shall appear, **we shall be like him**; for we shall see him as he is. - 1 John 3:2

The Gospels of John and Luke tell us what this "like Him" would be. After His resurrection Y'shua could enter a room with a closed door, which means His body was not subject to the laws of nature in the physical realm:

[26] And after eight days again his disciples were within, and Thomas with them: <u>then came Jesus, the doors being shut, and stood in the midst</u>, and said, Peace be unto you. - John 20:26

However, He could also eat, which means that His body (while in this form) maintained some form of physicality:

[40] And when he had thus spoken, he shewed them his hands and his feet.

[41] And while they yet believed not for joy, and wondered, he said unto them, Have ye here any meat?

[42] And they gave him a piece of a broiled fish, and of an honeycomb.

[43] And <u>he took it, and did eat before them</u>. - Luke 24:40-43

It looks as though Y'shua's spiritual (celestial) body was one which could transition in form to some sort of physicality when desired. This would be somewhat like the angels who spoke to Abraham, as they too ate:

[8] And he took butter, and milk, and the calf which he had dressed, and set it before them; and he stood by them under the tree, <u>and they did eat</u>. - Genesis 18:8

It appears that our next transition will be from a terrestrial body to a celestial one which will no longer be constrained by the material confines of this 3-D reality.

Obviously Y'shua could come and go from this dimensional reality, as He vanished before the eyes of men into a cloud:

[9] And when he had spoken these things, while they beheld, he was taken up; and a cloud received him out of their sight. - Acts 1:9

Two Trees, Two Kingdoms, Two Kings

The passages in Matthew, Mark, and Luke that reference new wine and new wine bottles might actually be an allusion to a deeper message about the change from our corruptible blood and our fleshly bodies to a new type of incorruptible life fluid and our new spiritual bodies The word for these "bottles" is Strong's #G779 ("askos") - *a leathern (or **skin**) bag used as a bottle*. It is therefore commonly referred to more accurately as wine skins (rather than wine bottles). In the following reference, the wine might represent our blood, and the wine skins might be symbolic of our fleshly bodies:

> [22] And <u>no man putteth new wine into old bottles</u>: else the new
> wine doth burst the bottles, and the wine is spilled, and the
> bottles will be marred: but <u>new wine must be put into new bottles</u>.
> - Mark 2:22

If this is showing us a typology of this change, it would be to say that the new life-force can not be put into the fleshly skin. It would spill out and mar the skin. It must be put into a new spiritual body.

Isaiah seems to echo the thought from the pages of our Old Testament in a prophetic picture of the coming days of the Millennial Kingdom where he correlates the new wine to God's servants in this future Kingdom:

> [8] Thus saith the LORD, As the <u>new wine</u> is found in the cluster,
> and one saith, <u>Destroy it not</u>; for a blessing is in it: so will I do for
> my servants' sakes, that I may not destroy them all.
>
> [9] And <u>I will bring forth a seed out of Jacob, and out of Judah an
> inheritor of my mountains</u>: and <u>mine elect</u> shall inherit it, and <u>**my
> servants**</u> shall dwell there. - Isaiah 65:8-9

Deuteronomy correlates the grape to blood by prophetically speaking of the "blood of the grape".

> [14] Butter of kine, and milk of sheep, with fat of lambs, and
> rams of the breed of Bashan, and goats, with the fat of kidneys
> of wheat; and thou didst drink the pure <u>blood of the grape</u>. -
> Deuteronomy 32:14

A change in our flesh and our blood to an incorruptible state will eventually be necessary to enter into God's Heavenly Kingdom:

> [50] Now this I say, brethren, that <u>flesh and blood</u> cannot inherit
> the kingdom of God; neither doth corruption inherit incorruption. -
> 1 Corinthians 15:50

[21] For I will cleanse their blood that I have not cleansed: for the LORD dwelleth in Zion. - Joel 3:21

The sin nature of the blood and the lust of the flesh are the two aspects of our being that seem to be the primary culprits responsible for the corruptible nature of our present bodies. Father may transform the flesh to a new more spiritual form which no longer lusts (a new wine skin), and cleanse the blood to remove the sin nature, transforming it to a new type of life-force. This may be the process of turning our corruptible terrestrial bodies into our new incorruptible celestial versions. Along with this transformation would be the renewing of the mind:

[2] And be not conformed to this world: but be ye **transformed** by the renewing of your mind, that ye may prove what is that good, and acceptable, and perfect, will of God. - Romans 12:2

While we are to begin this process here, we believe that the transformation of the body will bring completion to this mind renewal as well. Obviously, a mind that still thinks inappropriate thoughts could not be part of an incorruptible body. The renewal of the human mind to a more complete version of the mind of Y'shua, and the transformation of the body to a celestial state will put a new and more complete emphasis on the spiritual aspects of the Law, and the physical portion will have less and less meaning to us. There will apparently be a combination of terrestrial and celestial bodies present on the earth during the Millennial Kingdom. If that is the case, then all bodies may not be transformed until the end of that time frame. Maybe that is why Y'shua said that it is only when Heaven and earth vanish away that every jot and tittle of the Law is fulfilled:

[18] For verily I say unto you, **Till heaven and earth pass**, one jot or one tittle shall in no wise pass from the law, till all be fulfilled. - Matthew 5:18

That would then be the time when we step into eternity:

[1] And I saw a new heaven and a new earth: for **the first heaven and the first earth were passed away**; and there was no more sea. - Revelation 21:1

It is apparently at the conclusion of the Millennial reign when Heaven and earth pass away, signifying that God's Law has been fulfilled and is no longer needed in the form we now know it to be. We view the Millennial Kingdom as being the time when the transformation process for man is initiated and then ultimately concluded - when all mankind will be changed to identify fully with God's Will and Way and receive glorified bodies. When we exit this physical realm and time itself at the conclusion of this thousand year period, we must all be equipped for this with our new bodies:

> [50] Now this I say, brethren, that <u>flesh and blood cannot inherit the kingdom of God</u>; neither doth corruption inherit incorruption.

> [51] Behold, I shew you a mystery; We shall not all sleep, but <u>we shall **all** be changed</u>,

> [52] In a moment, in the twinkling of an eye, at the last trump: for the trumpet shall sound, and the dead shall be raised incorruptible, and we shall be changed.

> [53] For **this corruptible must put on incorruption, and this mortal must put on immortality**.

> [54] So when **this corruptible shall have put on incorruption**, and <u>this mortal shall have put on immortality</u>, then shall be brought to pass the saying that is written, **Death is swallowed up in victory**. - 1 Corinthians 15:50-54

Once man has been changed to the spiritual immortal state which is coupled with incorruptibility, such sin offerings will no longer be needed:

> [16] This is <u>the covenant that I **will make** with them **after those days**</u>, saith the Lord, I will put my laws into their hearts, and in their minds will I write them;

> [17] And their sins and iniquities will I remember no more.

> [18] Now <u>where remission of these is</u>, <u>there is no more offering for sin</u>. - Hebrews 10:16-18

The word for "remission" in this last verse is Strong's #G859 ("aphesis"). It not only means: *forgiveness or pardon of sins; remission of the penalty,* but actually includes the meaning of: *release from bondage or imprisonment.* Deliverance from this imprisonment would be the release from the bondage of our fallen state, both within and without. Once we have been redeemed in this manner the remission of sin seems to be complete.

We are shown in 2 Corinthians 3 that the ministration of the Spirit in the heart is given to us as Believers:

> [3] Forasmuch as ye are manifestly declared to be the epistle of

> Christ ministered by us, written not with ink, but with the Spirit of
> the living God; not in tables of stone, but in fleshy tables of the
> heart. - 2 Corinthians 3:3

However, at the end of the Millennial Kingdom (which Hebrews 10:16 above references as "AFTER those days"), the Law will be fully implemented in the hearts and minds of God's children. With the sin nature being removed, all thoughts are brought into conformity with the perfect ways of God. This is when we will have the full mind of Y'shua and will no longer have the propensity OR the capacity to sin. Our mind will be stayed on Father at all times. We will have left corruption behind and be united in essence with Him:

> [23] I in them, and thou in me, **that they may be made perfect
> in one**; and that the world may know that thou hast sent me, and
> hast loved them, as thou hast loved me. - John 17:23

After our change of body the entire sanctification of 1 Thessalonians will be completed and we will be perfected:

> [23] And the very God of peace **sanctify you wholly**; and I pray
> God your whole spirit and soul and body be preserved blameless
> unto the coming of our Lord Jesus Christ. - 1 Thessalonians 5:23

The sanctification process will be concluded, the body changed, and there will be no more need for temporal sacrifice to come into God's presence:

> [14] For by one offering **he hath perfected for ever them that are
> sanctified**. - Hebrews 10:14

The sacrifice of Y'shua will be fully realized at this time, and will have accomplished the end of its destined purpose – bringing perfection to mankind and restoring him to Father. There will be no further need for sacrifice. The work of the cross is finished when sanctification is completed. When the mind and body are no longer linked to corruption, remission of sin is concluded. At that time, reconciliation with the Father becomes a permanent reality rather than an interim positional status, as it is at present. Ultimate perfection is not just God forgiving and forgetting our sins in the present fallen state, it is when we leave the imprisonment of our 3-D existence and enter our INCORRUPTIBLE glorified state where there is no longer any capacity for sin in our lives. That is when there will no longer be any need for a sin offering.

When this has been accomplished in its entirety, no physical Temple will even be needed:

> [2] And I John saw <u>the **holy** city</u>, **new** <u>Jerusalem</u>, coming down from God out of heaven, prepared as a bride adorned for her husband. - Revelation 21:2

> [22] And I saw **no temple therein**: **for the Lord God Almighty and the Lamb are the temple of it**. - Revelation 21:22

What a day that will be! It is though quite distant from our present lives. Even the Millennial Kingdom is yet future. During the Millennial Kingdom the transition will be in progress, and men will be coming to the understanding they need to have. At that time the Temple will be reinstated, and the Law will be kept:

> [2] And many nations shall come, and say, Come, and <u>let us go up to the mountain of the LORD</u>, and to the house of the God of Jacob; and <u>he will teach us of his ways</u>, and <u>we will walk in his paths</u>: for **the law shall go forth of Zion**, and the word of the LORD from Jerusalem. - Micah 4:2

> [10] Thou son of man, shew the house to the house of Israel, <u>that they may be ashamed of their iniquities</u>: and <u>let them measure the pattern</u>.

> [11] And if they be ashamed of all that they have done, <u>shew them the form of the house</u>, and the fashion thereof, and the goings out thereof, and the comings in thereof, and all the forms thereof, and all the ordinances thereof, and all the forms thereof, and all <u>the laws thereof</u>: and <u>write it in their sight, that they may keep the whole form thereof</u>, and all the ordinances thereof, and do them.

> [12] **This is the law of the house**; Upon the top of the mountain **the whole limit thereof round about shall be <u>most holy</u>**. Behold, **this is the law of the house**. - Ezekiel 43:10-12

The Law which engenders holiness is expressed in the very pattern and form of the Temple, which some have come to view as a microcosm of Heaven itself. In fact, it is supposed (and we believe rightfully so) that the very fabric of creation and the ordering of the universe is actually interwoven with the Law of Heaven. The holiness and sanctity of the Tree of Life essence imprints all of creation (which God pronounced as being "very good"):

> [31] And God saw every thing that he had made, and, behold, it was <u>very good</u>. And the evening and the morning were the sixth day. - Genesis 1:31

It is likewise this same essence that was poured forth in the giving of the Law, which Paul says is holy and good:

[12] Wherefore the law is holy, and the commandment <u>holy, and just, and good</u>. - Romans 7:12

Knowing that the Law will be kept and the Temple will be reverenced with purification sacrifices during the Millennial Kingdom, we must step back for now and realize that we are not yet there. Therefore, with the absence of a Temple today, we must determine what aspects of the Torah instructions are to be observed in our walk of obedience in the Spirit while we await the Millennial age.

Testimony in the Ark

The finger of Father carved the ten most central and major commandments of His Law into stone tablets which He gave to Moses for the people. We believe these same stone tablets reside in the Ark of the Covenant yet today, and will become available once again for viewing by His people when the Ark is found:

[18] And he gave unto Moses, when he had made an end of communing with him upon mount Sinai, <u>two tables of testimony</u>, tables of stone, <u>written with the finger of God</u>. - Exodus 31:18

[16] And thou shalt <u>put into the ark **the testimony** which I shall give thee</u>. - Exodus 25:16

[4] Which had the golden censer, and <u>the ark of the covenant</u> overlaid round about with gold, <u>wherein was</u> the golden pot that had manna, and Aaron's rod that budded, and **the tables of the covenant**; - Hebrews 9:4

They were put there along with the book of the Law which likely contains the rest of the Law Father gave to Moses:

[24] And it came to pass, when Moses had made an end of writing the words of this law in a book, until they were finished,

[25] That Moses commanded the Levites, which bare the ark of the covenant of the LORD, saying,

[26] <u>Take this book of the law</u>, and <u>put it in the side of the ark of the covenant</u> of the LORD your God, that it may be there for a witness against thee. - Deuteronomy 31:24-26

Two Trees, Two Kingdoms, Two Kings

We cannot be sure today what might have been meant by "in the side of the ark", but it would have been associated in some form with the ark and would have been near the ten major commandments. Some believe this might have been the whole book of Torah which was written by Moses and constituted the entirety of Scripture for a time.

So we see that the Law of God was carved in "stone" by God. In a similar vein, the book of Deuteronomy makes a direct correlation between the word "rock" and God, both our God and the gods of others. We find it in several verses in chapter 32. Though they are not consecutive, we will list them together below:

> [4] He is the **Rock**, his work is perfect: for all his ways are judgment: a God of truth and without iniquity, just and right is he.

> [15] But Jeshurun waxed fat, and kicked: thou art waxen fat, thou art grown thick, thou art covered with fatness; then he forsook God which made him, and lightly esteemed the **Rock** of his salvation.

> [18] Of the **Rock** that begat thee thou art unmindful, and hast forgotten God that formed thee.

> [30] How should one chase a thousand, and two put ten thousand to flight, except their **Rock** had sold them, and the LORD had shut them up?

> [31] For their **rock** is not as our **Rock**, even our enemies themselves being judges.

> [37] And he shall say, Where are their gods, their **rock** in whom they trusted, - Deuteronomy 32:4, 15, 18, 30-31, & 37

Several chapters earlier, we saw Moses draw water from a rock for the people to drink:

> [15] Who led thee through that great and terrible wilderness, wherein were fiery serpents, and scorpions, and drought, where there was no water; who brought thee forth water out of the **rock** of flint; - Deuteronomy 8:15

Was this rock, from which water was drawn, God as well? Our New Testament book of 1 Corinthians shows us that typologically, this rock was indeed Divine:

> [1] Moreover, brethren, I would not that ye should be ignorant, how that all our fathers were under the cloud, and all passed through the sea;

[2] And were all baptized unto Moses in the cloud and in the sea;

[3] And did all eat the same spiritual meat;

[4] And did all drink the same spiritual drink: for they drank of that spiritual **Rock** that followed them: **and that Rock was Christ**. - 1 Corinthians 10:1-4

The typological significance in deriving physical water from the physical rock in Deuteronomy days is that of deriving the spiritual living water from our spiritual Rock Y'shua. Indeed He is the typological Rock of salvation of Deuteronomy 32:15 as well.

It seems more than coincidental to us that the Law was carved in stone, and that Y'shua is a typological rock. The word "rock" in 1 Corinthians 10:4 is Strong's #G4073 ("petra") - *a rock, a large stone*. Peter indicates that Y'shua is also the chief corner stone:

[6] Wherefore also it is contained in the scripture, Behold, I lay in Sion a chief corner stone, elect, precious: and he that believeth on him shall not be confounded.

[7] Unto you therefore which believe he is precious: but unto them which be disobedient, the stone which the builders disallowed, the same is made the head of the corner,

[8] And a **stone** of stumbling, and a **rock** of offence, even to them which stumble at the word, being disobedient: whereunto also they were appointed. - 1 Peter 2:6-8

When Y'shua took on human form, He carried forth the Law to man as the living Torah. He lived it, He breathed it, He walked in perfection within it. He came to fulfill it:

[17] Think not that I am come to destroy the law, or the prophets: I am not come to destroy, but to fulfil. - Matthew 5:17

Through keeping it flawlessly, He validated His worthiness to be the Lamb of God. By living the Law that was carved in **stone** (as well as all of the more minor precepts) without a single glitch, He was deemed fit to be a **chief corner stone** for all of mankind. His testimony of God's Law to mankind would be a **"stone of stumbling"**, and a **"rock of offense"** "unto them which be disobedient". How profoundly that applies to our day when we are told the Law is obsolete.

Two Trees, Two Kingdoms, Two Kings

It is also interesting to us that there are many teachings today which acknowledge the mercy seat of the Ark of the Covenant as being a type of Y'shua. Indeed the testimony resides in the Ark, even as it resided within Y'shua.

Peter testified of the relationship of Y'shua to the living God:

> [15] He saith unto them, But whom say ye that I am?
>
> [16] And Simon Peter answered and said, **Thou art the Christ, the Son of the living God**.
>
> [17] And Jesus answered and said unto him, Blessed art thou, Simon Barjona: for <u>flesh and blood hath not revealed it unto thee, but my Father which is in heaven</u>.
>
> [18] And I say also unto thee, That thou art Peter, and **upon this rock I will build my church**; and the gates of hell shall not prevail against it. - Matthew 16:15-18

The Greek word "petra" for "rock" in 1 Corinthians 10:4 above is derived from Strong's #G4074 ("Petros"), which is actually the Greek word for the name "Peter" found in this Matthew text. This is no small coincidence, since verse 18 indicates that Peter's testimony of the Father and Son's singularity of essence would be the foundation stone on which Y'shua would build His church! The word "church" here is Strong's #G1577 ("ekklēsia") - *a called out assembly, set apart, separated from.*

As a part of this church (ekklesia), we too are equipped with this testimony. We are to be called out from the world, set apart from it, and separated to understand and proclaim the Truth of God. His Law, as it was inscribed on the stone tablets and embodied in the Son, is the central pillar of this singular essence of Truth, the testimony on which the church is built. This testimony now resides within each of us as a result of the indwelling Holy Spirit which has written it on our hearts:

> [3] Forasmuch as ye are manifestly declared to be the epistle of Christ ministered by us, written not with ink, but with the Spirit of the living God; not in tables of stone, but in fleshy tables of the heart. - 2 Corinthians 3:3

We are then to pattern ourselves after Y'shua. We are to live and breathe the Law as He did, striving to abide within its precepts. We are to be lively stones, a holy priesthood:

> [5] Ye also, as <u>lively stones</u>, are built up <u>a spiritual house</u>, <u>an **holy**</u>

priesthood, to offer up **spiritual sacrifices**, acceptable to God by
Jesus Christ. - 1 Peter 2:5

We cannot be holy unless we understand the nature of holiness, and this holiness is the purity of essence of God which is wrapped around the Law of Father. In this 1 Peter text we see that sacrifices in the church today are to be of a spiritual nature. There was a hint of this as well in Samuel's words to Saul which we have covered more thoroughly previously:

[22] And Samuel said, Hath the LORD as great delight in burnt
offerings and sacrifices, as in obeying the voice of the LORD?
Behold, to obey is better than sacrifice, and to hearken than the fat
of rams. - 1 Samuel 15:22

While Saul thought he had obeyed God, he had altered what God had instructed in order to provide for animal sacrifice, and this was not pleasing to God. Samuel is clear in this passage that obedience to God's instructions (being a spiritual sacrifice of sorts) is much more important to God than any physical animal sacrifice.

Y'shua came to show us how to more effectively deal with the spiritual Law from above - to sacrifice in a spiritual manner. The animal sacrificial system was dependent on the physical presence of a Temple. It was performed on the physical altar of this physical Tabernacle/Temple where the Glory of God resided.

We believe that the destruction of the physical Temple after the resurrection of Y'shua demonstrated that it was time for the spiritual application to take the forefront for a time. Man would be unable to approach the Glory of God in the Temple for a time so the spiritual presence could be established through the Holy Spirit within. Until the expanded aspects of the spiritual Law are understood, embraced and enacted in the body of the church, there will be no more animal sacrifice. After the resurrection of Y'shua we now have a spiritual Temple within, a spiritual altar within, and even a spiritual ark within. This ark resides in the heart and houses the Law of God. Through obedience to His ways we offer continual spiritual sacrifices to Him, being a living sacrifice of holiness – our reasonable service:

[1] I beseech you therefore, brethren, by the mercies of God, that
ye present your bodies a living sacrifice, **holy**, acceptable unto
God, which is your reasonable service. - Romans 12:1

Being a living sacrifice involves a change of attitude – taking one out of the worldly focus, and looking toward the Heavenly. God desires not only obedience to the physical Law, but also a change of heart:

> [10] Create in me <u>a clean heart</u>, O God; and renew <u>a right spirit within me</u>. - Psalms 51:10

Spiritual sacrifice is born of a broken and contrite heart (a heart that is yielded totally to God). Thus we are shown in Psalms that we are to allow our inner man to be loosed from self-gratification (broken) and yielded to God's perfect Will for our lives (contrite):

> [16] For thou desirest not sacrifice; else would I give it: thou delightest not in burnt offering.

> [17] **The sacrifices of God are a broken spirit: a broken and a contrite heart, O God, thou wilt not despise.**

> [18] Do good in thy good pleasure unto Zion: build thou the walls of Jerusalem.

> [19] **<u>Then</u> shalt thou be pleased with the sacrifices of righteousness, with burnt offering and whole burnt offering: <u>then shall they offer bullocks upon thine altar</u>.** - Psalms 51:16-19

The contrite heart is one of penitence or sincere remorse for wrongdoing in God's eyes which entails an about-face from those wicked ways. This happens only when we are convicted by the Spirit that we need to turn from our disobedience to Father's ways and from our selfish desires to His purposes. Now that Y'shua has made spiritual purification possible, we must restore our spiritual relationship with God before our physical offerings are acceptable once again. This is the interruption in time when there is no physical Temple in existence. Once we (as a corporate people) have had an opportunity to begin to realize the spiritual application of the Law (a broken spirit and a broken and contrite heart) in our lives, <u>then</u> our physical sacrifices will be meaningful to Father once again (verses 18 and 19). This attitude will prevail during the Millennial Kingdom, so these physical sacrifices at the Millennial Temple of Ezekiel's vision will be pleasing at that time.

It is well acknowledged by Biblical scholars that the Millennial Kingdom unfolds in the later chapters of Ezekiel. The restoration of Israel is seen in Ezekiel 39:21-29, then Ezekiel has a vision of the Temple which will be built during those days. When this future Temple of Ezekiel is built for the Millennial Kingdom, man will once again approach the physical presence of God at the Temple, so animal sacrifice will resume on the physical altar of the new physical Temple:

[39] And in the porch of the gate were two tables on this side, and two tables on that side, to slay thereon the burnt offering and the sin offering and the trespass offering. - Ezekiel 40:39

This has caused much contention within today's church, as the words of Hebrews are brought to the forefront and hotly debated:

[11] But Christ being come an high priest of good things to come, by a greater and more perfect tabernacle, not made with hands, that is to say, not of this building;

[12] Neither by the blood of goats and calves, but by his own blood he entered in once into the holy place, **having obtained eternal redemption for us**.

[13] For if <u>the blood of bulls and of goats</u>, and <u>the ashes of an heifer</u> sprinkling the unclean, **sanctifieth to the purifying of the flesh**:

[14] How much more shall <u>the blood of Christ</u>, who through the eternal Spirit offered himself without spot to God, **purge your conscience from dead works to serve the living God**? - Hebrews 9:11-14

The blood of animals and the ashes of a heifer is to make the <u>flesh</u> acceptable (verse 13), yet the blood of Y'shua obtains our eternal redemption (verse 12) and purges the <u>conscience</u> so we can serve God properly (verse 14). The blood of animals deals with the outer man, and the blood of Y'shua deals with the inner man.

Conversely, if these passages are interpreted to mean that any animal sacrifice after the sacrifice of Y'shua on the cross is blasphemous, then the Temple of Ezekiel's vision must by its explicit wording fall into that category. This would mean that the literal prophetic words Ezekiel brought forth are heretical and their placement in our Bibles makes the Biblical text heretical. It is for this reason that many try to write off Ezekiel's words as being merely figurative. To do so appears to be a major stretch into error. All of the specific dimensions and details given in the six chapter span of his Temple teaching (chapters 40-45) do not lend to a figurative approach at all. Again, a misunderstanding of such wording can cause huge divisions and distort Scriptural intent. It is only when passages such as those of Hebrews are brought into alignment with those such as Ezekiel that the true meaning can be perceived. Biblical integrity of the Old and New Testaments must interlock.

CHAPTER 10

LIBERTY AND TRUTH

A number of things kept coming up as we felt that we were being drawn nearer and nearer to a fuller Truth of God's Word. One of those things was Paul's use of the word "liberty" in his writings. When we listened to standard instruction regarding Paul's epistles, we kept hearing that this liberty equated to freedom from the constraints of the Law. However, this just didn't fit the protocol of unified intent, and we suspected that this word "liberty" might have deeper implication than one would think at first glance. It prompted a question. How does Paul's use of this word "liberty" fit into the singularity of Tree of Life instruction?

Liberty – What it Is and What it Is Not

Being freed from the bondage of the penalty of sin, we are given a certain liberty of existence in the here and now, though we are cautioned not to abuse it:

> [12] So speak ye, and so do, as they that shall be judged by the
> law of liberty. - James 2:12

The word "liberty" in our James 2:12 context is: Strong's #G1657 ("eleutheria") - *freedom, liberty, <u>true liberty is living as we should, not as we please</u>*.

Though we will not prolong this segment by expounding on each use of the word "eleutheria" in our New Testaments, we will note for you that this Greek word is used ten times in nine verses of our New Testament text: Romans 8:21, 1 Corinthians 10:29, 2 Corinthians 3:17, Galatians 2:4, Galatians 5:1, Galatians 5:13, James 1:25, James 2:12, 1 Peter 2:16, 2 Peter 2:19. We will pull from some of these for your reference.

Our definition of liberty indicates "living as we should, not as we please". James correlates liberty with doing that which we should as well:

> [25] But whoso looketh into <u>the perfect law of liberty</u>, and continu-
> eth therein, he being not a forgetful hearer, but <u>a doer of the work</u>,
> this man shall be blessed in his deed. - James 1:25

Paul cautions that we are not to misconstrue this liberty:

> [13] For, brethren, ye have been called unto liberty; only use not
> liberty for an occasion to the flesh, but by love serve one another.
> - Galatians 5:13

Peter actually speaks of religious leaders becoming ensnared in the contra gospel and going astray. He tells us that these then teach their errant message to others, <u>promising liberty</u> but bringing those who hear and follow them into the bondage of corruption:

> [19] While they **promise** them **liberty**, they themselves are the
> **servants** of corruption: for <u>of whom a man is overcome, of the</u>
> <u>same is he brought in</u> **bondage**.
>
> [20] For if after they have <u>escaped the pollutions of the world</u>
> <u>through the knowledge of the Lord</u> and Saviour Jesus Christ, they
> are <u>again entangled therein</u>, and overcome, **the latter end is**
> **worse with them than the beginning**. - 2 Peter 2:19-20

This frightening passage stresses the reality that Believers who end up in iniquity due to the "liberty" espoused by the contra gospel can actually end up in a worse spiritual condition than they were in before belief. The abuse of liberty is seen here as corruption. Verse 19 tells us that bondage to this corruption is the consequence for one who has received the knowledge of the Lord, yet turns back from it to the corruption. Galatians warns us as well:

> [1] <u>Stand fast therefore in the liberty wherewith Christ hath made</u>
> <u>us free</u>, and <u>be not entangled again with the yoke of bondage</u>. -
> Galatians 5:1

Galatians 5:1 is often cited today to indicate that liberty stands in opposition to the yoke and bondage of the Law – that standing fast in liberty is to disengage from the Law. This is the bait and switch tactic of the contra spirit. The bondage spoken of by Paul here would not be the bondage of the Law, but the same bondage of sin and corruption that is referenced by Peter above. Therefore, he is in TOTAL agreement with Peter. Romans shows us that we will be servants to (or in bondage to) that which we yield ourselves to:

> [16] Know ye not, that to whom ye yield yourselves servants to

> obey, his servants ye are to whom ye obey; whether of sin unto
> death, or of obedience unto righteousness? - Romans 6:16

True liberty is Y'shua setting us free from the bondage of death so we can live in God's TRUE liberty. This liberty (living as we should instead of as we please) aligns with Father's precepts and liberates us from the bondage or (as Paul says here) the "law of sin and death":

> [2] For the law of the Spirit of life in Christ Jesus hath made me
> free from the law of sin and death. - Romans 8:2

Peter and Paul seem to be showing us that there is an unwritten law of sorts that bondage to sin is the byproduct of walking improperly in the liberty set before us. Therefore, we must learn to avoid being entangled again in the yoke of bondage that Peter warns of in the verses shown above. We must allow the Spirit to direct us from this iniquitous bondage into the TRUE liberty that was meant by Paul:

> [21] Because the creature itself also shall be delivered from the
> bondage of corruption into the glorious liberty of the children of
> God. - Romans 8:21

A bit later, Peter continues his warning by mentioning how many will twist Paul's words (along with other Scriptures) to allow them more flexibility than Father intends, and will fall from their steadfastness:

> [15] And account that the longsuffering of our Lord is salvation;
> even as our beloved brother Paul also according to the wisdom
> given unto him hath written unto you;

> [16] As also in all his **epistles**, speaking in them of these things; in
> which are some things hard to be understood, which they that are
> unlearned and unstable **wrest**, as they do **also the other scrip-
> tures**, unto their own **destruction**.

> [17] Ye therefore, beloved, seeing ye know these things before,
> **beware** lest ye also, being led away with the **error** of the wicked,
> **fall from your own stedfastness**. - 2 Peter 3:15-17

The knowledge and thorough understanding of Torah Truth should be a prerequisite for doctrinal structure, but unfortunately it is rarely given this consideration. It is far too easy to simply trust in and build on that which we have been taught and have known since childhood, and our pastors are not exempt from that path. Their time in seminary is intense, and they are expected to absorb the theologies they are taught, and pass them along to the churches they oversee. The demands and responsibilities of the material world limit both time and energy for their own personal contemplative study. This is a hardship on them which often necessitates a default mode of Biblical study. This default mode rests on the previous assumptions from past instruction rather than an honest and continual seeking of truth without preconceived biases. Sadly, this typically removes any potential and inclination for these chosen men of God to see that the teachings they have absorbed and pass on are in conflict with the totality of God's Truth. <u>Once a preconception sets in, it is difficult to see around it to the truth of the matter, and the contra spirit works hard to ensure that the truth is never found.</u> If that which they are initially taught is of itself contaminated and corrupt, then what they end up teaching their unsuspecting and trusting congregations is the same corrupted interpretations. This is precisely how the "good" of the Tree of Knowledge is cunningly embedded in God's work. It ever so alluringly replaces His true and perfect "good" with a version that is just slightly off kilter and has the potential to be intensely destructive.

As a result, many today have come to use the grace and liberty of God as an escape mechanism by which they free themselves from any perceived constraints. Verses like 2 Corinthians 3:17 are drawn from their context and used to provide validity for such liberal theology:

> [17] … where the Spirit of the Lord is, there is liberty. - 2 Corinthians 3:17

The context surrounding this verse indicates that this liberty is bound by the precepts of Father as written on our hearts by His Holy Spirit:

> [3] Forasmuch as ye are manifestly declared to be the epistle of Christ ministered by us, written not with ink, but with the Spirit of the living God; not in <u>tables of stone</u>, but in fleshy <u>tables of the heart</u>. - 2 Corinthians 3:3

This "liberty" is not meant to usurp or override the precepts that Father brought to man in Torah. That which is written on our hearts by the Spirit must be of the same essence as that which was written on the stone tablets by Father. There is no need to memorize all of the intricate ins and outs of the sacrificial aspects of Torah Law, because there is no Temple at this time. However, maintaining a sure footing with the precepts of Torah is a part of our walk that prepares us to properly apply Father's liberty. Though Father's precepts are written on our heart, our study of them keeps them front and center to our walk in the Spirit, and we will more readily identify them when prompted by the Spirit. We must learn to hear the still small voice that points to them in any given situation. If we choose to ignore this voice or replace it with the contra voice, we put ourselves in jeopardy.

A good familiarity with the Torah and the balance of Scripture will help us to know if the voice we are hearing is the right one. The right voice will not lead us astray and will uphold the precepts of the Father which He has brought to us in the Word. The essence is the same from Father to Son to Holy Spirit, and the Holy Spirit will not guide us to trample on the essence of these precepts in our walk. If we are being led to do so, it is not by the right spirit, as the Holy Spirit will not lead us into conflict with the precepts of the Father.

While we will never find justification through the keeping of the Law, neither are we to transgress it in our walk of faith. To develop such a pattern of transgression is to spite the Spirit of Grace provided for our salvation (Hebrews 10:29). It is important to be knowledgeable of Father's precepts so we can be sure the voice we are hearing is the right one. When we are told to separate Father's precepts from our walk with the Spirit, it opens the door for the wrong voice to take control. It is a very real and well-crafted net of deception to ensnare the Believer. When we are taught that the Old Testament is for the "Jews" and not for our use today we become very vulnerable to this net. As we fall prey to this ploy, we do away with the filtration system (the entirety of the Word) that is designed to help us see the gospel of error for what it is. It is a very brilliant plan. The subtlety of the adversary cannot to be underestimated and should not be ignored. The contra spirit replaces the Truth of the singularity of the Tree of Life Gospel message with the lie of the duality of the Tree of Knowledge gospel message, and when we have chosen to dispel Torah instruction, the error will not be seen and many will fall into this net. The instruction of God in Genesis to NOT eat of the Tree of Knowledge is for us today as well:

> [17] But of <u>the tree of the knowledge of good and evil, thou shalt not eat of it</u>: for in the day that thou eatest thereof thou shalt surely die. - Genesis 2:17

Though the contra gospel is profoundly disguised today, to eat of it is to eat of the Tree of Knowledge, and is still a deadly choice:

> [12] There is a way which seemeth **right** unto a man, but the end thereof are the ways of death. - Proverbs 14:12

Conversely, to partake of God's precepts is to rightly discern our liberty, and to choose instead the Tree of Life:

[44] So shall I keep thy law continually for ever and ever.

[45] And **I will walk at liberty**: **for I seek thy precepts**. - Psalms 119:44-45

[14] Blessed are they that do his commandments, that they may have right to the tree of life, and may enter in through the gates into the city. - Revelation 22:14

What Is Truth?

The Truth of the Father is ever present to all generations through His Word to mankind:

[5] For the LORD is good; his mercy is everlasting; and his truth endureth to all generations. - Psalms 100:5

[2] For his merciful kindness is great toward us: and the truth of the LORD endureth for ever. Praise ye the LORD. - Psalms 117:2

It was first given to man as the written Word of Torah where we find the Law:

[142] Thy righteousness is an everlasting righteousness, and thy law is the truth. - Psalms 119:142

[151] Thou art near, O LORD; and all thy commandments are truth. - Psalms 119:151

[17] **Sanctify** them through thy truth: **thy word is truth**. - John 17:17

John informs us here that God's Truth (which includes the Law) is critical for our sanctification. The whole Word of God is given to us as our filter of Truth, so the sanctification of God's children can proceed smoothly. Therefore, if we fail to properly comprehend the Torah as the basis for our filter of Truth, our sanctification process will almost certainly be hindered.

The Truth of the written Torah was brought forth as the living Torah in the Son when He came to walk among us:

[14] And the Word was made flesh, and dwelt among us, (and we beheld his glory, the glory as of the only begotten of the Father,) full of grace and truth. - John 1:14

[6] Jesus saith unto him, I am the way, the truth, and the life: no man cometh unto the Father, but by me. - John 14:6

> [17] For the law was given by Moses, *but* grace AND truth came
> by Jesus Christ. - John 1:17

The essence of Truth is consistent from Father to Son to Holy Spirit to man. As we begin to understand the spiritual application of the Truth through Y'shua's teachings and the impartation of the Holy Spirit, we see that the spiritual Truth can be even more demanding than the physical. As in the example of adultery mentioned before, it begins with the physical (as in Exodus) and applies an even stronger adherence to principal (as in Matthew):

> [14] Thou shalt not commit adultery. - Exodus 20:14

> [28] But I say unto you, That whosoever looketh on a woman to
> lust after her hath committed adultery with her already in his heart.
> - Matthew 5:28

The Holy Spirit or Comforter sent from the Father dwells within the Believer, revealing God's Truth, and leading the Believer to find it:

> [26] But when the Comforter is come, whom I will send unto you
> from the Father, even **the Spirit of truth**, which proceedeth from
> the Father, he shall testify of me: - John 15:26

> [17] Even the **Spirit of truth**; whom the world cannot receive, be-
> cause it seeth him not, neither knoweth him: but ye know him; for
> he dwelleth with you, and shall be in you. - John 14:17

> [13] Howbeit when he, the **Spirit of truth**, is come, he <u>will guide you
> into all truth</u>: for he shall not speak of himself; but <u>whatsoever he
> shall hear, that shall he speak</u>: and he will shew you things to come.

> [14] He shall glorify me: for <u>he shall receive of mine</u>, and shall
> shew it unto you.

> [15] <u>All things that the Father hath are mine</u>: therefore said I, that
> <u>he shall</u> take of mine, and shall <u>shew it unto you</u>. - John 16:13-15

We then are to walk in the Truth we are shown:

> [4] I have no greater joy than to hear that my children walk in truth.
> - 3 John 1:4

> [10] All the <u>paths of the LORD are mercy and truth unto such as
> keep his covenant and his testimonies</u>. - Psalms 25:10

It is important to walk in the Truth, as we will be judged by it:

[13] Before <u>the LORD</u>: for he cometh, for he cometh to judge the earth: he <u>shall judge</u> the world with righteousness, and <u>the people with his truth</u>. - Psalms 96:13

<u>This judgment will be implemented using God's version of Truth – NOT man's</u>. Since it is His verdict that counts, it is of great importance that we begin to see the "truth" from His jurisdictional point of view rather than from our own limited and biased perspectives, or those of any other human authority:

[6] <u>By mercy and truth iniquity is purged</u>: and by the fear of the LORD men depart from evil. - Proverbs 16:6

Conversely, if we do not perceive the Truth of Father's Law properly, iniquity may not be adequately purged, and we may be in trouble when we are judged:

[7] Yea, the stork in the heaven knoweth her appointed times; and the turtle and the crane and the swallow observe the time of their coming; but **my people know not the judgment of the LORD**.

[8] How do ye say, We are wise, and <u>the law of the LORD</u> is with us? Lo, certainly in vain made he it; the pen of the scribes is in vain.

[9] The wise men are ashamed, they are dismayed and taken: lo, **they have rejected the word of the LORD; and what wisdom is in them**? - Jeremiah 8:7-9

This last verse indicates that those who view themselves as wise are actually not wise in God's eyes if they have rejected His Word, and Romans tells us that the Law is the knowledge of sin:

[20] Therefore by the deeds of the law there shall no flesh be justified in his sight: for **by the law is the knowledge of sin**. - Romans 3:20

It stands to reason that it is extremely important to come to grips with the Truth of the Law so we will be able to identify what is and what is not sin and be properly purged of our iniquity. God has given us His Truth so we can know Him. Our discernment is skewed if we do not walk within it. His Truth is our exceedingly helpful friend, and the distortion of it is our worst enemy. Let us find it, embrace it, and walk in it!

Do We Love God's Truth?

How do we feel when we are shown our iniquity through the mirror of the Truth of the Law? Are we sorry we have let God down and rejoice to repent (turn away from the iniquity) as we seek forgiveness? If we do so, we know we love Father's Truth. If we are merely sorry we got caught, but really have no desire to turn from that which the Truth says is wrong, then we do not love Father's Truth. If we confront God's Truth and choose to ignore it, then not only do we not love Father's Truth, but we actually choose to walk in rebellion to it.

In a personification of charity (the greatest of the virtues) we see that it rejoices not in iniquity but in Truth:

> [4] Charity suffereth long, and is kind; <u>charity</u> envieth not; charity vaunteth not itself, is not puffed up,

> [5] Doth not behave itself unseemly, seeketh not her own, is not easily provoked, thinketh no evil;

> [6] Rejoiceth not in iniquity, but rejoiceth in the truth; 1 Corinthians 13:4-6

Love and charity are closely linked, and sometimes used synonymously. We cannot exhibit charity (or likely even love) properly (at least from God's perspective) if we are ignoring the Truth and walking in iniquity.

Only when we perceive Father's Truth properly and walk within it are we promised in the Word that He will be "<u>nigh unto</u>" us:

> [18] <u>The LORD is nigh unto all them that call upon him,</u> **<u>to all that call upon him in truth</u>**.

> [19] He will fulfil the desire of them that fear him: he also will hear their cry, and will save them. - Psalms 145:18-19

We have already mentioned that Father used Paul in 2 Thessalonians to caution man that if they failed to love His Truth (which includes His Law), that HE HIMSELF would present a delusion which would lead them to believe a lie:

> [10] And with all deceivableness of unrighteousness in them that perish; **because they received not the love of the truth, that they might be saved**.

> [11] And for this cause **God shall send them strong delusion, that they should believe a lie**:

> [12] That they all might be damned who believed not the truth, but had pleasure in unrighteousness. - 2 Thessalonians 2:10-12

These are hard words, but it shows us how important Father's Truth is to Him, and how important He intends it to be to us!

It amazes us that Father would have the Spirit provide for Paul such masterful artistry in his choice of words. Paul's epistles can be read and interpreted in two different ways. The one who loves Father's Truth of singularity can find it throughout Paul's writings. On the other hand, the way in which the Holy Spirit inspired Paul to write his epistles, they can easily be misconstrued. In today's churches, this is rampant. It takes commitment and diligent study to draw together the entirety of Scripture to uphold the unity of God's Truth throughout the text.

Matthew describes Y'shua separating the wheat from the chaff:

> [12] Whose fan is in his hand, and he will throughly purge his floor, and gather his wheat into the garner; but he will burn up the chaff with unquenchable fire. - Matthew 3:12

It seems Father has used Paul's words as a winnowing instrument to separate the chaff from the wheat. Those who love Father's Truth will make the effort to put "line upon line" and "precept upon precept" to harmonize the words of Paul to the rest of Scripture. Those who do not love Father's Truth will take the easy interpretation without balancing Paul's words with Torah, and will fall prey to the deception which comes from such interpretation. This interpretation is the default mode adopted by much of Christendom today. It isolates Paul's words from the context of the entirety of the Word, and inadvertently builds a deceptive doctrine around them. This is the thorny fruit which draws people into the lie, producing chaff.

Father knows that some have understood His Truth, but looked for ways around it so they don't have to follow it. That is not pleasing to Him!! However, He also knows that some have a true love for Him but have just never been exposed to or confronted with the greater fullness of His Truth. He cares enough to try to rescue such Believers from the deception they have come under. He will provide opportunities for awakening them to find His Truth. He may use a variety of teachings and studies, or work through life situations (which may include chastisements). Those who take the bull by the horns and dedicate their lives henceforth to properly discerning Father's Truth will be seen as wheat that is worthy to be gathered into the barn:

> [28] Because he considereth, and turneth away from all his transgressions that he hath committed, he shall surely live, he shall not die. - Ezekiel 18:28

Two Trees, Two Kingdoms, Two Kings

There is much more to becoming wheat than just a desire for Father's Truth, but that is the place to start. The rest is to be worked out in the individual's walk of faith. We can only hope we will be found worthy to be viewed as wheat when we stand before the Son of man:

> [36] Watch ye therefore, and pray always, that ye may be <u>account-ed worthy</u> to escape all these things that shall come to pass, and <u>to stand before the Son of man</u>. - Luke 21:36

Father knows who will be wheat and will guide them to His Truth in His time. That may well be why Paul then cautioned us to STUDY to show ourselves approved!:

> [15] **Study to shew thyself approved unto God**, a workman that <u>needeth not to be ashamed</u>, **rightly dividing the word of truth**. - 2 Timothy 2:15

Note here that **the WORD IS TRUTH**. Paul does not say that parts of the Word are Truth, he indicates that the Word as a WHOLE is Truth. Neither does he say the Word is composed of truths (plural). There is only one Truth, and the Word (our Bible) is a unified singular Truth throughout. By way of recall, the word "dividing" actually means: *to discern properly; equivalent to doing right; without perversion; to proceed on straight paths; hold a straight course; to teach the truth directly and correctly.*

This type of reference makes us wonder if even Paul may have realized Father would design the words of his epistles through the Holy Spirit as a test to the heart of the Believer - a test to see if the heart is fixed on the singular and complete Truth of the Heavenly realm, or if it can be swayed to the duality of the partial truths of the earthly:

> [10] And with all deceivableness of unrighteousness in them that perish; because they received not the love of the truth, that they might be saved.

> [11] And for this cause God shall send them strong delusion, that they should believe a lie:

> [12] That they all might be damned who believed not the truth, but had pleasure in unrighteousness. - 2 Thessalonians 2:10-12

We sense an urgency in coming to grips with the 2 Thessalonians passage above. It does NOT say "because they love not God", it says "because they receive not the love of the truth". Many believe they love God, yet they fail to (or even refuse to) receive a love for His Truth! It seems imperative that we develop a love for God's Truth so we will cling to it and seek it out throughout the entirety of the Word. Failure to properly love His Truth opens up the deception which then makes the Truth even more distant. Verse 12 indicates that a severe judgment follows this lack of love for His Truth and the delusion that results from it.

If we come to love Father's Truth, we will want to embrace it totally:

> [97] O how <u>love I thy law</u>! it is my meditation all the day. - Psalms 119:97

> [165] Great peace have they which <u>love thy law</u>: and nothing shall offend them. - Psalms 119:165

When God's children fully desire to understand and embrace the fullness of Father's Truth, He will eventually draw them to His Truth. If the desire for the things of this world is stronger than the desire to seek, find, and understand the fullness of Father's Truth, then the deception may be unavoidable.

The earthly (contra) version of the gospel message is more to the liking of the carnal nature, so the carnal portion of our being is quick to grasp it and run with it unless our heart of hearts has come to love Father's Truth enough to withstand the tempter's snare. If indeed Paul's words are God's test of our faithfulness to see who loves His Truth enough to stand on it in the New Testament as well as the Old, then unfortunately many will be in trouble when the ultimate results of the testing are tallied. Will we cling to our iniquities and the thorny fruit that condones them, or will we seek Father's Truth and be purged of our unrighteousness?

Athaliah Is Alive and Well Today

In 2 Kings 11 we find the story of Athaliah and her plan to destroy the royal seed:

> [1] And when Athaliah the mother of Ahaziah saw that her son was dead, she arose and destroyed all the seed royal. - 2 Kings 11:1

She was very close to succeeding. Had Jehosheba not snatched the child Joash (the last child of the royal seed) and hid him, Athaliah might have managed to achieve her goal:

> [2] But Jehosheba, the daughter of king Joram, sister of Ahaziah, took Joash the son of Ahaziah and stole him from among the

> king's sons which were slain; and they hid him, even him and his
> nurse, in the bedchamber from Athaliah, so that he was not slain. -
> 2 Kings 11:2

It is the same with the royal seed Gospel. There is a typological correlation of a more spiritual nature to Athaliah of this story. It is the spirit behind the adulterated gospel message which is propagated throughout the land today. With its fast and far-reaching tentacles, the contra message is threatening to destroy all that remains of the seed of the true Gospel message. The contra gospel is a message which promotes segregation of the Law from the Spirit of Grace; segregation of the written Torah of the Old Testament from the spiritual version as shown to us in the New Testament. It has almost managed to do away with the royal seed of the true Gospel message of singularity entirely. However there is a small remnant who understand the true Gospel message (the royal seed – the figurative Joash above) and steal it away from the corrupted interpretations which deny it. This remnant is depicted by the hero in our story above – Jehosheba who steals the true Gospel message away from those who want to destroy it, and protectively secures it.

The figurative Joash is the seed of the royal (true and Divine) Gospel message - the message of singularity of essence, a single Truth – the Shema of Truth of our unified God. The royal message is the revelation of the Truth, the <u>whole</u> Truth, and nothing but the Truth, while the adulterated version which Athaliah intends for us to receive is shades of Truth, partial Truth, and a little bit other than Truth, which creates total confusion, disorientation, and perversity in the walk of the Believer. This makes a great deal of sense when we realize that Athaliah is the daughter of Jezebel, the one whom the book of Revelation says seduces God's servants to commit fornication:

> [20] Notwithstanding I have a few things against thee, because
> thou sufferest that woman Jezebel, which calleth herself a proph-
> etess, to teach and to seduce my servants to commit fornication,
> and to eat things sacrificed unto idols. - Revelation 2:20

The word "fornication" is Strong's #G4203 ("porneuō") - *to prostitute one's body to the lust of another; to give one's self to unlawful sexual intercourse; to commit fornication; <u>metaphorically to be given to idolatry, to worship idols; to permit one's self to be drawn away by another into idolatry</u>*. While it can be physical sexual impropriety, it can also be spiritual impropriety (idolatry). John relates the wiles of Jezebel to luring God's children into dangerous waters. Likewise her daughter Athaliah has the spiritual effect of stealing away the seed of the true Gospel message. In this way she coerces God's children to become intimate with the contra version and with the spirit which presides over it – idolatry to our God.

We must figuratively strive to be as Jehosheba who steals away God's Truth from those who want to destroy it, and protectively secures this Truth. God's children are at risk! Likewise, as His children we have an obligation to be sure that the version of the gospel message we are hearing, receiving, and taking to heart is the version which is the Truth, the WHOLE Truth, and the NOTHING BUT the Truth.

James gave us an important observation in the first chapter of his epistle:

> [21] Wherefore lay apart all filthiness and superfluity of naughtiness, and <u>receive with meekness the **engrafted word**, which is **able to save your souls**</u>.
>
> [22] But be ye doers of the word, and not hearers only, deceiving your own selves. - James 1:21-22

The word "engrafted" in verse 21 is Strong's #G1721 ("emphytos") - *implanted*. It is derived from Strong's #G5453 ("phyō") - *to beget, bring forth, produce; to be born, to spring up, to grow*.

The true Word of harmonized Scripture is a Living book which will bring the seed of understanding to fruition and save the soul. If we try to dissect the seed into segments, how is the seed to grow and produce Life? By dissecting it, we do violence to the seed – the same seed that was designed to save our souls. The contra gospel does essentially that. Using distorted interpretations, it successfully splits the seed by dividing out various portions of the Word of God and segregating them from the rest. At this point the seed can no longer produce Life. It is our job to be Jehoshebas – to steal away the spiritual royal seed of singularity while it can still be found, and to secure that seed in our hearts. Joash was saved so he could benefit others. Likewise, the royal Gospel seed is preserved so it can be shared with others to benefit humanity. May we be about that process!

Epilogue

If segments of this book look familiar to you it may be because you value some of the same sources we use. Often we have brought forth the concepts presented in this book, and then have found these same concepts being expressed by others who provide ministry resources. Other times the concepts we have presented were expanded as a result of videos we have watched, audios we have heard, articles and books we have read, as well as conversations with our brothers and sisters in Messiah. Most importantly though, our inspirations were routinely conceived and expanded through the actual reading of the entire Biblical text. Seeds are sometimes planted during these times of viewing, listening, and reading, and the seeds planted by one ministry may mature when another waters them or when a Biblical passage seems to jumps off the pages. At times the concepts remain firmly entrenched long after we have forgotten the sources from which they were obtained in their original seed forms. Notes are made that are later referenced and found to be incomplete. Ideas flourish and the finished product may include aspects of a number of ministries rather than just one or two. Because compilation is such an overlapping process, we will rarely attempt to distribute such credit throughout the book. We regret that we cannot do justice to distributing credit where it is due, as we so appreciate all of these conscientious servants who are so faithful to feed their flocks so diligently.

We realize that the material in this book will be challenging to the reader who is under the influence of the contra gospel message. When determining to make a new beginning, there are many considerations. You may be excited to share with others and be surprised when they refuse to see what you try to present to them. For this reason, it may change relationships. We say this not to frighten you, but to forewarn you about what you might expect. We wish it could be a simple matter, but our trials prove who we are to the One who saved us. We pray that if your heart is telling you to make these changes you will be up to the challenge.

Please feel free to correspond. Our time is limited, but we will respond as opportunity presents itself. In the meantime may you be blessed as you evaluate what has been presented and come to a conclusion about making any needed changes in your walk, even as we and so many others have had to make also.

Correspondence pro or con is welcome at:

Bill and Karen Bishop – P. O. Box 64 – Glasgow, KY 42142